Richelieu

PROFILES IN **POWER**

General Editor: Keith Robbins

Richelieu

R. J. Knecht

An imprint of **Pearson Education**

Harlow, England · London · New York · Reading, Massachusetts · San Francisco
Toronto · Don Mills, Ontario · Sydney · Tokyo · Singapore · Hong Kong · Seoul
Taipei · Cape Town · Madrid · Mexico City · Amsterdam · Munich · Paris · Milan

Pearson Education Limited
Edinburgh Gate
Harlow
Essex CM20 2JE
England

and Associated Companies around the world

Visit us on the World Wide Web at:
www.pearsoneduc.com

First published 1991

ISBN 0 582 43757 1

British Library Cataloguing-in-Publication Data
A catalogue record for this book can be obtained from the British Library

Library of Congress Cataloging-in-Publication Data
A catalog record for this book can be obtained from the Library of
Congress

10 9 8 7 6 5 4 3 2 1
04 03 02 01

Produced by Pearson Education Asia Pte Ltd.,
Printed in Singapore

CONTENTS

v

. . . .

PREFACE

Cardinal Richelieu shares with Bismarck the distinction of being the only foreign statesman to have become part of the store of knowledge of the average educated English person. Why that should be is a matter for speculation. His achievement in itself is not a sufficient explanation: though substantial, it was no more important than those of some other statesmen whose fame has remained confined to their own countries. Nor did Richelieu's career impinge particularly on England's history. His role in defeating Buckingham's expedition to the Île de Ré hardly justifies the exceptional place he occupies in English historical thinking. Far more significant perhaps was the cardinal's assiduous cultivation of his own posthumous reputation. By commissioning historians to glorify his achievement and by committing his political ideas to paper, he did everything possible to ensure that he was not easily forgotten or underrated. But that begs a further question. Until the mid–twentieth century the cardinal was seen by Englishmen less as a hero than as a villain. Machiavelli, in their perception, was his closest cousin: a devil and a popish one at that. How did this come about?

The cardinal's popular reputation in nineteenth–century England probably owed more to fiction than history. In 1826 Alfred de Vigny, one of the pioneers of the romantic movement in France, published his historical novel, *Cinq–Mars*, in which Richelieu was portrayed as a cruel tyrant. Among English readers of *Cinq–Mars* was Edward Bulwer–Lytton, who was inspired to write a play in blank verse, called *Richelieu or the Conspiracy*. The author was not entirely hostile to Richelieu. He saw him as France's dictator but also her benefactor; a man with a dual character at once witty and sinister. He captured the interest of the famous actor Macready and tried to make him see Richelieu's dramatic potential with 'one leg in Comedy, the other in Tragedy'. Actors in those days took history seriously. Macready read *Cinq–Mars* and, on learning that de Vigny was in England, arranged to see him. 'He will be splendid in Richelieu,' de Vigny prophesied, 'and I will have much to tell him about this man whose intimate enemy I was during the time I was writing *Cinq–Mars*.' On 24 February 1838 Macready reported to Bulwer–Lytton: 'Count de Vigny gave me more than two hours on Thursday and brought the man Richelieu directly before me.' The instruction served Macready well. When Bulwer–Lytton's play was staged at Covent Garden in 1839 in the queen's presence it was much acclaimed. Frequent revivals ensued, and Henry Irving presented it at the Lyceum no less than four times. Thus did Richelieu become a well-known stage villain in England. He also became known to a wider public through the popular novels of Alexandre Dumas, particularly *The Three Musketeers*. In 1896 he reappeared in Stanley Weyman's popular novel *Under the Red Robe*, which was successfully dramatised at the Haymarket theatre. In the face of so much public exposure is it surprising that Richelieu became almost a household name this side of the Channel?

In recent years Richelieu has become known to sixth-formers and undergraduates less for his dramatic persona than on account of his frequent appearances among examination questions on early modern European history. Past generations of historians have presented him as the restorer of France's greatness following her disastrous civil wars and as the founder of that absolute monarchy which reached its zenith under Louis XIV. That picture remains broadly true, but modern research has toned it down in various ways. The attention of a new generation of historians has been focused on a number of hitherto neglected aspects: the nature of absolutism, the effectiveness of royal power in the provinces, the impact of the Thirty Years War on taxation, the causes of social unrest. Among the more notable contributions made in these fields are several studies of popular risings under Richelieu by French scholars. The nature of absolutism has been hotly debated by Porchnev, Mousnier and Beik. William Church has examined Richelieu's concept of 'reason of state'. The role of the *intendants* and the varying fortunes of the royal treasury have come under scrutiny from Richard Bonney. New light has been shed, notably by David Parker, on the revolt of La Rochelle and on the Huguenots in general. Joseph Bergin has shown that the basis of Richelieu's authority was more than the king's trust: it also rested on the systematic building up of a vast personal fortune, much of it comprising lands and offices in western France. The present work tries to incorporate these recent findings into a reassessment of Richelieu.

In presenting Richelieu to a readership mainly of sixth-formers, students and teachers, I feel that it is important to concentrate on his ministerial career: that is to say, his rise to power, the opposition he encountered, his aims and policies at home and abroad, his interest in the navy and overseas trade, his methods of government and the patronage of learning and the arts. To be concise and effective such a treatment must necessarily depart from the conventionally chronological and narrative treatment. Clearly, some observance of chronology is necessary, but this is done within each analytical section. The first three chapters ought to introduce Richelieu to those readers who are as yet unfamiliar with him. In preparing this book I have been much helped by Joseph Bergin, who has given me advice and lent me books not easily accessible. His recent book on Richelieu's private fortune has been an inspiration and his current research on the cardinal's rise to power will doubtless prove equally illuminating. I am most grateful to Keith Robbins for kindly inviting me to write this 'profile' and for much helpful advice; also to I A Shapiro and Susan Brock for their theatrical guidance. My greatest debt, as always, is to my wife for allowing Richelieu to take precedence over matters of even greater urgency.

Birmingham
3 February 1990

TO THE MEMORY OF MY PARENTS, JEAN AND ODETTE KNECHT

Chapter 1

RICHELIEU'S RISE TO POWER
(1585–1624)

Armand-Jean du Plessis, the future Cardinal Richelieu, was born on 9 September 1585, almost certainly in Paris. He was the youngest son of François du Plessis, *seigneur* de Richelieu, a nobleman from Poitou. Early in his career François committed a murder, but the legend that he escaped prosecution by going into exile is unfounded. He travelled to Poland in the entourage of Henri duc d'Anjou, who, after a brief spell on the throne of that country, succeeded to the French kingdom in May 1574 as King Henry III. François was appointed *prévôt de l'hôtel*, and as such was responsible for keeping law and order at court. In 1578 he was given the title of *grand prévôt de France* and created a knight of the Holy Ghost. This was a new order of chivalry with a fixed membership of one hundred, dedicated to honour the person of Henry III. François's duties often kept him in Paris, which probably explains why his son, Armand-Jean, was born there rather than at the family home in Poitou. As a member of the royal entourage, François became involved in some famous events of the Wars of Religion. He was among the first to declare for Henry IV and was accordingly confirmed in his office of *grand prévôt*. He took part in Henry's campaigns for the conquest of his kingdom, being present at the battles of Arques and Ivry. But he did not live to see Henry's final victory, for he died on 10 July 1590 at the age of 42.

Suzanne de la Porte, cardinal Richelieu's mother, was the daughter of François de la Porte, a well-to-do barrister in the Parlement of Paris. She married François du Plessis in 1569, bringing him a substantial dowry. She gave him five children: three sons – Henri, Alphonse and Armand-Jean – and two daughters, Françoise and Nicole. Suzanne was, it seems, unhappy in her relations with her mother-in-law. Financial difficulties also beset her after her husband's death. She was apparently driven to sell his collar of the Order of the Holy Ghost, but, as Dr Bergin has recently shown, 'very little is known about the economic position of the Richelieu family before the cardinal's rise to power'.[1] It is clear, however, that François du Plessis left his affairs in a state of confusion. His widow and later his children decided that their interest could best be served by repudiating his inheritance. It thus became a bankrupt estate and his creditors were left free to recoup their loans by selling it off. In 1603 Suzanne was allowed to take 22,000 *livres* out of the estate.[2]

Following the death of her husband, Suzanne lived at the manor of Richelieu in Poitou; it was here that her third son, Armand-Jean, spent his childhood. In 1594 his uncle, Amador de la Porte, took him to Paris which had recently submitted to King Henry IV. As peace returned to the capital, its schools reopened and Armand was admitted to the famous Collège de Navarre. The course offered by the college comprised three main subjects: grammar, arts and philosophy. Young noblemen usually studied only the first two, leaving philosophy to students who wanted to become priests or scholars. Armand was by all accounts a diligent student. An early biographer states that 'his thirst for praise and fear of criticism were such as to keep him fully stretched'.[3]

Once Armand had completed his courses in grammar and arts, his mother called a family council. It was decided that he would become a soldier. He was given the title of marquis du Chillou and allowed to carry a sword. He moved from the home of his uncle Amador to that of a *parlementaire,* called Bouthillier. At the same time he joined the Academy of Antoine de Pluvinel, a finishing school for young noblemen. This taught not merely physical exercises, fencing and riding but also deportment, alertness of mind and body, elegance and honourable conduct. Courtly manners and dress were also part of the Academy's curriculum. Armand always showed a strong liking for the martial arts; but an unexpected turn in the fortunes of the Richelieu family diverted him from the military career that had been mapped out for him. The reason was his family's need to retain control of the bishopric of Luçon.

It had become the custom in sixteenth-century France for the Crown to bestow important ecclesiastical benefices, such as bishoprics and abbeys, on faithful servants, even if they were laymen. Thus in 1584 Henry III had given the see of Luçon to François du Plessis and for the next half century it was handed down according to the wishes of the Richelieu family. The first bishop chosen by François was his uncle, Jacques, who never resided. The second was François Yver, *curé* of Braye, who was merely a caretaker until such time as Armand's brother, Alphonse, who had been promised the see, completed his studies. But in 1602 he declined the dignity, preferring instead to become a Carthusian monk. Rather than lose the see of Luçon and its revenues as a result of Alphonse's decision, the Richelieu family called on Armand to step into his shoes. Without hesitation he complied: 'Let God's will be done!,' he wrote to his uncle. 'I shall accept everything for the good of the church and the glory of our name!'[4]

The switch in Armand's career necessitated a readjustment of his education. He left Pluvinel's Academy and returned to the Collège de Navarre to study philosophy. He allegedly 'threw himself into controversy with so much application and assiduity that he gave it regularly eight hours a day for four years'. This intensive period of study has been blamed for permanently damaging his health.[5] In 1604 he held a public debate at the Collège de Navarre. By this time he had been formally nominated bishop of Luçon, but, being under the canonical age, he required a papal dispensation before he could be consecrated. Such dispensations were not uncommon, and cardinal du Perron was asked by Henry IV to obtain it. Meanwhile, Richelieu (as we shall call him from now on) obtained an exemption from the university's residence requirements. Soon afterwards he left for Rome in the hope of speeding up his dispensation. He reached the Holy City in January 1607 and was introduced to Pope Paul V by the French ambassador. He apparently dazzled everyone, including the pope, by his eloquence and extraordinary memory. It is also alleged that he became fluent in spoken Italian and Spanish. Having obtained his dispensation, he was consecrated in Rome on 17 April 1607.

Soon afterwards the new bishop returned to Paris and wound up his studies. On 29 October he became a bachelor of theology (not a doctor, as historians have sometimes suggested). A few days later he was admitted to membership

3

of the Sorbonne.[6] He was now ready to advance his career at court, but in January 1608 he fell gravely ill. For several weeks he endured bouts of fever and severe migraines. Throughout life Richelieu was bedevilled by what he called his 'wretched head'. By Lent 1608 he had recovered sufficiently to accept an invitation to preach at court, but he found it less immediately receptive of his talents than he had hoped, so he retired to his diocese. Since 1583 the Richelieus had drawn income from the see without giving anything in return. Their three successive episcopal nominees had been non-resident and the cathedral and episcopal palace had fallen into disrepair.[7]

Richelieu began by giving himself a home worthy of his status. He acquired servants, furniture and plate, and within a few months boasted of being taken for a man of substance. In the meantime, he was formally installed as bishop and promised to serve his flock faithfully. More important was his revitalization of the diocesan clergy in accordance with the rules laid down at the Council of Trent. A synod held at Luçon produced a series of ordinances reminding the clergy of their duties. They were to stay away from fairs and abstain from trade and from games of chance. All were to be tonsured and decently dressed. They were to show respect when administering the sacraments and observe strictly the liturgy of the mass. This was to be celebrated at times convenient to the faithful. Taverns were to be closed during services. Every Sunday parish priests were to teach the catechism and recite the Lord's Prayer and the Ten Commandments in French, not Latin, so that everyone could understand. The faithful were to be encouraged to take communion once a month or, at least, on the four main feast-days of the Christian year.

Richelieu made great efforts to revive religious devotion in his diocese. He wrote a small book, called *Instruction du Chrétien,* which aimed to present the Christian truths intelligibly to all.[8] Although largely untouched by the more ascetic aspects of the Counter-Reformation, his beliefs were none the less sincere. 'He devoutly believed in the Roman Church's great mission and repeatedly sought to improve its institutional functioning and to abet its religious purposes.'[9] The *Instruction du Chrétien,* published in 1618, was widely read in France and translated into several languages.

As bishop of Luçon, Richelieu carried out many pastoral visitations. These were more than routine inspections. The clergy were required to prepare for his coming by organising sermons and prayer meetings. In his concern to improve the quality of his diocesan clergy Richelieu carefully controlled new appointments. He was among the first French prelates to take seriously the Tridentine directive for the creation of seminaries. In 1609 he bought a house next to his cathedral for use as a seminary. Although seminaries existed elsewhere in France, they did not become numerous till after 1650.[10]

Richelieu, then, was a model bishop, but running a poverty-stricken see could not satisfy his ambition. It was but a stepping-stone from which he hoped to return to Paris and the royal court at an appropriate moment. The assassination of Henry IV on 14 May 1610 gave him a chance of escape from his provincial backwater. The king's son and heir, Louis XIII, was only nine at the time and, therefore, too young to rule. The queen mother, Marie de' Medici, was appointed regent until Louis reached the age of majority, fixed at thirteen for a French king. The change of regime was viewed apprehensively by the French, many of whom remembered only too vividly the civil wars that had followed in the wake of Francis II's minority and the regency of Catherine de' Medici. In June 1610, as provincial governors prepared for a possible renewal of unrest, Richelieu returned to Paris. He called on members of the administration, doubtless in a bid to win favour, and preached in a few Parisian churches. But no one seemed interested in employing him. Sully and other ministers of the late king still ran the government and the time was not yet ripe for newcomers.[11] So Richelieu returned to his diocese, whence he kept in touch with events in the capital and tried to ingratiate himself with people in high places by offers of assistance and cringing professions of loyalty.

Late in 1613 Richelieu returned to Paris and made contact with the regent's Italian favourite, Concino Concini, who had just become a marshal of France. He and his wife, Leonora Galigaï, were among the earliest recipients of the many pensions and offices that Marie had showered upon her entourage following her husband's death. Within a few months Concini had become marquis d'Ancre, governor of Péronne, Roye and Montdidier, lieutenant-general of Picardy and first gentleman of the bedchamber. His meteoric rise was extremely unpopular among the French nobility, but Richelieu was careful to conceal any contempt he may have felt for the Italian upstart. 'Monsieur', he wrote to Concini, 'as I always honour those whom I have promised to serve, so do I confirm my assurances to you; for I would rather demonstrate the reality of my affection on important occasions than offer you merely its appearance at other times.'[12]

Marie de' Medici, it has been claimed, was a more effective ruler than past historians have suggested, and tried as far as possible to continue the policies of Henry IV.[13] Such a view is difficult to uphold in face of the factual evidence. She was a devout Catholic and a friend of Spain, and her policies proved so unpalatable to Henry IV's chief minister, Sully, that he resigned from office in January 1611. He was replaced by a commission of three 'greybeards' – Brûlart de Sillery, Villeroy and Jeannin – who, as members of the *noblesse de robe,* lacked the authority needed to keep the upper nobility in order. Sully's fall was followed by 'a loosening of the purse strings, an outpouring of pensions and gifts that was unprecedented since 1594'.[14] Between 1610 and 1614 the regent spent nearly 10 million *livres* bribing the magnates. What made the situation even worse was the control exercised over her patronage by Concini's wife, Leonora. The regent's generosity to the great nobles may have bought four years of domestic peace, but in 1614 this ceased to be true. The government had to face a series of aristocratic rebellions, which began with the revolt of Henri, prince of Condé. He argued in a manifesto that only a meeting of the Estates-General could save the state from collapse. During the negotiations that followed, Condé objected not only to Concini's control of patronage but also to the regent's policy of marrying her son, Louis XIII, to the Spanish infanta, Anne of Austria. To counter the threat of open revolt, the government came to terms with Condé at St Menehould (15 May 1614). The Spanish marriage was deferred till the king's majority, the Estates-General were summoned to Sens in August and Condé received 450,000 *livres* to cover the cost of his rebellion. Richelieu's Memoirs indicate that he did not think highly of either side in the crisis. 'This was such a wretched time,' he writes, 'that the great nobles who were regarded as the ablest were those who were busiest in stirring up trouble; and the disorders were such . . . that the ministers looked to saving their own skins rather than ensuring the good of the state'.[15]

Control of the elections to the Estates-General was crucial to the survival of the regency. Royal letters sent to the governors early in June required them to summon the three estates of their respective areas. *Cahiers* were to be drawn up and deputies chosen from men of integrity and intelligence, sincerely interested in the well-being of the king and his subjects. Such a man was the bishop of Luçon. On 24 August he was chosen as one of two representatives of the clergy of Poitou. During the following weeks he helped to draft the clergy's *cahier de doléances* which in its completed form was to reflect many of his opinions, notably on the need for decorum in religious services, obedience to the Tridentine decrees, an improved education for priests and a ban on duelling.[16] By late September the government had postponed the meeting of the Estates-General until after the king's majority and moved its venue to Paris.

Louis XIII's majority was proclaimed at a *lit-de-justice* on 2 October with Condé and most of the other disaffected nobles in attendance. The first act of the new king was to renew edicts condemning blasphemy, protecting the Huguenots, banning duels, outlawing leagues and decreeing the pacification of the kingdom. Meanwhile, the deputies to the Estates-General had begun to arrive in Paris. Some idea of the issues facing them may be gathered from the many pamphlets that circulated at the time. Those produced by the clergy were aimed primarily at refuting arguments regarding the power of the king advanced by the Third Estate and also at gaining official acceptance for the decrees of the Council of Trent. Pamphleteers drawn from the nobility were anxious to defend aristocratic privileges against the encroachments of royal officials. As for pamphleteers of the Third Estate, they wanted the people to be freed from excessive taxation, violence and business restrictions.[17]

Although the estates met separately, they understood the need for a consistent programme of reform. Consequently they kept in touch with each other by exchanging delegations. Richelieu acted as spokesman for the clergy in its dealings with the other two estates. Thus he invited the Third Estate to swear to work for the glory of God, the service of the king and the relief of the people. He also intervened in a quarrel between the nobility and the Third Estate over a proposal to suspend the *droit annuel.* A highly controversial issue was an article presented to the Third Estate on 15 December urging the Estates to declare as a fundamental law that the king of France was sovereign in his state and that no power on earth, whether spiritual or temporal, had any sway over his kingdom. This was a serious challenge to papal authority and was vigorously resisted by the clergy. Other important issues also occupied the clergy's attention. They called for a serious review of government expenditure, for the suppression of the *droit annuel,* and for the decrees of the Council of Trent to be applied to France.

The Estates-General were formally closed at the Hôtel de Bourbon on 23 February 1615. This was only the second joint meeting of the Estates since the opening session, and its purpose was for each estate to present its *cahier* to the king. The government was clearly anxious to avoid contentious speeches, and the queen mother is known to have influenced the choice of speakers. Thus it was almost certainly with her approval that Richelieu was picked to speak for the clergy. He began by focusing attention on the Crown's financial difficulties. It was necessary, he said, to reduce the amount of useless gifts, to curb tax exemptions and to raise the material and moral condition of the clergy. The French church, he went on, was 'deprived of all honour, robbed of its wealth, denied authority and profaned'. Because it was being hampered in its mission many souls were being lost for whom the king would have to account to God. Four remedies were available: first, he could give the clergy a share in governing the kingdom. This had the endorsement of history: in the past all nations, both pagan and Christian, had given a leading role in state affairs to the clergy. Being celibate and therefore free from worldly interests, clergymen were well fitted for this role. Secondly, the church should be exempted from taxation, its only lawful contribution being prayer. Thirdly, it must be defended from the attacks of lay judges and others. Huguenots who resorted to violence should be severely punished; peaceful ones should be left in peace. Lastly, if the king would only seek inspiration from the Gospel, 'the reign of reason' would be established: justice would regain its integrity, evil would be punished and good rewarded, the letters and the arts would prosper, the state's finances would recover and religion would flourish anew. Finally, turning to Marie de' Medici, Richelieu poured out an encomium: 'Happy is the prince,' he exclaimed, 'to whom God has given a mother filled with love for his person, zeal towards his state and experience in the conduct of affairs.' But Marie's task was not yet done. 'You have achieved a great deal, Madam,' Richelieu declared, 'but you must not stop now.' He urged her by listening to the plea of the Estates to add the title of mother of the kingdom to the glorious one she already held of mother of the king.[18] At the start of Richelieu's speech the hubbub in the hall had been great; by the end it had largely subsided. He had won attention by his eloquence and was warmly applauded for his performance. He was followed by the spokesmen for the nobility and Third Estate. In his reply the king thanked the deputies for their efforts and promised to give close attention to their requests.

Many members of the Third Estate wanted the meeting to last till the *cahiers* had been answered, but on 24 March they were ordered home. The government explained that answers would take a long time to prepare. In fact, the wishes of the Estates-General were largely disregarded by the government; for they had been called not to reform the kingdom but to foil the prince of Condé and gain approval for Marie's policies. As Richelieu commented later:

> The Estates ended as they had begun. The proposal to hold them had been under a specious pretext, without any intention of taking advantage of them for the service of the king and public, and the conclusion was without fruit, the whole assembly having no effect except to overburden the provinces with the tax they had to pay to their deputies, and to let the whole world see that it is not enough to know evils if one does not have the will to remedy them.[19]

Marie's main concern after the Estates-General had met was to take the court to Bordeaux to conclude the two Spanish marriages: that of Louis XIII to the Infanta Anne of Austria, and that of his sister, Elizabeth, to the future Philip IV of Spain. She tried to clear the way by negotiating with Condé, but he broke off the talks. After retiring to his lands, he tried to stir up the Huguenots, who viewed the Spanish marriages with apprehension; but only the duc de Rohan, who bore the regent a personal grudge, allowed himself to be drawn into dissidence: he gathered an army in south-west France to block the court's progress. On 10 September, as the court stopped at Poitiers, Condé and his associates were proclaimed guilty of *lèse-majesté*. Richelieu, who had returned to his diocese in the meantime, paid his respects to Louis XIII and his mother during their stay in Poitiers. But he did not follow the court to Bordeaux and, therefore, did not witness the marriage of Louis XIII and Anne of Austria on 28 November. However, he was kept informed of events at court by his friends and was gratified to learn that he had been chosen to serve as Anne's almoner.

During the court's sojourn in Bordeaux the political situation in France deteriorated sharply. Condé planned to march south and join forces with Rohan. By January 1616, however, the prince was ready to negotiate. The Spanish marriages had taken place in spite of his opposition and he had failed to gain wide support in France. On 3 May the peace of Loudun was signed between the Crown and the rebels, who again received large bribes of money and offices from the government. As Richelieu reflected sadly, a show of force by the Crown might have resulted in a cheaper settlement. Be that as it may, the treaty marked the triumph of the peace party at court. Condé had been empowered by the treaty to countersign royal warrants, and it was widely believed that Concini's much-hated supremacy was at an end. But Marie was not so easily parted from her favourite. In May she secured the appointment of Claude Barbin, one of his creatures, as *contrôleur des finances*. A month later Concini himself was made lieutenant-general of Normandy and given the fortresses of Caen, Pont-de-l'Arche and Quilleboeuf.

Richelieu, who had looked to the Concinis for advancement, welcomed these developments. He returned to Paris, assured Marie of his devotion, and was soon able to prove it by going to Bourges and persuading Condé to return to court. But the prince continued to be a focus of opposition. His residence at the Hôtel de Gondi became an alternative court to which enemies of the Concini regime flocked in large numbers. On 1 September Condé was arrested. His fellow-conspirators, however, fled from the capital and regrouped at Soissons. A renewal of civil war seemed imminent, but on 6 October another settlement was patched up. Only the duc de Nevers refused to comply. He seized a château belonging to La Vieuville, who promptly demanded justice from the king. This led to the resignation of the Keeper of the Seals, du Vair. His place was filled by Mangot, who gave up his post of secretary of state. On 30 November Richelieu was chosen to fill the vacancy.

As secretary of state Richelieu was given special responsibility for war and foreign affairs. His first task was to deal with the aristocratic rebels at home. He raised three armies under the duc de Guise, the comte d'Auvergne and marshal Montigny respectively. They went into action in February, but Richelieu had to watch his commanders closely as they were often slack at imposing discipline on their men. Absenteeism was rife in the army and the secretary of state had to send stinging rebukes to his commanders. He also tried to ensure that the troops were paid on time, a perennial problem of early modern warfare. Though clear and concise, Richelieu's orders were not always obeyed, especially if they ruffled aristocratic sensibilities. Thus he had trouble persuading his subordinates that he really did intend that all fortresses which surrendered should be razed to the ground.

In foreign affairs, Richelieu was not especially successful at this stage of his career. As he soon discovered, France's international standing was at a low ebb in 1617. He needed to reassure France's former Protestant allies – England, the United Provinces and the German princes – that Marie de' Medici's recent flirtation with the Habsburg powers did not mean that they were being deserted. French envoys dispatched to the various courts to explain her policies were not always able to counter the propaganda that emanated from rebellious French nobles or Huguenots. In Italy, Richelieu suffered two major setbacks. In the summer of 1616 the duke of Savoy invaded Montferrat, which belonged to Mantua, a protégé of Spain. The Spanish governor of Milan retaliated by overrunning Piedmont, whereupon the duke of Savoy asked France for help. Fortunately for Richelieu, the king of Spain was willing to negotiate. The bishop accordingly offered his good offices to the duke if he would evacuate Montferrat. Peace seemed imminent when, in December, the French marshal Lesdiguières, acting on his own authority, drove the Spaniards out of Piedmont. Richelieu publicly disavowed his action, while accepting its consequences: Piedmont had been freed, Spain had been taught a lesson and the duke of Savoy evacuated Montferrat.

A more serious humiliation suffered by Richelieu stemmed from a conflict between Venice, France's traditional ally, and the Archduke Ferdinand of Styria. Venice looked to the Swiss cantons of Berne and Zürich for mercenaries, but they required French permission to pass through the territory of the Grisons, a small republic bound by treaty with France. Richelieu, who was as yet unwilling to provoke the Habsburgs, refused the necessary permission and offered the Venetians his mediation. But they asked Spain to intervene. Deeply wounded by this snub, Richelieu blustered in vain. He warned the Venetians of Louis XIII's displeasure. 'He is weak at present, it is true,' he said, 'but he is not so weak that in time his kingdom will not recover its former vigour and impose the respect that belongs to him by right.' For the present, however, the bishop had brought only ridicule upon himself and his nation.

In mid-April the Crown seemed on the verge of crushing the latest aristocratic uprising. The duc de Mayenne, who had been holding Soissons, asked for terms. Barbin and Richelieu wanted to force an unconditional surrender upon the duke. However, they were overtaken by events at court, where Concini's arrogance, dictatorial ways and open contempt for Louis XIII were becoming daily more intolerable to the young monarch. Even the king's personal security began to seem at risk, as Concini set about fortifying Quilleboeuf in Normandy. Towards the end of 1616 Louis XIII began to seek advice from a small circle of friends who would meet each night before his *coucher*. The chief of this informal council was Charles Albert de Luynes, a petty nobleman from Provence. In 1611 he had become Keeper of the King's Birds, in January 1615 governor of Amboise, and in 1616 captain of the Louvre. This last office entitled him to occupy a room directly above the king's, which were connected by means of a secret staircase. Charming and elegant, Luynes soon gained a strong influence over the king.[20]

On 17 April Concini returned to Paris determined to crush his enemies at court. Luynes urged the king to flee, but Louis refused to take such an undignified course. He had the authority but not the power to arrest Concini and send him for trial. It was therefore decided to lure the favourite into a trap with the connivance of baron de Vitry, captain of the king's guard. On 24 April, as Concini entered the courtyard of the Louvre, a gate was closed immediately behind him so as to isolate him from his armed escort. He was then shot at point-blank range and killed. On receiving news of the assassination, Richelieu expressed surprise that the king's friends had been strong enough to mount such an enterprise. He promptly went to the Louvre to congratulate the king on his deliverance, but Louis, it seems, was not inclined to welcome him. According to one version of the events, Louis was standing on a billiard table surrounded by a crowd of enthusiastic courtiers as the bishop arrived. 'Well, Luçon, here I am rid of your tyranny,' cried the king. 'Go, Monsieur, go. Leave this place.' In his Memoirs, Richelieu gives a different account. The king, he states, wished him well, saying that he did not hold him responsible for Concini's bad counsels. Luynes then invited him to keep his seat in the king's council as well as his offices. What is certain is that Richelieu lost his ministerial post in a reshuffle that returned to power Henry IV's old ministers: Villeroy, Jeannin, du Vair and Sillery. He also ceased to be a royal councillor.

Soon afterwards the king banished Marie de' Medici to Blois and Richelieu accompanied her as president of her council. For the second time he found himself exiled from the capital, and seven long years were to pass before his return. His ambition, however, was irrepressible. Within a few days of his arrival in Blois, he wrote to Luynes a detailed account of the queen mother's journey. Thereafter, he kept the favourite regularly informed of all that was happening in her entourage. 'I promise the king on my own head', he wrote, 'to stop all cabals, intrigues and plots, or if I cannot do so to warn him in good time so that he can find a remedy.'[21] By acting as a self-appointed government spy Richelieu evidently hoped to regain the king's confidence, but he only succeeded in arousing everyone's distrust. He himself became aware of this. 'I am the most wretched of men,' he wrote, 'without having deserved it. If I had not thought that I would be protected from envy and anger by the support you know about, I would never have embarked on this ship.'[22] He would confound his enemies, he said, by proving his complete devotion to the king. For the present, however, he decided to withdraw from public life. On 11 June 1617 he left Blois without giving notice. He later explained that he had tried to forestall a letter from the king ordering him back to his diocese. Be that as it may, Marie was furious. She pressed him to return and begged Louis XIII and Luynes to rescind the alleged order. 'To banish the bishop of Luçon,' she declared, 'is to bear witness to the fact that I am no longer being treated as a mother but as a slave'.[23] On 15 June Louis ordered Richelieu to stay in his diocese for the time being 'so as to perform the duties of his office and exhort his flock to obey God's commands and his own'.[24]

The dictatorship of Concini had merely given way to that of Luynes. As Bouillon remarked, the inn was the same, only the sign had changed. Luynes got Concini's fortune and offices, but much property was retained by Concini's widow, Leonora. To acquire this as well, Luynes had her tried on a trumped-up charge of witchcraft. She was found guilty and executed, and her property given to Luynes. In September the new favourite married into one of the noblest houses in France. At the same time, he kept a close watch on Marie and her circle. Some of her letters were intercepted, and Louis XIII was persuaded that a plot was being hatched against his authority. Luynes took appropriate action, one of his first victims being Richelieu, who, on 7 April, was banished to Avignon, then an autonomous papal enclave within France.

On 22 February 1619 Marie staged a dramatic escape from the château of Blois with the connivance of the duc d'Épernon. He was accused by the government of kidnapping her and threatened with the appropriate punishment, but Richelieu offered to mediate between the queen mother and the government. His offer was accepted, and Richelieu left Avignon. His talks with Marie and Épernon at Angoulême resulted on 12 May in a treaty under which Marie received the governorship of Anjou and Épernon was pardoned. The settlement was widely acclaimed as a triumph for the bishop. Louis XIII and Marie were publicly reconciled at Couzières on 5 September, but the queen mother refused to return to court unless she was re-admitted to the council. As Luynes would not concede this, a new crisis developed. Louis decided on a show of force. On 7 August he defeated Marie's army at Les Ponts de Cé, near Angers. Three days later a new treaty was signed confirming the Angoulême settlement. Louis and his mother then staged another public reconciliation, this time at Brissac, whereupon Marie returned to Angers, while Louis marched south to restore Catholicism in Béarn and annex this independent state to the French kingdom.

The conquest of Béarn was accomplished with so much ease that Louis XIII was encouraged to further exploits. A militant Huguenot reaction centred upon an assembly at La Rochelle in the spring of 1621 triggered off another royal campaign in the south-west. It began with the siege of St Jean d'Angély, which surrendered on 23 June. More royal gains at the expense of the Huguenots followed during the summer, but the siege of Montauban later in the year brought discredit on Luynes, who by now had become Constable of France and Keeper of the Seals. He was extremely unpopular, especially among the high nobility, and rumours that the king was disenchanted with him were rife. Thus Luynes's death from fever on 15 December was hailed by many as a deliverance.[25] However, it did not bring about a change of policy, as many had expected: the war against the Huguenots was resumed in 1622.

The death of Luynes left the administration headless. There was no one in Louis XIII's entourage who could take his place and enjoy the king's trust. Marie de' Medici was ruled out by her recent record. Behind her stood Richelieu, who had already attracted the attention of shrewd foreign observers, but Louis regarded him as an ambitious schemer. 'There goes the double-dealer,' he once said as Richelieu walked by. On another occasion Louis pointed him out, saying: 'There is a man who wants to join my council, but I cannot allow it after all the harm he has done me.'[26] Louis remembered the bishop's close association with Concini and also his role in Marie's recent revolts. Everyone knew that he was responsible for her recent diplomatic successes, while his ability and ambition were feared at court. He wanted to be a cardinal, and Marie worked hard on his behalf. Louis XIII and Luynes had given his candidature their official backing, but unofficially they had warned against the dangers of promoting him.[27] Consequently, Richelieu was not among the new cardinals created in January 1621. However, following Luynes's death, the king became more favourably disposed towards him and asked the pope to elevate him. On 5 September 1622 Richelieu was made a cardinal. As a new career lay before him, he decided to rid himself of any responsibility that might stand in its way. The pastoral duties of a bishop could not be easily accommodated within a busy ministerial career. So Richelieu resigned his see of Luçon, while reserving for himself a pension of 5,000 *livres* out of its revenues. He also ceased to be Marie's Grand Almoner.[28]

Louis XIII respected his father's old ministers, but their ranks had thinned. Villeroy had died in 1617. Jeannin was eighty, as was the new Keeper of the Seals, De Vic. Chancellor Sillery was no younger. The secretaries of state, except Sillery's son, Puysieulx, were second-rate figures. The head of the king's council, the cardinal de Retz, was but a figurehead. There remained two men of sufficient stature: the prince of Condé and the finance minister Schomberg. Condé had been released from captivity and admitted to the council, but his stormy past was not easily forgiven and he had a potentially dangerous claim to the throne. Schomberg was able and honest, but he failed to control state expenditure. In January 1623 he was replaced by La Vieuville, who buttressed himself by forming an alliance with the queen mother. To achieve this, however, he had to pay a high price: on 29 April 1624 Richelieu was admitted to the king's council.[29]

. . .

NOTES AND REFERENCES

1. Bergin J 1985 *Cardinal Richelieu: Power and the pursuit of wealth*. New Haven, CT, p. 13.
2. Ibid., pp. 23–34.
3. Carmona M 1983 *Richelieu: l'ambition et le pouvoir*. Paris, p. 26.
4. Lacroix L 1890 *Richelieu à Luçon: sa jeunesse, son épiscopat*. Paris, p. 35n.
5. Hanotaux G 1899 *Histoire du cardinal de Richelieu*. Paris, vol. I, p. 77 n. 2.
6. Ibid., vol. I, pp. 82–5; Marvick, E W 1983 *The Young Richelieu: a Psychoanalytic Approach to Leadership*. Chicago, p. 247 n. 93.

7. Avenel D L M (ed.) 1853 *Lettres, instructions diplomatiques et papiers d'état du Cardinal de Richelieu.* Paris, vol. I, p. 24; see below, p. 196.
8. Hanotaux, *Histoire du cardinal de Richelieu* vol. I, p. 109.
9. Church W F 1972 *Richelieu and Reason of State.* Princeton, NJ, p. 86.
10. Delumeau J 1977 *Catholicism between Luther and Voltaire: a New View of the Counter-Reformation.* London, p. 32.
11. Hanotaux, *Histoire du cardinal de Richelieu* vol. I, p. 136.
12. Avenel, Lettres, i. 121–22.
13. Hayden J M 1974 *France and the Estates General of 1614.* Cambridge, pp. 15–16.
14. Bonney R 1981 *The King's Debts: Finance and Politics in France, 1589–1661.* Oxford, p. 76.
15. Richelieu, *Mémoires* i. 57.
16. Hanotaux, *Histoire du cardinal de Richelieu* vol. I, p. 151.
17. Hayden *France and the Estates General of 1614,* pp. 107–10.
18. Ibid., p. 159; Richelieu, *Mémoires* i. 340–65.
19. Ibid., i. 367–68.
20. Marvick E W 1986 *Louis XIII: the Making of a King.* New Haven, CT, pp. 134–38.
21. Hanotaux, *Histoire du cardinal de Richelieu* vol. II, p. 216.
22. Ibid., vol. II, p. 218.
23. Carmona, *Richelieu,* p. 307.
24. Ibid.
25. Lublinskaya A D 1968 *French Absolutism: the Crucial Phase, 1620–1629.* Cambridge, p. 195.
26. Chevallier P 1979 *Louis XIII,* Paris, Fayard, pp. 270, 273.
27. Carmona, *Richelieu,* p. 389.
28. Ibid., p. 402.
29. Bonney, *The King's Debts,* p. 112.

Chapter 2

RICHELIEU AS CHIEF MINISTER

The council to which Richelieu was admitted by King Louis XIII on 29 April 1624 was the *Conseil d'en haut,* the highest policy-making body in France. We shall call it the council of state. It formed part of the king's council, which also comprised three lesser councils (*Conseil d'état, Conseil des finances* and *Conseil privé*). These councils had their distinctive responsibilities – namely, administration, finance and justice – but they overlapped a good deal, both functionally and in their personnel. Membership of the council of state was less flexible than historians have sometimes supposed. Apart from the king, its members, who were called ministers, included the chief minister, the chancellor or Keeper of the Seals, the minister of finance (*surintendant des finances*) and at least one secretary of state. A number of secretaries were also present who noted down decisions or supplied information when required. Other people might be invited from time to time for consultation.

The competence of the council of state was all-embracing, though much of its time was spent discussing political matters. As the business reaching it grew in quantity, so the councillors found it necessary to devote certain days to certain kinds of business. The council was chaired by the king, who was always present in theory. Sometimes, however, when his absence was inevitable, his place would be taken by his mother or the chancellor. All decisions, however, were taken by 'the king in his council'. He alone could decide, and he was free to disregard the council's advice, even if it was unanimous. His decisions were embodied in decrees which he signed and a secretary countersigned. They had the force of law; no authority other than the king could cancel or modify them.[1]

A rigid protocol governed sittings of the council of state. The king sat at the head of the table in an armchair, while the ministers sat on folding stools in accordance with a strict order of precedence. The highest ministers of state sat nearest the king, the rest according to their respective dates of admission to the council. Richelieu, being a cardinal, posed a problem. As the 'new boy', was he to sit furthest from the king, or was he to take precedence over lay members? The constable Lesdiguières strongly objected to Richelieu passing before him. But jurists pointed out that since the fifteenth century cardinals had taken precedence over laymen. So Richelieu was allowed to sit nearer the king than the chancellor or the constable. This cannot have made him popular.[2]

When Richelieu joined the council, the Chief Minister was La Vieuville, who had been finance minister since January 1623. He was well qualified for the post, but lacked a firm power base within the central government. He had formed an alliance with d'Aligre, Keeper of the Seals, and, more importantly, with the queen mother. But the price he had paid for Marie's support was Richelieu's admission to the council. From this time onwards he was threatened by a possible alliance of Richelieu and d'Aligre. La Vieuville, however, brought about his own downfall. As Richelieu later remarked, the minister was 'like a drunkard who could not take a step without stumbling'. He incurred massive unpopularity by his policy of financial retrenchment and managed to alienate the king, the queen mother and Gaston d'Orléans at the same time.[3] By assuming too much power and making mistakes in foreign policy, he exposed himself to the vitriolic abuse of Fancan, Richelieu's propagandist. On 12 August 1624 La Vieuville offered to resign, but the king preferred to arrest him. Next day, Richelieu was appointed Chief Minister.

.   .   .

THE CHIEF MINISTER AND THE KING

As Chief Minister, Richelieu had wide-ranging responsibilities. He gave detailed instructions to ambassadors, military commanders and provincial governors. He maintained a huge correspondence with bishops, nobles, office-holders and *intendants*. In June 1626 he was discharged from hearing private grievances so that he might concentrate on really important matters of state. In the council of state his was the preponderant voice. He conveyed ministerial advice to the king or the regent. After 1630 he tended to deal mainly with foreign affairs, leaving domestic policy to others. He did not attend the lesser councils but was kept informed by the chancellor of their decisions. Richelieu disclaimed any financial knowledge and left the details of the financial administration to experts, but he did not hesitate to ask for a review of financial policy.[4]

Richelieu was not the first chief minister, nor might he be the last. As a cardinal, he had an advantage over his lay predecessors, Concini and Luynes. Behind him stood the church which would not readily tolerate an attack upon its main representative in the council. But this would not have saved Richelieu if the king had turned against him for some reason. Louis, as we have seen, had serious misgivings about admitting Richelieu to his council in the first place. But under pressure from his mother he had changed his mind and soon he came to appreciate the cardinal's outstanding qualities.

Louis was a conscientious monarch, who saw himself as God's lieutenant on earth with a responsibility to his subjects. At the same time, he realised that he could not rule alone: he needed someone to shoulder the increasingly onerous tasks of government and to advise him. Richelieu undertook both tasks skilfully and reliably. He never allowed power to go to his head to the extent of forgetting that he was and ever would be second in command to the king. He explained his policies to Louis carefully, allowing him to think that the decisions were his own. The cardinal's tact paid off: the king became his friend. In 1626, the cardinal, finding himself under extreme pressure, offered to resign. Louis urged him to think again: 'everything, thank God, has gone well,' he wrote, 'since you have been [in the council]. My trust in you is complete, and it is true that I have never found anyone whose service has pleased me as much.'[5]

Richelieu, however, was never the king's favourite, and it was always on the cards that such a person would seek to get rid of him. Fortunately for Richelieu, Louis was unlikely to fall under a feminine spell, for he never showed much interest in women.[6] He did, however, respect his mother, who was probably the only woman to be a potential threat to Richelieu. Far more dangerous generally were Louis' male companions.

He had four favourites in turn after the fall of Luynes: Toiras, Barradat, Saint-Simon and Cinq-Mars. None, however, was capable of standing up to Richelieu. Only Cinq-Mars was rash enough to try, and the attempt cost him his life. Louis, in fact, never allowed any favourite to dominate him. One man, however, stood in a category of his own. This was Gaston d'Orléans (Monsieur), who, as the king's brother and heir to the throne (until the birth of the future Louis XIV on 5 September 1638), was immune from prosecution. He could not be tried, imprisoned or executed, and, if he chose foreign exile, he had to be lured back in case France's enemies might make use of him. Fortunately for Richelieu, Louis was jealous of Gaston, who was Marie de' Medici's favourite son and had all the social graces that he himself so signally lacked. But Gaston remained a thorn in Richelieu's flesh throughout his ministry.

It seems that over the years a genuine bond of friendship was formed between the king and his chief minister. The poor health which they shared seemed to deepen their mutual understanding and dependence. Louis fell victim to bouts of enteritis early in his reign and was eventually reduced to a walking skeleton riddled with consumption. In 1630 he nearly died of an abscess, and Richelieu feared for his own survival. As he wrote to his friend Schomberg, if the king had died, his own life and work would have been extinguished by the hatred of his enemies. Louis was well aware of this. 'You give all to my service,' he wrote, 'and many *grands* resent you on my account; but rest assured that I will never abandon you.'[7]

For a long time historians tended to assume that Richelieu virtually governed France alone, but, like any other senior minister, he needed assistants. Richelieu, however, went one step further: he ensured that his assistants were also his 'creatures': that is to say, men tied to him by obligation and affection.[8] And, as far as possible, he picked them from his own family. As he himself gathered offices and wealth, the du Plessis and the La Portes acquired positions of political and ecclesiastical power as well as social prestige. Richelieu's brother became a cardinal, one niece a duchess and a cousin a marshal of France. Countless offices were held by more distant relatives. By planting members of his family in such positions of power and influence the cardinal naturally strengthened his own personal security.

Among friends who owed their careers to Richelieu the Bouthilliers are especially noteworthy. Their family had played an important part in his life since childhood. In September 1628 Claude Bouthillier became secretary of state, and in May 1629 he succeeded to the department of foreign affairs. In 1632 his son Léon, comte de Chavigny, became secretary of state for foreign affairs, while his father and Claude de Bullion became finance ministers. They remained the cardinal's loyal creatures till his death. At the same time they obtained from him favours for their own families, such as higher incomes, advantageous marriages and offices with pensions. Though Claude de Bullion was older than Richelieu and belonged to a rich and influential family, he attached himself to the cardinal between 1624 and 1630, and, as finance minister, worked hard to satisfy Richelieu's heavy wartime demands.[9]

Among the most diligent of Richelieu's assistants were the four secretaries of state. Traditionally, their role was to read to the king his correspondence, prepare replies at his dictation and keep extracts of the letters. Each would attend the council of state in monthly rotation. Even in the sixteenth century the secretaries had tended to specialise, each being made responsible for a cluster of provinces. By the seventeenth century, however, two had become particularly associated with war and foreign affairs. In March 1626 the distinction was formalised.[10] The secretaries in the course of their daily duties received a vast amount of miscellaneous information from all over the kingdom and abroad, and one of their duties was to pass it on to the king, the chief minister and any other appropriate minister. But they were far more than conveyors of information. Because they were so well informed, their advice was frequently sought and they took an active part in conciliar debates.

The secretaries of state were also valuable as intermediaries between the king and the chief minister, who were sometimes separated by circumstances. Louis XIII nearly always had a secretary with him who would transmit his commands to colleagues. Chavigny's reports were invaluable to Richelieu, for they kept him abreast of the king's notorious mood changes. 'If the king continues to keep his disposition on the plate where it is now,' he wrote on 3 September 1638, 'His Eminence should have no difficulty in proposing whatever he pleases to him, for His Majesty will not make any opposition to following his advice, and I see that at this moment he is out of that distrustful mood which he expressed in the past.'[11] As secretary of state for foreign affairs, Chavigny had two main duties: first, to supervise all royal correspondence between governments and their ambassadors; secondly, to influence foreign policy decisions.

François Sublet de Noyers, who became secretary of state for war in 1636, was an indefatigable worker. Over a period of seven years he prepared some 18,000 letters and dispatches. Although, like other secretaries, he attended to a wide variety of business, military affairs were his main preoccupation. He occupied the unenviable ground between the army commanders, who constantly asked for money, and the finance ministers, who tried to avoid paying it. Louis XIII did not care for him, but Richelieu trusted him. 'I have so much faith in what comes from Monsieur de Noyers,' he once wrote, 'that it is not necessary for him to send me musters and troop reviews which he well knows that I never see. It is sufficient that he take the trouble to write me what is happening.'[12] Sublet was duly rewarded by Richelieu. He became superintendent of royal buildings, and, as such, kept watch on the Louvre. He was also *concierge* of Fontainebleau. In 1642 he acquired a library for Richelieu and also prepared his last will and testament.

. . .

RICHELIEU'S POWER BASE

Richelieu was much too astute politically to rely on the king's trust alone for his ministerial survival. He had experienced civil unrest and had seen great noblemen hold out against the Crown from within powerful provincial redoubts. As political adviser to Marie de' Medici he had drawn up a statement pointing out the advantages of Nantes as a fortified town as against Angers. Once he had become chief minister he set about acquiring his own provincial base by collecting governorships in western France.

Provincial governors were powerful figures. In the early sixteenth century they had been princes of the blood or members of the highest nobility who had provided the king with a network of 'viceroys' through which he might rule his kingdom. During the Wars of Religion, when the central government had all but collapsed, they had often behaved as semi-autonomous rulers leading private armies. By becoming a governor Richelieu could achieve four objectives: first, establish his own authority within a province or town; secondly, enlarge his sphere of patronage; thirdly, acquire fortresses which might prove useful against his enemies; and fourthly, stop such persons obtaining the same governorships for themselves.

Richelieu concentrated his governorships, both of provinces and towns, in western France. He began with Le Havre (October 1626) and spent the rest of his life turning it into France's strongest fortified town. Lesser governorships soon followed (Harfleur, Montvilliers, Pont-de-l'Arche, Honfleur). Late in 1626 he gained control of Brouage under the nominal governorship of Marie de' Medici. In October 1629, he was appointed lieutenant-general in Brouage, Oléron and Ré. At the same time he became captain and governor of the island and fortress of Oléron. In December 1630 Richelieu became governor of Ré, Aunis and La Rochelle in place of Toiras who was compensated with a marshal's baton. In 1632 Richelieu obtained Nantes. Finally, he accepted the governorship of Brittany at the request of the provincial estates. Of all his governorships, this was the most important as it carried rights and prerogatives dating back to the days of the independent dukes. Such a powerful concentration of governorships, all of them acquired in less than six years, point to Richelieu's 'determination and ability to build a power base for himself beyond the court and the council chamber'. To this must be added all the governorships (for example, Brest and Calais) acquired by members of his family or close political associates which served to extend his own power.[13]

Until recently little was known about the cardinal's private fortune. Historians tended to assume that his power rested exclusively on his master's trust and that his political ambitions were wholly dedicated to the service of the state. In the words of C V Wedgwood: 'he remained always what he had always sought to be, not a rich and powerful man, but the servant of the state, or, in the words which had decked his cradle, "Armand for the King".'[14] However, evidence has come to light which obliges one to correct this judgement.[15] In spite of his disclaimer of any financial expertise, Richelieu understood perfectly the adage that 'power is money'. As chief minister, Richelieu had a salary of 40,000 *livres,* but his unofficial income was much more important. This was partly derived from the provincial governorships which he acquired. A governor's salary was fixed at 6,000 *livres,* but he had concealed revenues as well. Representative estates, towns and corporations commonly purchased a governor's favour and goodwill with substantial gifts in cash or kind. He might also share in the proceeds of taxation or raise illegal taxes of his own. He might blackmail financiers or exact bribes from officials and others seeking his patronage. No governor left behind any account books. But it is known that Richelieu received a pension of 720,000 *livres* from the Breton estates. He must also have profited from his many town governorships. Le Havre, La Rochelle, Nantes and Brouage were thriving Atlantic ports anxious to capture his favour.[16]

Early in 1626 Richelieu was appointed *Grand maître et surintendant général du commerce,* and in January 1627 the office of Admiral of France, held by Montmorency, was suppressed. The cardinal asked that no salary should be attached to his new office. This should have saved the Crown 35,000 *livres* a year, but Richelieu profited from the office in ways undreamed of by his predecessor. Louis XIII conferred upon him the right to a share of the proceeds of all shipwrecks, flotsam, jetsam and the confiscation of ships and merchandise at sea. He was also allowed to take the proceeds of permits French ships had to take out before setting sail. In December 1628 he was given for life the anchorage fees charged in French ports. Lastly, in February 1631, he was empowered to nominate all naval officials and, in effect, to pocket the yield from the sale of such offices. By the late 1630s the known revenues of the *Grand Maître* varied between 200,000 and 240,000 *livres* a year.[17]

Richelieu was also a great purchaser of land. His father had died bankrupt, but his brother, Henri (unfairly dismissed by past historians as a spendthrift), had done a great deal to redeem the family lands. Thus Richelieu inherited a nucleus in Poitou which might serve as the foundation for a much larger holding. He set about doing so by patiently stalking noble families burdened with mounting debts. But his purchases were not indiscriminate: he concentrated them in two regions of western France: Anjou-Poitou and Aunis-Saintonge, where his personal domination was assured by his governorships, his office of *Grand Maître* and his important purchases of royal domain. His investments in land were 'part of a concentrated strategy aimed at capturing all the important sources of power and control in those regions'. In 1621 Richelieu had managed to purchase the family estate of Richelieu which he added to the lands he had inherited from his brother, Henri. As yet they did not constitute a significant holding in the province. In July 1626, however, he bought Faye for 127,500 *livres* and this marked a breakthrough in his campaign to establish himself as the leading landowner in Anjou-Poitou. In August 1631 Louis XIII conferred the status of a *duché-pairie* on the *seigneurie* of Richelieu, turning Richelieu into a 'cardinal-duc'. Along with this new title, he acquired powers expressed in a ducal court of justice. In May 1631 he had been empowered by the king to build a walled town at Richelieu and to hold regular markets and fairs there. He also built a handsome château close by and persuaded his rich clients to set up houses in the town. In the last decade of his life, Richelieu added five more estates to his holding in this part of France. The most important of these was the Montpensier seat of Champigny, which in the 1630s had been held by Gaston d'Orléans for his granddaughter, the future 'Grande Mademoiselle'. Altogether the cardinal spent 1,294,000 *livres* on lands in Anjou-Poitou. In Aunis-Saintonge, his largest purchase was Fronsac, which cost him 600,000 *livres* and made him a duke twice over. Altogether his investments in land in this part of France amounted to 1,863,000 *livres*. Elsewhere in France, the cardinal acquired lands primarily for resale or exchange. Some were in the Paris area, where he spent a long time looking for an ideal rural retreat until he settled on Rueil. When Richelieu died the lands still in his possession were worth about 5 million *livres*. 'No other figure,' writes Bergin, 'during the entire ancien régime, not even Mazarin, ever succeeded in amassing singlehandedly such vast holdings in land.'[18]

Other forms of investment much exploited by Richelieu were rights pertaining to the royal domain and *rentes*. Between 1627 and 1634 the cardinal spent about 2,500,000 *livres* on domain, mainly in Anjou-Poitou and Aunis-Saintonge. His acquisition of domain at Brouage served to tighten his hold on that region. It also gave him a share of the lucrative salt-tax. Taken together, his rights at Brouage and La Rochelle yielded more revenue than the totality of his lands. In February 1634 the Crown suddenly decided to revoke the rights (*droits aliénés*) which it had been selling assiduously since the 1610s, but the cardinal was handsomely reimbursed to the tune of more than 1,500,000 *livres* in cash. Most of this sum he chose to reinvest in *rentes*. At his death Richelieu's domain investments were worth 1,378,000 *livres*. The income he derived from them rose from 60,000 *livres* in 1628 to 120,000 in 1633. In 1636 the total was 200,000 and, in 1642, 190,000. Among his most lucrative rights was his share of the salt-tax of Brouage, which yielded an annual income of 100,000 *livres* between 1635 and 1642. Excluding his admiralty rights, this was the largest single contribution to the cardinal's income in his last years. 'Despite occasional mistakes and errors of judgment,' writes Bergin, 'few men during the entire ancien régime can have speculated in royal domain so unremittingly and to such good effect.'[19]

By contrast, the cardinal's holdings in *rentes* were few. They were one of the Crown's favourite methods of raising revenue. New flotations were the subject of much feverish speculation: as the market became saturated, *rentes* were bought, sold and exchanged for much less than their nominal value. Yet Richelieu's holdings were limited in number. Four out of five were disposed of in his lifetime to patronise and finance certain religious enterprises and individuals. Unlike so many other *rentiers,* the cardinal seems to have been paid his due by the Crown.[20]

Richelieu's wealth also included ecclesiastical benefices. Pluralism – the holding of more than one benefice by a single individual – was widespread at all levels of the church hierarchy below the rank of bishop. Another common practice was the granting of benefices *in commendam*. This enabled persons other than professed members of religious orders to become titular abbots or priors. Even laymen could be *commenditaires*. Not only did they exercise a large measure of control over the affairs of the religious houses concerned, but they also drew the lion's share of the revenues. The granting of benefices *in commendam* was in the king's gift and his court was the clearing-house for their disposal. As cardinal, Richelieu had a particular incentive for accumulating benefices: it was universally recognised that a cardinal's dignity required the support of a considerable endowment of benefices.

Richelieu was 'one of the best beneficed churchmen in all of French history.'[21] Until 1621 his benefices were all in Poitou, but three years later he acquired St Pierre de Chalons in Champagne, and thereafter his geographical horizons widened. In

1629 he obtained five major abbeys, including Cluny, which the Guise family had held for almost a century. By the mid-1630s he had decided to unite all the Benedictine and Cluniac houses in France into a single, reformed congregation under the aegis of the Maurists. As part of this plan, he gained control of the congregation of Chezal-Benoît in August 1634 and had himself nominated 'abbot, chief and general administrator' of its five abbeys. Late in 1635 he became 'abbot-general' of Cîteaux and Prémontré. Richelieu ended his life in possession of fifteen abbeys, four priories and the generalship of Chezal-Benoît. His collection of benefices was the largest hitherto amassed by a single individual in French history. Only a handful produced an income of less than 10,000 *livres* a year. Like most other benefice-holders, Richelieu drew his revenues through fixed-term leases which offered him a predictable income while relieving him of many administrative and economic risks. In 1634 his annual income from benefices stood at 240,000 *livres*.[22]

Richelieu's vast wealth generated a complex administrative machine, but no hard and fast distinction was drawn between his private and public affairs. Just as his personal secretaries would perform a wide range of public duties, so royal officials helped to run his private affairs. Among the most important of his personal secretaries were Michel Le Masle, prior of Les Roches, and Julius de Loynes, *sieur* de La Ponterie. The cardinal also had his own council, which examined the accounts of his many receivers and dealt with appeals from them and others. Two high-ranking churchmen, Henri de Sourdis, archbishop of Bordeaux, and Léonor d'Étampes, bishop of Chartres and later archbishop of Rheims, helped Richelieu in various ways. Sourdis, for example, directed work on the château of Richelieu, while Étampes supervised the cardinal's household and his building projects at Rueil and at the Palais-Cardinal. Nearly all Richelieu's possessions were in the hands of revenue-farmers, bound to him by short-term contracts. One of them was with three Protestant bankers whom he apparently employed continuously for ten years.[23]

Important lessons may be drawn from a study of Richelieu's wealth. There was nothing haphazard about the way in which he built it up. From the start of his ministerial career, he was remarkably single-minded in gathering offices, lands, domain, benefices and *rentes*. Wherever possible he tried to enhance his revenues. As his power grew, so did his ability to appoint members of his own family and friends to positions of influence. Two objectives were uppermost in his mind: first, to raise his status and that of his house to the level of the highest aristocracy; secondly, to form a compact territorial base capable of buttressing his political authority. Richelieu certainly depended on retaining the king's trust, but he evidently did not rely on it exclusively. He had seen too many favourites fall to rely on anything less solid than wealth. He used it to protect him from the vagaries of fortune. That is doubtless why he chose to concentrate his offices and lands in western France. By degrees he made himself the master of France's Atlantic coast and much of its hinterland. Several major fortresses and an entire fleet fell under his control. Whether he would have dared to use them against the Crown is a matter for conjecture, but the possibility was there.

Richelieu was passionately devoted to the state. But can he still be regarded as a visionary statesman animated by a selfless devotion to France and her king? Far too much premeditation governed the construction of his fortune to suggest a lofty idealism free from self-interest. It may be suggested that Richelieu left the running of his private affairs to underlings with a better grasp of finance than he professed to have. But the evidence suggests otherwise. 'Routine matters of administration,' Bergin writes, 'he left to those employed for that purpose, but the decisions which shaped the history of his wealth were his alone.'[24]

. . .

NOTES AND REFERENCES

1. Mousnier R 1970 *La plume, la fauçille et le marteau*. Paris, PUF, pp. 141–78.
2. Battifol L 1934 *Richelieu et le roi Louis XIII*. Paris, Calmann-Lévy, pp. 14–16.
3. Bonney R 1981 *The King's Debts*. Oxford, Clarendon, pp. 110–12.
4. Bonney R 1978 *Political Change in France under Richelieu and Mazarin, 1624–1661*. Oxford, Oxford University Press, pp. 7–8.
5. Chevallier P 1979 *Louis XIII*. Paris, Fayard, pp. 282–84; Battifol *Richelieu et le roi Louis XIII*, pp. 72–99.

6. Chevallier *Louis XIII*, pp. 284–85.
7. Ibid., p. 286.
8. Ranum O 1963 *Richelieu and the Councillors of Louis XIII*. Oxford, Clarendon, pp. 28–9.
9. Ibid., pp. 30–44.
10. Ibid., p. 55.
11. Ibid., p. 81.
12. Ibid., p. 113.
13. Bergin J 1985 *Cardinal Richelieu: Power and the Pursuit of Wealth*. New Haven and London, Yale University Press, pp. 80–94.
14. Wedgwood C V 1962 *Richelieu and the French Monarchy*. London, p. 49.
15. Bergin, *Cardinal Richelieu*, pp. 1–12.
16. Ibid., pp. 91–4.
17. Ibid., pp. 94–118.
18. Ibid., pp. 119–57. The quotation is on p. 140. See below, p. 196.
19. Ibid., pp. 158–80. The quotation is on p. 195.
20. Ibid., pp. 180–84.
21. Ibid., p. 197.
22. Ibid., pp. 196–242.
23. Ibid., pp. 41–68.
24. Ibid., p. 68.

Chapter 3

RICHELIEU'S TRIUMPH

In 1624 Richelieu was a stalking-horse for the queen mother, Marie de' Medici. It was not simply to aid his advancement that she had pressed the king to admit him to the council; it was in the expectation of using Richelieu to strengthen her own position at the heart of the government. Being proud and ambitious, she longed to regain the authority she had wielded as regent between 1610 and 1617. Nor was she disappointed at first, for Richelieu was shrewd enough to realise that he needed her support. He gave the utmost attention to the opinions she voiced in the council. He would communicate important matters to her before they came up for discussion and would consult her as well as the king. But Marie was a less sophisticated political animal than the cardinal. She was a devout Catholic who prayed for the triumph of the Counter-Reformation and for the victory of the Austrian and Spanish Habsburgs over their Protestant enemies, the Dutch and the German princes. As from 1624, she was the standard-bearer of the *dévots* – those Frenchmen who believed that peace with the Habsburgs was the essential prerequisite to the eradication of heresy at home. Richelieu, as a cardinal, was naturally expected to fall in with these views. But experience had already taught him that religion and politics were not always reconcilable. Though deferential towards the queen mother, he was not so slavishly her creature as to sacrifice his political judgement for the sake of his relations with her.[1]

The marriage of Louis XIII's sister, Henrietta Maria, with Charles, Prince of Wales, was the first item of foreign policy which Richelieu had to deal with as chief minister. It involved negotiations with a Protestant power, but this did not upset

Marie. For she wanted the marriage desperately, and the *dévots* believed – mistakenly, as it happened – that it would benefit the cause of English Catholicism. The dispute between France and Spain over control of an Alpine valley, called the Valtelline, was altogether different, as it occasioned an armed confrontation between France and the Papacy to whom Spain had entrusted her forts in the valley. The support given by the *dévots* to the papal nuncio, Cardinal Barberini, when he visited Paris was the first instance of open opposition to Richelieu's anti-Spanish policy. He was accused of heretical sympathies simply because he preferred to temporise with the Huguenots as long as the Valtelline dispute remained unsettled. An agreement between Louis XIII and the Protestant town of La Rochelle in February 1626 was the signal for a flood of pamphlets, mostly of foreign origin, accusing Richelieu of making peace with the Huguenots in order the more freely to assist foreign Protestants in their struggle against the Habsburgs.

The opposition to the cardinal found its natural leader in Louis XIII's younger brother, Gaston, who was commonly called 'Monsieur'. Historians generally have not given him a good press. They have presented him as unprincipled, dissipated and cowardly, albeit a much livelier person than the king. One historian has suggested that Gaston may have genuinely held the quasi-liberal views which he aired in a number of public pronouncements.[2] Whether or not he sincerely believed in a limited monarchy must remain an open question. What is certain is that he and his high-born friends and their ladies continually plotted to overthrow Richelieu till the end of his life. Of course, Gaston was in a strong position to do so, for he was not only the king's brother but also the heir to the throne, at least till the future Louis XIV was born, in September 1638. His mother, who doted on him, anxiously pressed him to marry Marie de Bourbon-Montpensier, but he did not like her. Nor was the king particularly enthusiastic, as she was connected with the powerful house of Guise. Even so, he gave his consent to the marriage, whereupon a group of noblemen, including the Condés and the comte de Soissons, rallied to the defence of Gaston's celibacy. It was known as the party of 'aversion to the marriage'. But the chief opponent of the Montpensier marriage was the queen,

Anne of Austria. She was assisted by one of her ladies, the duchesse de Chevreuse, an arch-intriguer whom Richelieu aptly nicknamed 'the devil'. She put pressure on Gaston's former tutor, the maréchal d'Ornano, to rally supporters at home and abroad. Foolishly, he asked some provincial governors if they were prepared to offer Gaston protection should he be forced to leave the court. His moves were reported to the king, who had him arrested in May 1626.

Believing that Richelieu was to blame for their troubles, Gaston and his friends laid plans to threaten, kidnap or even assassinate him. Louis gave the cardinal an armed escort. He also prevailed upon his brother to submit. On 31 May Gaston formally promised to be loyal to the king and to inform on any future plots. His word, however, was worthless. Within a short time, he was again at the centre of a conspiracy, involving this time the young count of Chalais. The plot was betrayed and Chalais arrested. Gaston thought of fleeing the kingdom, but was again persuaded to fall into line. On 31 July he was given the duchy of Orléans and the county of Blois in apanage along with a large annual pension. In exchange for these bribes he married Marie de Montpensier on 6 August, much to his mother's satisfaction. Thirteen days later Chalais was executed; on 2 September Ornano died of natural causes. The duchesse de Chevreuse was banished by the king to Poitou, but she preferred to leave the kingdom and settled in Lorraine, an independent duchy soon to become a notorious haven for Richelieu's enemies.

A consequence of these dramatic events at court was the fall of the chancellor, d'Aligre. On 1 June Michel de Marillac was appointed Keeper of the Seals, and eight days later the marquis d'Effiat took his place as finance minister. Despite many domestic and foreign problems, the years from 1626 to 1630 saw serious attempts at administrative reform. The old notion that the government was split between Marillac, who wanted reform, and Richelieu, who wanted war, is no longer tenable. At least in 1626 and 1627 Richelieu shared the same objectives as Marillac and d'Effiat. In addition to a general plan of reform he tried to restore stability to the king's finances by creating the first budgetary surplus since Sully's ministry. Along with a curtailment of expenditure, the cardinal envisaged a redistribution of taxes, but, being a pragmatist, he had to temper the application of reform so as to accommodate his other political aims.[3] Yet some significant changes were introduced, notably the abolition of the offices of Constable and Admiral of France in January 1627. Financial as well as political reasons lay behind this move. The finance minister needed greater control over military and naval expenditure than would have been possible if the two offices had survived. Richelieu also wanted to build up France's naval strength, hence his self-appointment as *Grand maître, chef et surintendant général de la navigation et commerce de France*. Other reforms proposed in an Assembly of Notables (December 1626 to February 1627) found expression in the famous *Code Michau* which Marillac drew up in 1629.

· · ·

THE DAY OF DUPES

From April 1624 until November 1630 France was ruled in effect by a triumvirate made up of the king, his mother and cardinal Richelieu. But in November 1630 Louis XIII was forced against his will to drop one member of the trio. Was it to be his mother or the cardinal? He made his choice on what has come to be known as 'The Day of Dupes'. It was to be the watershed of Richelieu's ministerial career.

Marie de' Medici was extremely jealous of the political influence she wielded as the king's mother. But she was also stupid and highly susceptible to the tittle-tattle of courtiers. Richelieu, as superintendent of her household, had taken care to introduce many of his kinsmen and friends into it, but he could not easily exclude from Marie's entourage members of the royal family or of the upper nobility, many of whom heartily detested him. But relations between the queen mother and the cardinal remained more or less equable until the siege of La Rochelle. Contemporaries noticed that, after Richelieu had triumphed over the Huguenots, he appeared less respectful towards her and less inclined to seek her advice. Hearing that she had complained of his behaviour, he hastened to reassure her. 'I protest before God,' he wrote on 30 April 1628, 'that I am as much concerned to please you as I am to achieve my salvation. . . . You have told Monsieur that you are being treated like a bauble (*marotte*). You can imagine what a fatal dagger-blow this is to one who has never thought of anything other than your honour and glory.' Marie's reply was reassuring: 'I beg you not to believe that there has been any alteration in the affection that I have always felt for you or that anything might cause me to change.'[4] But whatever Marie might say, she could not accept the idea that her erstwhile creature was now more influential than she was. He even dared to stand up to her in the council. The clearest sign of a rift between them was given at Fontainebleau, in September 1629, following Richelieu's return from his victorious campaign against the Huguenots of Languedoc. The cardinal, it seems, was publicly snubbed by Marie, whereupon he offered to resign as minister and as superintendent of her household. Louis XIII managed to patch things up, but, as the papal nuncio noted, the queen mother continued to harbour 'the same hatred' of the cardinal as before.

If jealousy was the mainspring of Marie's resentment of Richelieu, more rational considerations animated some of her allies. Foremost among these were Michel de Marillac, Keeper of the Seals, and Cardinal Pierre de Bérulle.[5] Marillac was at the peak of a long and distinguished career as a magistrate. A devout and austere Catholic, he had once served the Catholic League, while his family played a prominent part in the French Counter-Reformation. For five years he and Richelieu were on excellent terms, but in 1629 Marillac opposed the cardinal's policy of armed intervention in Italy. As for Bérulle, he was the founder of the Oratoire and the author of several mystical works. In 1627 he had been given the red hat at the instance of Richelieu and Marie. He frequently assured the cardinal of his devotion, but candour was not, it seems, a dominant feature of his character or conduct. His political views certainly departed from those of Richelieu. After the fall of La Rochelle, for example, he wanted a religious crusade against England. Richelieu, as a realist, had no time for Bérulle's brand of politics. He found him an embarrassment and was about to send him to Rome as ambassador, when Bérulle suddenly died (on 2 October 1629).

Both Marillac and Bérulle believed that Richelieu should devote his efforts to rooting out heresy at home rather than to fighting Spain, which they regarded as the champion of Catholicism. Whenever Richelieu spoke of the king's honour and prestige in Europe and of the need to check the growth of Spanish power, Marillac pointed to the unsettled state of France: the revolts of nobles and peasants, the general misery and the state's chronic insolvency. Late in 1628 Marillac and Bérulle opposed Richelieu's intervention in the Mantuan succession crisis. They believed it would lead to war with Spain. While the king continued to endorse Richelieu's policy, Marillac and Bérulle won over the queen mother.

As long as Richelieu remained alongside the king, he could be reasonably certain that his policy would carry the day. But, ironically, the war in Italy which he had unleashed brought about his temporary separation from the king. Early in 1630, as Louis XIII planned to lead his army across the Alps, he was persuaded not to do so as long as his brother remained in exile abroad. Louis consequently remained in France to negotiate his brother's return, leaving Richelieu in charge of the invasion of Italy. His capture on 29 March of Pinerolo, a strategically important place in Savoy, raised a major question of policy: should France provoke a war with Spain by keeping Pinerolo, or should she hand it back as part of a peace settlement?[6] Richelieu believed that France should retain Pinerolo, whatever the risks, in order to maintain her influence in Italy and, in a famous memorandum addressed to Louis, he laid out the arguments for and against such a course. It was for the king to decide.

Louis, by this time, had brought his brother back to France and was, therefore, free to join Richelieu. He was in favour of keeping Pinerolo, but would not finally commit himself until he had obtained the approval of his queen and queen mother. He asked Richelieu to negotiate with Marie, but she found excuses for not doing so. Eventually, the French court fell into two camps: while the two queens and Marillac were in Lyons, Louis and Richelieu supervised military operations from St Jean-de-Maurienne. On 25 July, however, the king fell ill and returned to Lyons, leaving Richelieu behind with the army. The cardinal had reason to fear that Louis would fall under the influence of Marie and Marillac. As plague threatened his safety, he too went to Lyons. His return on 28 August brought together the cast-list for the final showdown between himself and his enemies. Marie, it seems, was strangely divided in her attitude to the cardinal. It fluctuated wildly from day to day and she turned to various spiritual remedies as if to assuage her tormented conscience.

No final decision about policy had been reached by 22 September, when Louis XIII developed a high fever. His chances of survival seemed nil, and Richelieu's anxiety grew as the prospect of Monsieur succeeding to the throne loomed larger each day. On 30 September, however, the king's condition suddenly improved. Richelieu expressed his relief to Effiat: 'I pray God to send me death out of his grace rather than allow us to fall back into the state through which we have passed.'[7] But an even more testing time awaited the cardinal.

Early in October Louis had recovered sufficiently to undertake the journey to his beloved Île-de-France. He left Lyons accompanied by Richelieu on 16 October, but four days later, at Roanne, news reached him of the Treaty of Regensburg.[8] As this required a conciliar debate, Louis ordered Richelieu to wait for the arrival of the queen mother and the council while he himself continued on his journey to Paris. At the council meeting, which Marie chaired in her son's absence, Richelieu and Marillac clashed over the treaty: Richelieu wanted it repudiated whereas Marillac was in favour of endorsing it. Curiously, Marie sided with Richelieu, which made him think that he was back in her good books. But, as a contemporary pointed out, she was a Florentine to whom the art of dissimulation was second nature. She had apparently extracted a promise from Louis during his recent illness that on returning to Paris he would dismiss the cardinal. On reaching La Charité-sur-Loire, she wrote reminding him of this promise. But Louis continued to promise Richelieu his support. 'Be assured,' he wrote, 'of my affection which will always be as you would wish it to be.'

By 9 November the king, the queen mother and the cardinal were all in Paris at their respective residences. The stage was set for the Day of Dupes, one of the most dramatic episodes in French history. In describing it most historians have drawn on a history by Vittorio Siri, who owed his information to Louis XIII's favourite, Claude de Saint-Simon, father of the famous memorialist. They have also used various contemporary memoirs. But, as Pierre Chevallier has shown, these sources contain inaccuracies and disagreements.[9] They are not even agreed about the date of the Day of Dupes, some choosing 10 November and others the 11th. It is by no means certain that Claude de Saint-Simon was always an eye-witness of the events he described. A far more reliable account of what happened may be pieced together from the dispatches of foreign ambassadors who were in Paris at the time. They offer incontrovertible evidence that the Day of Dupes was spread over two days: Sunday 10 November and Monday 11 November.

On 10 November Louis XIII attended morning mass at Notre-Dame. Then, in the afternoon, he presided over a council meeting at the Luxembourg palace, his mother's residence. Marie, Richelieu and Marillac were all present. They decided to appoint the latter's brother, marshal de Marillac, as commander of the French army in Italy. Immediately afterwards Marie threw off her mask. In her son's presence, she told Richelieu that for more than a year she had lost faith in him and that she no longer needed his services as superintendent of her household. His dismissal entailed that of all his relatives and friends. The king, hoping no doubt that he would again be able to patch up relations between his mother and the cardinal, advised Richelieu to take formal leave of Marie the next day before joining him at Versailles.

On Monday 11 November at 11.30 a.m. Richelieu returned to the Luxembourg to take formal leave of the queen mother. He found the doors closed against him, but, being well acquainted with the layout of the palace, he managed to reach her room by way of the chapel. Marie and the king were engaged in conversation when the cardinal suddenly appeared. 'Are Your Majesties talking about me?' he asked. 'Yes,' replied the queen haughtily. Then, exploding with anger, she said that she could no longer conceal her hatred of the cardinal or suffer his arrogance. She ordered him to go, adding that she never wanted to see or hear of him again. Richelieu, in reply, blamed his own bad fortune. No disgrace, he said, could be worse for him than the loss of Her Majesty's protection. He begged the king to let him retire since he had become hateful to his mother and had nothing to hope for. According to one account, Marie told her son that either she or the cardinal would have to leave the court, while Louis told Richelieu that he would continue to use his services and would never banish him. The cardinal, however, had been shattered by Marie's diatribe. He knelt and sobbed and, before leaving the room, kissed the hem of her dress.

As news of his dismissal spread through the palace, a joyful crowd gathered around the queen mother. She announced that Marillac was Richelieu's successor.

After he had returned to his residence at the Petit-Luxembourg, Richelieu was advised by cardinal de La Vallette to keep the king in his sights. Otherwise, he said, Louis would soon forget him and succumb to the influence of his enemies. The warning proved unnecessary, for the king summoned Richelieu to Versailles. This was unusual, for Versailles was then only a modest country retreat to which the king liked to escape from the cares of state; the council never met there. When Richelieu arrived that evening, he threw himself at the feet of Louis and thanked him, calling him 'the best of all masters'. The king, for his part, called the cardinal 'the most loyal and most devoted servant in the world'. He blamed a cabal for his mother's attitude and promised to protect the cardinal from its intrigues. After giving him a room under his own roof, Louis dismissed his entourage and talked to the cardinal alone for four hours. The gist of their conversation is known, as Richelieu reported it to two of his creatures. He once again offered to resign, but the king would not listen. 'I order you absolutely,' he said, 'to remain and continue directing my affairs; that is my irrevocable decision.' Later that evening, Louis presided over a council meeting. A notable absentee was Marillac, who, unlike his fellow ministers, had been ordered to go to Glatigny, a village near Versailles. Realising what this meant, he spent part of the night burning his papers. At the council meeting, Louis announced Marillac's dismissal and his replacement as Keeper of the Seals by M. de Châteauneuf, one of Richelieu's creatures. Soon afterwards, Marillac was arrested and imprisoned at Caen. He was later transferred to a prison at Châteaudun, where he died in 1632. Meanwhile, an order was sent to Italy for the arrest of his brother, marshal de Marillac, who was eventually tried and executed.

Louis XIII, whose firmness throughout these proceedings belies the portrait painted of him by contemporary memorialists, informed his mother of the decisions taken at Versailles. She could not believe her ears and would have gone post haste to Versailles had she not been strongly dissuaded. The atmosphere in her entourage turned suddenly from joy to despair, and she soon found herself deserted by those who, only the day before, had flocked to congratulate her.

Richelieu's triumph was now widely interpreted as the victory of the *bons Français* over the Spaniards who were accused of having engineered the attempted *coup d'état*. But his triumph was not yet assured. For a large question mark still hung over him: would Marie ever accept him? And if not, could he continue serving the king? Louis had not yet abandoned hope of a reconciliation and, in December, he almost succeeded with the help of the nuncio, Bagni. Marie agreed to see Richelieu at council meetings, but would not have him run her household.

Soon afterwards an event occurred which precipitated the queen mother's fate. Her son, Gaston, had so far followed the wind. After rejoicing with his mother at the Luxembourg, he had assured Richelieu, on 6 December, of his friendship and protection. But Monsieur allowed himself to be manipulated by two of his creatures, Puylaurens and Le Coigneux. They were infuriated by a decision of the king's council to defer the implementation of promises made to them by Richelieu. On 31 January 1631 Gaston went to the Palais Cardinal. Accusing Richelieu of bad faith, he declared himself no longer bound by his assurance of 6 December. As Richelieu tried to exculpate himself, Gaston broke off the interview, saying that he would defend himself, if attacked. He then left Paris for Orléans. Soon afterwards, the court moved to Compiègne, where a council meeting considered the new crisis. Richelieu, speaking last, looked at four possible solutions. The one he professedly favoured was that he himself should stand down, but his fellow-ministers preferred his fourth option, which was to destroy the opposition by banishing the queen mother. The king acted accordingly. He placed Marie under house arrest and ordered her banishment to Moulins. Several members of her household were also expelled or imprisoned. On 23 February the king left Compiègne without even taking leave of his mother. He was never to see her again.

On 18 July, Marie escaped from Compiègne. She made for the border town of La Capelle, where she had been offered asylum by an enemy of the cardinal, but her plan was foiled, leaving her no option but to seek refuge in the Spanish Netherlands. From here she lodged a formal complaint against Richelieu with the Parlement of Paris, demanding his trial. But on 12 August Louis XIII went to the Parlement. He denounced his mother's petition as libellous, declared her advisers guilty of *lèse-majesté*, forbade all dealings with them and ordered the confiscation of Marie's revenues. This marked the final breach between mother and son. She was to die in exile at Cologne in 1642.

The queen mother's banishment removed a serious threat to Richelieu's tenure of power. It would be wrong, however, to assume that his relations with the king were henceforth cloudless. Gaston d'Orléans remained a threat for at least as long as he was heir to the throne. Richelieu also had to be wary of the king's male favourites and of the queen. He could not assume Louis's continued support. It had to be worked for. As he himself admitted, the four square feet of the king's study were more difficult to conquer than all the battlefields of Europe.

. . .

RICHELIEU THE MAN

Two contradictory portraits exist of Richelieu. One is of a bloodthirsty tyrant, who caused his enemies to be imprisoned or executed, and who imposed his tyranny on a weak and unwilling monarch. The other is of a statesman of genius who restored France's greatness after her civil wars. It is claimed that he invented or revived the idea of France's 'natural frontiers', laid the foundations of absolute monarchy and promoted the centralisation of the kingdom. Neither portrait is now accepted without serious qualifications by historians.

Physically, Richelieu is well known, thanks largely to the portraits painted by Philippe de Champaigne. Tall and slim of stature, he had a long face with refined features: a high forehead, arched brows, large brown eyes, a long, thin and slightly curved nose, a well-shaped mouth and a strong chin beneath a pointed and neatly trimmed beard.

However, the cardinal's handsome looks were not matched by good health. Richelieu suffered from splitting headaches for much of his life. Periodically, he succumbed to fevers. In November 1632 he fell gravely ill on a journey to Bordeaux. An abscess on the bladder stopped him urinating. A surgeon cured the trouble, but it returned in 1635. The cardinal found travel difficult, even by litter, and feared that he would soon be bedridden. But surgery again came to the rescue: it relieved the pain but left Richelieu depressed. 'If I have been regarded hitherto as a sound diamond,' he wrote to the king, 'I now regard myself as an Alençon diamond that is no stronger than glass.' He also suffered from haemorrhoids. So painful were they in May 1634 that he anticipated having to be carried to Paris on a stretcher. In June he thanked the king for certain kindnesses 'which are the only things apart from the grace of God which enable me to put up with the continual troubles of my miserable health'. 'My rheumatism,' he added, 'is still affecting one side or other of my body, but only slightly; it is now in my jaw but I am treating it as best I can with small remedies.' The cardinal also suffered from chronic insomnia. He would wake up about 2 a.m. and work with a secretary till 5 a.m. Sometimes he would be read to in the early hours.[10]

Richelieu's enemies spread the story that every month he shut himself up in a room with a servant and a doctor and spent two or three days shouting, foaming at the mouth and hiding under beds. This story falls into the same kind of gossip as the story of Hitler chewing carpets. But Richelieu was certainly highly strung. The cool, self-controlled exterior which he usually presented to the world concealed an exceedingly nervous temperament. Bad news had to be broken to him gently. He would shed tears at the drop of a hat, causing Marie de' Medici to comment contemptuously: 'he cries whenever he wants to'. Sometimes Richelieu would hide his emotion by taking to his bed. He was also prone to melancholia. His friend, the bishop of Lavaur, wrote: 'He had a melancholic spirit and was infected by the weakness of black bile.'[11] His health understandably preoccupied him. His household included a physician, an apothecary and a surgeon, who were kept on their toes. Richelieu was bled once a week and given an enema daily. His drug bill was large: in 1635 it amounted to more than 1,401 *livres*.[12]

The cardinal led a frugal life. He liked to eat meals alone and was content with two courses per meal. Afterwards he would relax. At Rueil, he would take a walk in the gardens. He liked to listen to music, though he could not give much time to it. His chief form of relaxation was conversation. He was a countryman at heart, disliking the noises and smells of Paris. He much preferred the suburbs; above all he enjoyed 'the solitude of Rueil'. Richelieu was a loner. He disliked giving audiences and incurred unpopularity by giving as few as possible.

Many people found the cardinal intimidating. He often seemed cold and haughty, and he admitted himself that he was not always able to give people the courteous treatment their condition demanded. Yet on occasion he could be affable and charming. In 1629 the people of Montauban, whom he had just defeated in a military campaign, were amazed by his 'sweetness and modesty' which belied the awesome reputation that had preceded his coming. His friends regarded the portrait of him painted by hostile pamphleteers as a grotesque distortion. Shyness, of which Richelieu often complained, may partly explain his coldness towards strangers. To his close friends he could be warmly affectionate. Thus, when Father Coton arrived unexpectedly after a long absence, Richelieu broke off an audience with two ambassadors to throw himself around his friend's neck and kiss him effusively. He was popular with his servants, whom he treated kindly and generously. Desbournais, his *valet de chambre,* who had entered his service at the age of 17, stayed with him to the end of his life.[13]

Everyone who came into contact with Richelieu was impressed by his intelligence. 'Reason,' he wrote, 'must be the universal rule and guide; all things must be done according to reason without allowing oneself to be swayed by emotion.' His numerous memoranda to the king reveal his precise appreciation of state problems. He would go straight to their heart, balancing the arguments for and against a particular course of action. At the end he would leave the king to decide but would usually state a preference. Firmness was the quality he placed second to reason as essential to good statesmanship. 'Government,' he wrote, 'needs masculine virtue and an unshakeable firmness.' He did not allow himself to be moved from a decision once he had convinced himself of its correctness. Yet he was cautious by nature, admitting that he had always lived to regret decisions taken in anger. He advised French ambassadors abroad to show reserve and calm. His firmness was often construed as severity, for he believed that law and order could only be maintained by repression. People, in his view, remembered punishments longer than rewards. This was especially true of the French, who were naturally undisciplined. Yet he did not believe in violence for its own sake. 'A government,' he said, 'cannot survive where no one is satisfied and everyone is treated violently. Rigour is very dangerous where no one is contented.' Richelieu sometimes favoured moderation. 'It is far preferable,' he said, 'that men should return to their duty by themselves than by force, which is a remedy that God and men only use in default of the first.' The king, not Richelieu, was directly responsible for the most sensational beheadings of the reign.[14]

Catholic zealots, angered by Richelieu's willingness to allow the Huguenots freedom of conscience, accused him of being a Protestant, even an atheist. The charge is patently absurd. In so far as it is possible for us to know, Richelieu had a faith. His daily routine was punctuated by devotions. He prayed each morning and evening and attended mass daily. Each Sunday he went to confession and took communion. When he celebrated mass himself – only on important feast days and on feasts of the Virgin – he did so with 'exemplary reverence'. At Easter he would take a retreat in a monastery. Religious scruples caused him to seek dispensations from Rome. Thus he was authorised to take part in conciliar debates which might lead to 'effusions of blood'. He was also released from the priestly obligation of reading his breviary each day. Instead, he was to repeat the office of the Cross. Richelieu was ever conscious of mortality. 'We are like boatmen,' he said, 'who turn their backs on the places they are trying to reach; we try to distance ourselves from the thought of death, yet we do nothing but march towards it.'[15]

Richelieu, for all his political preoccupations, still found time to deal with religious matters. His household was full of churchmen. All his chamberlains became bishops, as did some of his confessors. Among the latter was Jacques Lescot, a distinguished theologian, who became one of the foremost reforming prelates. Richelieu's close friend, Father Joseph, was reputed as a preacher, missionary, reformer and author of spiritual works. He had a room that communicated with the cardinal's and had assistants, who were all Capuchins like himself. Among Richelieu's other close friends were two Jesuits, Georges Fournier and Jacques Sirmond, Henri de

Sourdis, archbishop of Bordeaux and Charles-François Abra de Raconis, to whom we are indebted for one of the best pen portraits of the cardinal. He held strongly ultramontane views and was among the first opponents of Jansenism. In 1636 he became bishop of Lavaur. Another friend of the cardinal was the Englishman Richard Smith, who founded a convent of English nuns – the *Dames anglaises* – in Paris.

Throughout his ministerial career Richelieu continued to be interested in church reform. He frequently discussed the establishment of seminaries, as laid down by the Council of Trent, with St Vincent de Paul, who opened one in Paris in 1642. He also persuaded the general of the Oratorians to set up seminaries in several houses of his order. Another of Richelieu's major preoccupations was finding worthy candidates for the episcopate. He found several among members of his entourage, but also asked others, including St Vincent, to recommend names. His efforts resulted in the saintliest bench of French bishops of the century. Finally, as Richelieu made plain in his *Testament politique,* he was keenly interested in the reform of religious houses. He urged the Benedictines and Cistercians to observe their rule and encouraged reform among the mendicants. But he was especially interested in female conventuals. Thus it was with his support that Father Joseph founded the nuns of Notre-Dame du Calvaire whose idea it was that Louis XIII should dedicate his kingdom to the Virgin Mary. Richelieu was also a close friend of the Carmelites of the rue St Jacques. Finally, he shared with Father Joseph an interest in foreign missions. In the words of the bishop of Lavaur, 'his zeal for the Glory of God was boundless'.[16] However, as a monastic reformer he achieved little, for he placed his authority behind groups of uncompromising reformers in each order. They provoked a strong opposition among the majority of monks by their use of force. In the end the opposition, led by the abbot of Clairvaux and supported by Pope Urban VIII, won the day, leading to a reaction in 1643, which one historian has called the 'Fronde of the monks'.[17]

Despite his onerous ministerial responsibilities, Richelieu found time to write theological works. According to his confessor, he 'devoted to this not only what remained to him of hours in the day, but also usually a great part of the night'.[18] His religious writings show a solid grounding in the Catholic faith. Although his magnificent library contained mystical works by St John of the Cross and St Teresa of Avila, he was not inclined towards mysticism himself. 'He did not possess to any degree that sense of spiritual sinfulness that is so striking among the mystics, who were always so worried about the impurity brought by pride into the motives of the finest deeds.' Richelieu regarded mystics as dangerous, and gave practical expression to this belief by committing the abbé of St Cyran to prison at Vincennes in May 1638. Several chapters of Richelieu's unfinished *Traité de la Perfection du Chrétien* were directed against St Cyran. 'Contemplation,' wrote the cardinal, 'is far more liable to deceive than action. . . . It is very dangerous in matters of faith to follow new paths, to have a particular devotion. . . . On this basis many do not think of themselves as truly devout unless they set up a new order.' Throughout his life Richelieu preferred to adhere strictly to the decrees of the Council of Trent.[19]

Richelieu's private life was free from scandal. His enemies tried to add licentiousness to the many charges they levelled at him. They claimed that in his youth he had enjoyed certain *voluptés*. It was rumoured that he had lived 'rather familiarly' with Madame Bouthillier, and that she had given him a son. But no documentary evidence bears out this allegation. Even less likely is the story that Richelieu was the lover of Queen Anne of Austria. As a historian has recently written: 'Every posthumous rumor of Richelieu's sexual indiscretions has been thoroughly canvassed and dismissed.'[20] The cardinal, it seems, did not have a very high opinion of women. 'These animals,' he said of them, 'are very strange. One sometimes thinks they must be incapable of doing much harm, because they are incapable of doing any good; but I protest on my conscience that there is nothing so well able to ruin a state as they are.'[21]

Richelieu was not an austere person. He did not wear a monk's habit under his red robes. He was the richest man in France and lived extravagantly. He bought lands, built fine houses and collected works of art. His household was comparable in size and splendour to that of the greatest nobleman. It comprised courtiers, secretaries, servants, soldiers and pages.[22] His enemies claimed that when he left his residence the street outside was so crowded with coaches that onlookers shouted 'Vive le roi!' by mistake. Yet, in spite of all this magnificence and of Richelieu's efforts to glorify his achievements and perpetuate his name, he could appear modest. If he were praised to his face, he would look away or seem uninterested. His private lifestyle was simple. All this serves to demonstrate that Richelieu was a complex personality full of subtleties and apparent contradictions.

Few statesmen of the past have been so reviled as Richelieu. He has been called vain, faithless, arrogant, sly, vindictive, cruel, grasping and much else besides. He was far from perfect and did not always live up to the fine sentiments he expressed in writing. In the pursuit of his ambitions he could be calculating and sickeningly obsequious. In following his ideals he could be ruthless. He may not always have been straight in his political dealings, and his dedication to the greatness of Louis XIII and France may not have been as single-minded as his admirers have affirmed. He systematically amassed one of the largest private fortunes of the ancien régime. Nor did he have any scruples about using his power and influence to promote his kinsmen. His vices, however, may have been outweighed by his virtues, not the least by his resignation in the face of abuse. 'Whatever one does,' he wrote, 'the public will not do you justice. Great men who serve the state are like men sentenced to death. The only difference is that the latter are punished for their sins and the former for their virtues.'[23]

. . .

NOTES AND REFERENCES

1. Battifol L 1934 *Richelieu et le roi Louis XIII*. Paris, Calmann-Lévy, p. 101.
2. Dethan G 1959 *Gaston d'Orléans, conspirateur et prince charmant*. Paris.
3. Bonney R 1981 *The King's Debts*. Oxford, Clarendon, pp. 130–32.
4. Chevallier P 1979 *Louis XIII*. Paris, Fayard, p. 361.
5. Ibid., pp. 353–53; Pagès G 1937 'Autour du "Grand Orage": Richelieu et Marillac: deux politiques' in *Revue historique* 179: 64–7.
6. Ibid., p. 82.
7. Chevallier *Louis XIII*, p. 373.
8. See below, p. 96.

9. Chevallier *Louis XIII* pp. 379–81.
10. Battifol L *Richelieu et le roi Louis XIII,* pp. 23–5; Deloche M 1912 *La maison du cardinal de Richelieu.* Paris, Champion, pp. 197–201; Marvick E W 1983 *The Young Richelieu.* Chicago, Chicago University Press, pp. 121–122.
11. Battifol *Richelieu et le roi Louis XIII,* p. 25.
12. Deloche, *La maison du cardinal de Richelieu,* pp. 201, 208.
13. Battifol, *Richelieu et le roi Louis XIII,* pp. 33–7.
14. Ibid., pp. 30–1.
15. Ibid., pp. 45–7, 50–1.
16. Darricau R 1985 'Richelieu et les hommes d'église' in *Richelieu et le monde de l'esprit.* Paris, Imprimerie nationale, pp. 265–76.
17. Briggs R 1989 *Communities of Belief: Cultural and Social Tensions in Early Modern France.* Oxford, Clarendon, pp. 204–5; Elliott J H 1982 *Richelieu and Olivares.* Cambridge University Press, p. 75.
18. Blet P 1972 'La Religion du Cardinal' in A. Adam *et al. Richelieu,* Paris, Hachette, p. 172.
19. Orcibal J 1948 'Richelieu, homme d'église, homme d'État, à propos d'un ouvrage recént' in *Revue d'histoire de l'église de France* XXXIV: pp. 94–101.
20. Ibid., pp. 51–3; Marvick, *The Young Richelieu,* p. 101. But in 1605 'Monsieur de Lusson', who was almost certainly Richelieu, was treated for 'gonorrhoea inveterata' by the king's physician. See Bergin, J., 1991 *The Rise of Richelieu* New Haven, CT p. 58.
21. Huxley A 1941 *Eminence Grise.* London, Chatto & Windus, p. 130.
22. Deloche, *La maison du cardinal de Richelieu, passim.*
23. Battifol, *Richelieu et le roi Louis XIII,* p. 50.

Chapter 4

RICHELIEU AND THE HIGH NOBILITY

Richelieu, in the opening section of his *Testament politique*, recalls some of the promises he made to Louis XIII. One was to employ all the industry and authority which the king cared to give him 'to abase the pride of the nobles'.[1] It would be wrong, however, to deduce from this statement that the cardinal was hostile to the nobility as such. Other parts of the *Testament politique* show a high regard for the Second Estate. It is described as 'the nerve of the state' and is seen as the backbone of the army. Richelieu deplored the erosion suffered by the nobility's economic position as a result of the inflation of venal offices. He urged the king to promote its revival in various ways: for example, by appointing only noblemen to governorships, military commands and court offices.[2] In his own personal affairs Richelieu was 'a perfect example of aristocratic values'. He devoted much attention to raising his family to the heights of aristocratic splendour and imitated the *grands* in every respect, save their fractious political conduct. He acquired lands, titles and palaces to rival the greatest of them and arranged marriages for his relatives with members of ancient families. His niece, Claire Clémence de Brézé, married the future 'Grand Condé' in 1641.[3]

Richelieu, then, placed a high value on the nobility, believing sincerely that it had an important contribution to make to the life of the nation. But he also believed passionately that all nobles, even the highest, should abstain from political intrigues and be loyal to the Crown. This view, however, which is understandable enough today, did not accord well with the concept of service to the king which the French aristocracy had inherited from its feudal past. Nobles regarded themselves as vassals rather than subjects;

they saw their service to the king as personal and voluntary. The king in their view shared in the quality of nobility: he was *primus inter pares*. Their relationship with him rested on mutual obligations of honour and fealty. At the same time, clientage was very important to the nobility. A nobleman commonly sought advancement by attaching himself to the service of another, more influential member of the same estate.[4] Thus some nobles at the court of Louis XIII tied themselves to the destinies of Gaston d'Orléans, Louis XIII's turbulent brother, who dragged his clients into a series of plots against Richelieu and his policies.[5]

The earliest of these plots stemmed from a proposal, backed by Richelieu, for the marriage of Gaston with Mademoiselle de Montpensier. This was strongly opposed by a group of nobles with ramifications as far afield as Holland and England. As the opposition grew, Louis ordered a number of arrests. The first was that of marshal d'Ornano (6 May 1626) on a charge that his seditious advice had impaired relations between the king and his brother. He was clapped in prison and died a few weeks later of natural causes, much to the regret of Richelieu, who would have liked to make him stand trial.[6] On 13 June the king's half-brothers, César and Alexandre de Vendôme, were arrested. But the most famous detention was that of the comte de Chalais on 8 July.

He was incarcerated at Nantes, where the court was in residence at the time, and charged with *lèse-majesté*. A special court was set up to try him and a verdict of guilty was swiftly reached. Chalais was the grandson of the famous sixteenth-century marshal Monluc, author of the *Commentaires*, and his mother pleaded for her son's life by reminding the king of the services rendered by her family to former kings of France. However, Louis and Richelieu were unmoved. On 19 August Chalais was executed in the most gruesome way. In the absence of the regular executioner, a convict was persuaded to act in his place. As no axe was available, a sword was used instead. But the convict did not know how to use it. After hacking at his victim's head more than fifteen times, he had to finish him off with twenty-nine blows from a cooper's mallet.[7] Richelieu approved of the rigour that had been displayed. In a memorandum to the king written shortly after Chalais's death, he warned him of the consequences of allowing plots against himself to succeed. Not only would

Louis lose his most devoted servant, he would also destroy the confidence of others in the king's protection and they would seek safety elsewhere.[8]

Two other measures were taken against the turbulent nobility in 1626. In February the king banned duelling, and in July he ordered the destruction of all castles situated at a distance from the kingdom's frontiers.[9] Duelling become a veritable craze in the sixteenth century. It had been condemned by the Council of Trent and various laws had been passed in France (for example, in 1566 and 1579) against it, but all to no effect. Richelieu had personal reasons for disliking duels. His father had killed a man in one and his eldest brother had died in another. The edict of February 1626 imposed heavy penalties on duellists. Challenging to a duel was to be punished by the loss of offices, confiscation of half the culprit's property and his banishment for three years. A duel which did not end fatally was punishable by loss of noble status, infamy or death according to circumstances; a fatal duel was to be treated as *lèse-majesté*. It was to protest against this edict that the comte de Bouteville, victor of twenty-two duels, staged another between six participants in the Place Royale on 14 May 1627. It left one dead – the equally famous Bussy d'Amboise – and one seriously wounded. Bouteville and his cousin, des Chapelles, one of the participants in the duel, fled from Paris, but were soon captured and thrown into the Bastille. Bouteville, however, was no mere duellist: he belonged to the illustrious family of Montmorency-Luxembourg, so that his trial was bound to have profound political significance. The duc de Montmorency and the prince of Condé appealed to the king's clemency, as did the comtesse de Bouteville and other aristocratic ladies. Speaking of the countess, who was three months pregnant, Louis XIII said: 'I pity the woman, but I must defend my authority.' For this reason, Bouteville and his cousin were duly executed on 22 June 1627 in the Place de Grève. Reflecting on this event, Richelieu wrote: 'it is impossible for a noble heart not to feel sympathy for this poor young nobleman whose youth and courage evoked deep compassion.' But the rivers of blood which the nobility drew from the duels had given the cardinal the strength to overcome his feelings and to strengthen the king's resolve to act in the state's interest.[10]

The death of Bouteville shocked public opinion so much that Richelieu's propaganda machine had to be used to justify it. An official pamphlet, entitled *Les Paroles de la France à la noblesse française*, presented duelling as an offence against God, the king and the French nation. Another in the form of a letter from a Dutchman argued that duelling among French noblemen played into the hands of France's chief enemy, Spain. While they were slaughtering each other, Spain was preparing to dominate the world. In a third pamphlet, the ghost of Bouteville advised his former companions to avoid his example: 'Be wise at my expense, take advantage of my loss and renounce this unfortunate custom of duelling which a fury has brought into France out of hell to destroy souls and bodies and to weaken the kingdom in the interest of its foes.'[11]

How far did Richelieu succeed in stamping out duelling? His *Mémoires* would have us believe that he and the king had won a notable victory over the aristocracy. This may have been true for a time. No duels are mentioned in the *Mercure françois* for the years that immediately followed Bouteville's execution. Maybe they did not take place or were carefully concealed. By 1629, however, Richelieu chided his master for his slackness in applying his laws, especially the edict on duels. The next decade undoubtedly saw a revival of duelling at court. In 1631 Montmorency and Chevreuse drew their swords in the king's garden at Monceau. They were soon separated and banished to their country seats. Within weeks they were back at court. In May 1634 Louis XIII renewed the edict of 1626, complaining that 'the abuse is once more getting the upper hand over the laws'. A widely publicised fatal duel took place in 1638 and many more in February 1639. Realising the futility of punishing all the violators of the 1626 edict, Louis pardoned them in 1638 and 1640. In his final years Richelieu again faced up to the problem of duelling. He wrote about it in the *Testament politique* and ordered a new ordinance, which was published after his death, in 1643. The preamble admits that neither clemency nor severity had proved effective against the evil. Thus Richelieu cannot be given credit for the eventual disappearance of duelling.[12]

At the Assembly of Notables of 1626–27 Richelieu tried to increase royal control of the nobility. Aristocratic unrest occupied an important place in the agenda for the meeting.

On 2 December both Richelieu and Marillac argued the case for more effective means of suppressing revolts. Marillac explained that even if guilt was proven in Chalais's case, this was not always true. Where proof was lacking, the Crown was within the law in acting on conjecture. Richelieu said that expenditure on state security was justified even when economies were necessary. He suggested, as a means of winning the notables' backing, a reduction of penalties for disobedience balanced by their speedier application. However, it is doubtful if he really intended any leniency. His marginal comment to the proposal points to his true state of mind:

> Kings are kings only as long as their authority is recognized and they demonstrate their favour. They are unable to ensure the effects of these unless they are strictly obeyed, since disobedience by one individual is capable of arresting the course of a plan whose effects will benefit the public. Obedience is the true characteristic of the subject.[13]

After lengthy debates the notables agreed to all the cardinal's proposals, including the destruction of castles away from the frontiers.

Not all Richelieu's acts during the assembly were hostile to the nobility's interests. A number of the concessions requested by the Second Estate in a lengthy remonstrance were incorporated in the *Code Michau*. They reveal a genuine concern for the plight of the nobility. But the cardinal would not allow it to dabble in affairs of state as of right. Politics were exclusively for the king and his ministers to decide.

In January 1629, five months before the Peace of Alès ended Huguenot resistance to the Crown, Richelieu submitted an important memorandum to the king, suggesting ways of tightening up the effectiveness of his authority in domestic and foreign affairs. Controlling the great nobles and limiting their seditious activities were among the cardinal's major preoccupations.[14] He approached the problem cautiously. With regard to Monsieur, he advised the king to satisfy him as far as possible without prejudice to the state. He should give favours to the *grands* and support them where necessary so as to deter them from lending their services to other princes. At the same time Louis needed to step up his efforts to enforce his laws. Crimes against the state had to be punished with extreme harshness, otherwise it would not survive.

The Day of Dupes, vitally important as it was in confirming Richelieu's hold on the government, did not set a term to aristocratic plots aimed at his overthrow.[15] These continued until the last months of the reign. Even after their flight abroad in 1631, Marie de' Medici and Gaston d'Orléans retained the sympathies of many important persons in France. They were also able to disrupt Louis' control over his subjects as well as his relations with foreign powers. As heir to the throne, Monsieur commanded a large, if indeterminate, following within the kingdom. French opinion was also sharply divided over the justice of the self-imposed exile of Gaston and his mother. During 1631 many pamphlets arrived in Paris, supporting their cause. On 30 March Louis issued a declaration, condemning as guilty of *lèse-majesté* all who had advised his brother to leave the realm, followed him into exile or raised troops on his behalf. Gaston for his part published a letter to the king on 1 April justifying his exile as the result of the ill-treatment he and his mother had suffered. This was followed, on 30 April, by a much longer letter, commonly referred to as Gaston d'Orléans's Manifesto, which heaped all the blame for France's troubles on Richelieu. The logical riposte to this charge was that the cardinal's policies were those of the government only because Louis XIII had approved them. This, in essence, was Louis' reply to Gaston: the criticisms he had levelled at royal policy did not deserve a detailed reply. The king, however, wished to make one point clear:

> I know the qualities and capacity of those whose services I employ, and God has given me the grace to understand my affairs better than those who mistakenly attempt to interfere by discussing them. It is neither for you nor them to censure my actions and those of the men whom I employ in my service. You have no power over them; on the contrary, it is up to me to cause your followers to be punished if they do wrong.[16]

One of the principal victims of the Day of Dupes was Marshal Louis de Marillac, who, as commander of the French army in Italy, was in a position to bring troops into France and stir up trouble. There is not a shred of evidence that such a move ever crossed his mind, but Richelieu decided to take no chances. The marshal was arrested and brought back to France for trial by a special court. The judges were carefully picked by Richelieu himself and, when they seemed disinclined to convict the marshal, he transferred the court to his own house at Rueil, doubtless so as to intimidate them. The outcome, in spite of the marshal's stout defence, was never in doubt. He was sentenced to death on 8 May 1632 and two days later beheaded in the Place de Grève. Significantly, the records of his trial were destroyed by royal command.[17] Marillac's execution had been intended as an example to others who might be tempted to challenge Richelieu's authority. It would have served this purpose more effectively perhaps if the marshal had not been an innocent victim. The sheer iniquity of his fate stirred deep feelings of resentment towards the cardinal. Chanteloube, one of Marie de' Medici's pamphleteers, voiced a widespread sentiment when he wrote:

> To-day it is generally accepted that it is just to imprison anyone because of the slightest wish of a favourite (for all know that these acts do not come from the king). Every suspicion is cause for imprisonment; every imprisonment is authorized by the judges. Every pretext is a crime; every crime is subject to condemnation; every condemnation is for not less than life. Whoever displeases a favourite is put in prison, and whoever is in prison must be executed to justify the act of him who caused him to be imprisoned. Are these maxims of state or of hell?[18]

Socially, Marillac was not particularly exalted. The same cannot be said of the cardinal's next major victim: Henri duc de Montmorency. He belonged to one of the most high-ranking houses which had given France over the centuries five constables, two grand masters, seven marshals, five admirals and two great chamberlains. Henri was a prince of the blood, Henry IV's godson and brother-in-law to the prince of Condé. As governor of Languedoc he lived almost like a king in the south of France. Potentially, of course, he was dangerous since his province bordered on Spain, France's chief foreign enemy. But for a long time his loyalty was not in question. He was not pleased when Richelieu eased him out of the Admiralty of France. Nor did he take kindly to the execution of his cousin, Bouteville. But his relations with the cardinal remained amicable enough thereafter: in September 1630 he offered Richelieu a refuge in Languedoc when his survival was threatened by Louis XIII's grave illness.

In 1631, however, serious trouble broke out in Languedoc as a result of Richelieu's efforts to introduce *élus* into the province, a move deeply resented by the local estates as a breach of their traditional privileges. Montmorency did not oppose the *élus*, but negotiated a compromise satisfactory to both sides. It was agreed that royal commissioners, not *élus*, would apportion taxation which would be levied only with the estates' authority. But there remained enough unease in the province for the queen mother and Gaston d'Orléans to stir up trouble for the government. Montmorency found himself under pressure from the bishop of Albi and other local supporters of the royal exiles to support their cause. The duke was informed that Gaston would soon march at the head of an army supplied by Spain and the duke of Lorraine. By July 1632 he had decided to throw in his lot with Monsieur. The risks attached to such a course were great and Montmorency talked of offering his services to Gustavus Adolphus should the conspiracy fail.[19]

In mid-June 1632 Gaston d'Orléans led a small army into France from Luxemburg and made his way south so as to join Montmorency in Languedoc. He issued a proclamation protesting his loyalty to the king while calling on all Frenchmen to free him from the cardinal's tyranny. Richelieu was denounced as

> a disturber of the public peace, enemy of the king and the royal family, destroyer of the state, usurper of all the best offices in the realm, tyrant over a great number of persons of quality whom he has oppressed, and generally all the people of France whom he has overburdened.

Gaston hoped that Dijon would open its gates to him, but they remained shut. Meanwhile, Montmorency threw down the gauntlet by ordering the arrest of the king's commissioners at the Languedoc Estates. On 22 July he was invited by the Estates to join them in an 'indissoluble union for the execution of the king's service and the relief of the province'. In effect, this was a declaration of civil war. On 12 August Louis

XIII condemned all who aided Gaston directly or indirectly as rebels, guilty of *lèse-majesté*.

On 1 September Montmorency and Gaston, who by then had joined forces, met the royal army commanded by marshal Schomberg at Castelnaudary. A swift engagement ensued, in the course of which Montmorency was badly wounded and taken prisoner. His capture proved a serious embarrassment to Richelieu. The duke was patently guilty of high treason and nothing short of his death would satisfy the cardinal's stringent criteria for maintaining order in the kingdom. But, as one of the most important nobles, his trial and execution were bound to cause an explosion of anger among his own kind. Legally, the duke could insist on being tried by his peers in the Parlement of Paris, but he was tried by the Parlement of Toulouse. Where state interest was at stake, Richelieu had no time for legal niceties. Every effort was made within France and abroad to ensure Montmorency's reprieve. Intercessors on his behalf pointed out that he was still in his prime and capable of performing notable services to the king. They pointed to the greatness of his name, his personal qualities and illustrious connections. A crowd gathered outside the archbishop's palace, where the king was in residence, shouting: 'Pardon him, pardon him, have mercy on him.' Even the captain of the king's guard threw himself at Louis' feet, pleading for mercy. But the king snapped back: 'No pardon shall be granted him. He must die.' Montmorency, the last of his line, was accordingly executed in the courtyard of the town hall of Toulouse. He showed great fortitude till the end.[20]

Meanwhile Gaston d'Orléans had come to terms with the king at Béziers, but on 6 November, one week after Montmorency's death, he again fled the kingdom on the excuse that he had been cheated. He had signed the Béziers agreement, he said, in the expectation of saving Montmorency's life. The dashing of that hope had stained his honour. Louis replied that the duke's death was legal in view of his crimes. He was determined to prevent the ruin of his subjects by 'these miserable revolts'. Early in 1633 Richelieu pressed home charges against Gaston's followers. The Parlement of Dijon found them guilty of *lèse-majesté*. Their property was confiscated and, in their absence, they were executed in effigy.

On 19 January a royal declaration stiffened the existing legislation in respect of royal officials guilty of *lèse-majesté*. This was specifically aimed at Le Coigneux, President of the Parlement of Paris, who had repeatedly accompanied Monsieur into exile. As time passed, however, it became clear that Gaston would not be enticed back by such harsh measures. So Richelieu changed his tactics. On 16 January 1634 Louis XIII promised Gaston and his friends, excluding Le Coigneux and a few others, an amnesty if they would return to France within three months. Early in October Gaston and many of his followers, weary of exile, reappeared in France. On 21 October Louis XIII and Gaston were reconciled at St Germain-en-Laye in an emotional scene. Puylaurens, who had taken a major part in secret negotiations that opened the way to this event, was pardoned. Before the end of October Louis forgave all Gaston's hostile acts and pardoned all who had followed him into exile, except Le Coigneux. Their property, offices and titles were restored. Gaston and Richelieu were also reconciled, at least publicly. But the cardinal continued to keep a close watch on Monsieur's activities, administering rebukes to him when necessary.[21]

After France's declaration of war on Spain in May 1635 Richelieu had to watch the French nobility even more closely than before. Any hint, however slight, of treasonable intent needed to be acted upon without delay or too much regard for the letter of the law. Among the first of Richelieu's wartime victims was Louis Clausel, *seigneur* de La Roche, who tried to suborn the duc de Rohan, commander of the French forces in the Valtelline, in the interest of Spain. Rohan, however, seized Clausel and informed Richelieu, who took personal charge of his prosecution. He was condemned by default in October 1635 and executed in November after being tortured. The cardinal argued that Clausel had justified the extra-legal proceedings taken against him by his threat to the state's security. Another nobleman, Adrien de Montluc, comte de Cramail, was more fortunate. He merely expressed defeatist sentiments and urged the king to make peace. Richelieu, fearing his influence with the king, threw him into the Bastille without charge. 'If one does not check factions,' he wrote to the king, 'crushing them at birth when their beginning is so weak that those who are unaware of their nature do not realize that they should be feared, they will grow again and gain strength in an instant in such manner that it is impossible later to resist their violence.'[22] As always, Richelieu was a powerful advocate of the pre-emptive strike. Cramail remained in prison till after Richelieu's death.

In the summer of 1638 the cardinal was shocked to learn that the French army besieging Fuenterrabía had been routed by the Spaniards. His disappointment turned to anger when he found that negligence was to blame. The prince of Condé accused the duc de La Valette of persistently refusing to storm Fuenterrabía, even after its defences had been breached. The duke was quoted as saying that he had paid his troops himself and would use them sparingly. He had even been caught smiling during the retreat. Instead of trying to rebut these charges, La Valette fled to England, where he remained till after Richelieu's death. The cardinal, meanwhile, decided to make an example of him. Normally he should have been tried by his peers in the Parlement of Paris; instead, a special court was set up at St-Germain-en-Laye under chancellor Séguier, who could be relied upon to secure a conviction. When the First President of the Parlement objected, Louis XIII put him firmly in his place: 'I wish to be obeyed,' he said, 'and I give you to understand that all privileges are founded only on bad usage. I do not wish to hear them spoken of.'[23] Eventually, La Valette was found guilty of treason and on 8 June he was executed in effigy in the Place de Grève.

Aristocratic opposition to Richelieu continued, in spite of his severity, almost till the end of his life. In 1642 his authority was seriously threatened by the king's favourite, Henri Coiffier de Ruzé, marquis de Cinq-Mars, whom Richelieu had himself introduced to Louis. At the time, the cardinal imagined that the handsome young man would satisfy the king's emotional need for a favourite without posing a threat to his own ministerial position. But Cinq-Mars had political ambitions which came to the fore after the king had become infatuated with him. At the age of nineteen he was appointed *Grand Écuyer de France* (Master of the Horse) – hence the name 'Monsieur le Grand' by which he was generally known at court. Although besotted with him, Louis was not blind to his faults and sometimes reproached him for his profligacy and dissolute ways. The relationship between the two men was punctuated by emotional tantrums reminiscent of 'lovers' tiffs'. Richelieu was forced at times to intervene, much to the annoyance of Cinq-Mars who began to think that his influence with the king would gain from the cardinal's removal.[24] Cunningly, he tried to detach Louis from Richelieu by playing on the king's disenchantment with the war which was bringing so much suffering to his subjects. He urged Louis to take charge of France's foreign policy. It is possible that in the early 1630s Louis had tried to reach an understanding with Spain behind Richelieu's back. Now it seems that he was ready to try again.[25] For it was widely believed that Richelieu would never make peace, since war made him indispensable to the king.

By working for peace, Cinq-Mars identified himself with a very popular cause in France. He could count on the support of Gaston d'Orléans and all his friends. They included the duc de Bouillon, who held Sedan, and François de Thou, son of the famous historian of that name, who acted as go-between. The plotters sent an emissary to Spain with a draft treaty. They offered to assist a Spanish invasion of France in return for military and financial help. Their aim was initially to overthrow Richelieu; then to make peace with Spain on the basis of a mutual restitution of all conquests. At the same time, France was to abandon her Protestant allies. On 13 March 1642 a treaty was signed with Olivares.[26] Richelieu's assassination may also have been planned by Cinq-Mars, though he always denied this. According to the memoirs of Montglat, Cinq-Mars horrified Louis XIII by suggesting the cardinal's murder. The king objected that it would cause his excommunication. The memoirs may not be taken as Gospel truth, but a letter subsequently written by Louis to chancellor Séguier suggests that the king's loyalty to Richelieu may not have been unshaken. He confessed that he might have complained at times of Richelieu and allowed Cinq-Mars to speak his mind. 'But,' wrote Louis, 'when he went so far as to tell me that it was time to be quit of my said cousin and to offer to do the deed himself, I was filled with horror and revulsion at his wicked thoughts.'

How Richelieu discovered the plot is not clear. His many spies may have got wind of it, but it may have been revealed to him by the queen, Anne of Austria, whom the conspirators had taken into their confidence at an early stage.[27] The text of the Spanish treaty certainly fell into the cardinal's hands. By 11 June he had enough evidence to act against the conspirators. Louis XIII was informed at Narbonne the next day. Though much disturbed by the news, he ordered the arrest of Cinq-Mars, de Thou and Bouillon. As for Gaston d'Orléans, he was promised a royal pardon if he would reveal all he knew. On 7 July he admitted his complicity, but placed the blame for what had happened on Cinq-Mars. Bouillon also came to terms with the king by dint of placing Sedan under French protection.

The chief conspirators, Cinq-Mars and de Thou, were tried in Lyons by a special court presided over by Séguier. Richelieu kept in close touch with the proceedings from a house nearby. On 12 September the two accused were found guilty of treason and sentenced to death. The cardinal wanted Cinq-Mars to be interrogated under torture even after his sentence, but his judges spared him this ordeal after he had assured them that he had nothing more to confess. That same day, he and de Thou were taken in a coach to the place des Terreaux where, in front of a huge crowd, they were beheaded. As in the case of Chalais, the execution was bungled by an amateur. 'Monsieur le Grand,' wrote Richelieu, 'died with constancy and some affectation of despising death; he continued to be haughty even on the scaffold . . . . M. de Thou died showing more anxiety, but with great devoutness and humility.'[28]

The principal plotters were no more, but Richelieu was uncertain of the king's attitude. Louis' hands were not as clean as he would have liked. Bouillon believed that it was with the king's consent that Cinq-Mars had approached him, while de Thou affirmed that it was with Louis' approval that he had negotiated with Spain. The cardinal needed some assurance that his position would not be undermined again. Under threat of resignation he persuaded the king to dismiss four members of his guard, who had been closely associated with Cinq-Mars. The king also promised in writing never to take another favourite from outside the council. Over policy Louis endorsed Richelieu's views: he undertook to reject any peace treaty that would deprive France of her conquests. But if the king and the cardinal seemed outwardly in accord, their personal relations suffered as a result of the Cinq-Mars affair. Louis' last letter to the cardinal is surprising by its coolness.[29]

On 4 December Richelieu died. For several months, till 14 May 1643, Louis XIII ruled alone. He caused public surprise by retaining the services of the cardinal's associates; he also adhered to his policies. But in his attitude to the nobility, he showed more clemency. Thus he allowed aristocratic exiles to come home and freed the prisoners in the Bastille. Great figures from the past reappeared, including the duc de Vendôme and the comte de Cramail. Gaston d'Orléans left Blois to resume his place at court. As La Rochefoucauld tells us, the court was filled 'with all those who had suffered under cardinal Richelieu'. Many were animated by a strong desire for revenge: they wanted to recover their former positions and to dispossess Richelieu's kinsmen and friends of their property and offices. The stage was set for a new round of aristocratic turbulence. The *Fronde des princes* which erupted six years later showed that Richelieu's humbling of the *grands* had succeeded only in the short term. The programme of the *Frondeurs* of 1649 was essentially the same as that of the plotters of 1642. They wanted to remove the king's chief minister (in this instance, Mazarin) and make peace with Spain. Above all, they wanted to reverse the trend of recent years which had excluded them from what they saw as their rightful place as the king's 'natural' advisers.[30]

· · ·

NOTES AND REFERENCES

1. André L (ed.) *Testament politique* 1947 Paris, Laffont, p. 95.
2. Ibid., pp. 218–29.
3. Bergin J 1985 *Cardinal Richelieu: Power and the pursuit of wealth*. New Haven, CT and London, Yale University Press, pp. 119–20.
4. Ranum, O A 1963 'Cardinal Richelieu and the Great Nobility: Some Aspects of Early Modern Political Motives' *French Historical Studies* III: 184–204; Church, W F 1972, *Richelieu and Reason of State*. Princeton, NJ, Princeton University Press pp. 176–78.
5. Dethan G 1989 *Gaston d'Orléans: conspirateur et prince charmant*. Paris, *passim*.
6. Constant J-M 1987 *Les Conjurateurs: le premier libéralisme politique sous Richelieu*. Paris, Hachette, pp. 34–6.

7. Ibid., pp. 12–14.
8. Avenel DLM 1856 *Lettres, instructions diplomatiques et papiers d'état du Cardinal de Richelieu*. Paris, vol II, pp. 265–68.
9. Isambert F A 1822–33 *Receuil général des anciennes lois françaises depuis l'an 420 jusqu'à la révolution de 1789*, vol. XVI, pp. 175–83, 192–94.
10. *Testament politique*, pp. 102–3.
11. Constant *Les Conjurateurs*, pp. 49–51.
12. Herr R 1955 'Honor versus Absolutism: Richelieu's fight against dueling' *Journal of Modern History* XXVII: 281–85.
13. Church *Richelieu and Reason of State*, p. 185 (Avenel *Lettres*, ii, 321).
14. Ibid., iii, 179–213.
15. See above, pp. 34–41.
16. Church, *Richelieu and Reason of State*, p. 209.
17. Mongrédien, G 1961 *La Journée des Dupes*. Paris, Gallimard, pp. 104–28.
18. Church, *Richelieu and Reason of State*, p. 232.
19. Tapié V-L 1984 *France in the Age of Louis XIII and Richelieu*. Cambridge, Cambridge University Press, pp. 304–6.
20. Mongrédien, *La Journée des Dupes*, pp. 129–49.
21. Church, *Richelieu and Reason of State*, pp. 319–21.
22. Ibid., p. 324; Avenel, *Lettres*, v. 330–31.
23. Church, *Richelieu and Reason of State*, p. 327.
24. Tapié, *France in the Age of Louis XIII and Richelieu*, pp. 417–19.
25. Elliott J H 1984 *Richelieu and Olivares*. Cambridge, Cambridge University Press, p. 147.
26. Elliott, J H 1986 *The Count-Duke of Olivares: the Statesman in an Age of Decline*. New Haven, CT and London, Yale University Press, pp. 634–35.
27. Chevallier P 1979 *Louis XIII.*, Paris, Fayard, p. 596.
28. Ibid., p. 620.
29. Ibid., p. 628.
30. Bonney R 1978 'The French civil war, 1649–53' *European Studies Review* VIII: 71–100.

Chapter 5

RICHELIEU AND THE HUGUENOTS

France in the early seventeenth century needed to solve a religious problem. This was the existence within the state of two religions: Catholicism and Protestantism. Today this would not be seen as a problem, for politics and religion are commonly deemed to be separate spheres of human activity. A single nation may contain several faiths, and they do not even need to be Christian. This would have been inconceivable in seventeenth-century France. The king was regarded by his subjects in general as God's lieutenant on earth. His coronation or *sacre* was a religious ceremony in which he was anointed with a sacred balm. It enabled him to take communion in both kinds like a priest, and he was held to possess miraculous powers of healing. He bore the title of 'Most Christian King' and his most important duty was to defend the Catholic faith from its enemies. His coronation oath included a promise to extirpate heresy from his kingdom. Yet his subjects, in the early seventeenth century, included many Protestants or Huguenots, who were heretics in the eyes of the Roman church. What is more, they had their own political and military organisation within the state. To many Frenchmen, particularly the Catholic clergy, this was an intolerable state of affairs. National unity was to them indivisible, their motto being 'one king, one law, one faith', and they longed for the time when the Huguenots would return to the Catholic fold or be forced back into it.

The Huguenots were only a minority of Frenchmen. No exact figure can be given, but it has been estimated that they numbered some 1.2 million about 1600 or between 5 and 6 per cent of the population of France as a whole. Most of them lived in the south within a crescent stretching from La Rochelle in the west to Valence in the east. Some significant communities existed in Normandy, the Orléanais and around Chartres, but they were isolated. The same was true of Huguenots in the Île-de-France and Picardy. Elsewhere, Protestantism was rare. Although Huguenot villages existed, Protestantism was, in general, more strongly entrenched in towns than in the countryside. Some towns in the south were completely Protestant (namely, Montauban, La Rochelle, Millau, Castres, Nérac and Clairac). In other towns (for example, Nîmes and Montpellier), where Protestants were in a majority, they belonged for the most part to the upper echelons of society.

Within the crafts and trades there were denominational differences that are not always easily explained: thus leather and textile workers tended to be Protestant, while workers engaged in building or in dispensing food and wine were usually Catholic. Many Huguenots held offices, both judicial and financial, which they commonly purchased and which gave them a considerable hold over the royal administration in areas where they were dominant. Like their Catholic counterparts, Huguenot office-holders avidly acquired *seigneuries* whenever they had the chance. Around 1,600 nobles and lesser nobles (*hobereaux*) loomed large within the Huguenot communities. A few belonged to the highest nobility, which had once sat in the king's council, and now had to be content with functions at court or important provincial posts. They included the families of Bouillon, Rohan, Châtillon, La Force and La Trémoille. They owned fine residences in Paris and châteaux in the countryside. They could raise private armies, if necessary, from among their numerous tenants. But there were many lesser nobles, who, without being rich, commanded great influence locally in the Protestant church or *temple*, the consistory, the town council or provincial council. They were often veterans of the Wars of Religion, but their religious convictions were not always firm. Some were tempted to give up their faith for the material advantages attached to serving the Crown.[1]

It is sometimes assumed that the Edict of Nantes, issued by King Henry IV in 1598, solved the religious problem in France by granting a measure of toleration to the Huguenots.[2] In fact, the problem survived at least till the edict was revoked by Louis XIV in 1685. It consisted of four separate documents (ninety-two general articles, fifty-six secret articles and two royal warrants) and its purpose was to provide all the king's subjects with 'a general law, clear, precise and absolute to be applied in all the disputes that have arisen amongst them ... and establish a good and lasting peace'.[3] Three categories of Huguenot worship were allowed: first, on the estates of noblemen with tenurial rights of justice; secondly, at two sites in each *bailliage* to be determined by royal commissioners; and thirdly, wherever Huguenots could prove that their faith had been openly practised in 1597. The edict also made it possible for them to acquire any office of state and to enter any profession or occupation. They were granted access to all schools, universities and hospitals. Special tribunals, called *chambres de l'édit*, comprising Protestant and Catholic judges, were to try lawsuits involving Huguenots. The secret articles expanded on the general edict and dealt with exceptions. As for the royal warrants, they allowed the Huguenots a limited military and political independence. The first provided for the payment of Protestant pastors out of public funds and the second set aside a sum of 180,000 *écus* per annum over eight years for the payment of garrisons in about fifty Huguenot fortified towns (*places de sureté*) scattered through western and southern France. The Huguenots were also allowed about 150 emergency forts and eighty other forts, to be maintained at their own expense.[4]

The Edict of Nantes fell short of what many Protestants would have liked. It did not put their church on the same footing as the Catholic one. Huguenots could only worship in certain specified places. Thus, in all cathedral cities, *temples* could only be built in the suburbs. What is more, the edict called for the restoration of Catholicism wherever it had been suppressed by the Huguenots. It provided for the rebuilding of Catholic churches that had been destroyed, the reopening of monasteries and convents, and the restoration of property confiscated from Catholic clergy. Protestant books could only be published freely in towns controlled by the Huguenots; elsewhere they were subject to censorship. It is misleading to suggest, as is often done, that the Edict of Nantes created 'a state within the state', for the royal warrants on which the claim rests were only personal promises by Henry IV; they did not bind his successors.[5]

Clause 82 of the general articles banned Protestant political assemblies, both national and provincial. Colloquies and provincial synods were allowed, but only for religious purposes. Nor was any Huguenot corporation permitted: all Huguenot property had to be individually owned. At best, the edict made the Huguenots a privileged group within the realm, but even this was enough to upset many Catholics.

Before the Edict of Nantes could become effective it had to be registered by the various parlements, and this did not prove easy. In February 1599 Henry IV urged the Parlement of Paris to accept it. 'What I have done,' he said, 'is for the sake of peace; I have established it outside my kingdom and now wish to ensure it inside. You ought to obey me if only because of my position, and the obligation which is shared by my subjects and particularly by you of my parlement.'[6] Three weeks later the Parlement registered the edict, and the other parlements followed suit, though not with any alacrity. Rouen held out till 1609. In the provinces commissioners sent out to enforce the edict met with resistance from Catholic extremists. The siting of towns where Protestant worship was to be allowed proved contentious.

Implementing the edict was a herculean task which took many years to complete, and even then constant vigilance had to be exercised in its defence.[7] Although officially described as 'perpetual' and 'irrevocable', it was never intended to be a permanent settlement. Its own phraseology pointed to its temporary character: 'God has not seen fit that my subjects should *as yet* worship and adore Him under one form of religion.' This was an opinion shared by Catholics and Huguenots alike; each side was convinced that sooner or later it would convert the other. While Huguenots continued to express their revulsion from transubstantiation and other Catholic doctrines, Catholic pamphleteers argued that Protestantism in France had only survived because of royal clemency. 'The Catholic faith,' one of them stated, addressing the Huguenots, 'is the fundamental law of the state, the religion of our fathers and our kings; yours is merely suffered as is an abscess on the body of France.'[8]

Richelieu was well acquainted with the Huguenots, having been brought up in Poitou, a province where they were well represented. His first public statement about them was made

at the time of his installation as bishop of Luçon in 1609.
Addressing his flock, he declared:

> I know that there are some here who are separated from
> us in faith. I hope in return that we may be united
> in love. I will do everything in my power to achieve
> this, which will benefit them as well as ourselves and
> be agreeable to the king whom we must all seek to
> satisfy.[9]

Yet, in spite of these conciliatory words, Richelieu's relations
with the Huguenots in his diocese were not always smooth.
He required them to move to another site, when they started
to build a church near his cathedral, and offered them an
indemnity. They refused and appealed to the government,
but in the end they had to give way. They also accused
Richelieu of harassing them in various ways: by insisting
on being saluted as he passed in front of their church, by
dismissing a 'good old man' from his post of sergeant because
of his faith, and by re-baptising people who had already been
baptised as Protestants. But Catholics, too, had grievances, if
a memorandum of 1608 from a royal secret agent in Poitou
is to be believed. Although in a majority, they were not always left to worship in peace by their Huguenot neighbours.
The bishop and his clergy complained to the king several
times about damage done by them to churches and other
religious edifices. Another source of irritation to Catholics
was the refusal of Huguenots to pay certain taxes. Writing
to a Huguenot nobleman in 1609, Richelieu deplored the
churlishness of Huguenots with whom he had tried to live
in peace.[10]

In May 1611 a Protestant assembly met at Saumur. The
regent, Marie de' Medici, asked the delegates through her
representatives to appoint six spokesmen to defend their
interests at court and then to disperse. But they would not
listen. Instead, they declared their assembly to be permanent and sent various demands to the regent. These were
so extreme, according to Richelieu, that, even if the king's
council had been Protestant, they could not have been satisfied.[11] The talks between the assembly and the regent lasted
four months. Eventually, the delegates at Saumur agreed to
disband but on terms that were distinctly harmful to the
kingdom's political unity. They returned to their respective

provinces, according to Richelieu, bent on 'disturbing the peace of the state and on fishing in troubled waters'.[12]

Richelieu always drew a clear distinction between religious nonconformity and political sedition. He did not believe that the Huguenots should be forced to become Catholics, yet he was equally sure that they should not be allowed to disobey the Crown. Thus he was indignant when a Protestant minister went unpunished after telling the chancellor that if the Huguenots were denied a permission they had requested, they would simply take it. 'This insolent man,' he wrote, 'should have been arrested. He could have been released later as a mark of the king's goodness after his power and authority had been affirmed.'[13] Richelieu stated his position unequivocally in his closing address to the Estates-General of 1614. Huguenots who resorted to violence, he said, should be severely punished; the rest should be left in peace. 'We desire only their conversion,' he added, 'and we wish to promote it by our example, teaching and prayers. These are the only weapons with which we want to fight them.'[14]

As a bishop, of course, Richelieu had a bounden duty to attempt the conversion of heretics. He did so by encouraging missionary activity and by writing against the Huguenots. He introduced the Oratorians and Capuchins into the diocese of Luçon, giving them every facility to preach. The Capuchins were especially successful. In October 1622 they converted many Huguenots in Poitou, even within the estates of the dowager of Rohan, where the mass had not been said for sixty years.

Richelieu's personal contribution to the struggle against heresy was a book entitled *Les principaux points de la foi de l'Église catholique*. He wrote this at the priory of Coussay after the fall of Concini, when he ceased to be a minister. It was a reply to a work written by four pastors of Charenton in defence of the Protestant faith which had been sent to the king and had circulated widely. In his preface, Richelieu indicated that his purpose was to cure the Huguenots, not to harm them. He hated only their doctrines, not their persons, for whom he felt nothing but goodwill. The pastors of Charenton, he argued, had every reason to be grateful to the kings of France; they should thank them instead of complaining about them. Their faith was hated, not for the reasons cited by them, but for others which they concealed.

The Catholic church, its clergy and others whom they accused of crimes were innocent. Richelieu's book is divided into nineteen chapters: fourteen contain point-by-point replies to the charges of the pastors; the other five set out to explain why the Protestant faith 'must be abhorred by everyone'. The Reformation, according to Richelieu, had revived ancient heresies, opened the door to all the vices and shaken the foundations of princely authority.[15]

A few Catholic voices urged Louis XIII to follow his father's example by postponing the religious unification of his kingdom, but this view was not shared by the clergy at the Estates-General of 1614. They wished to see a ban imposed on Protestantism or the *religion prétendue réformée*, although they were prepared to accept the Edict of Nantes as a temporary political necessity. But they believed that it should be enforced in Huguenot areas and were horrified by a report on the situation in the small independent *comté* of Béarn, where ecclesiastical property remained in heretical hands and Catholic worship was still banned. The Estates-General accordingly demanded the restoration of Catholicism in Béarn and even the complete annexation of that territory to France.[16] At an assembly of the French clergy, held in Paris in 1617, the bishop of Macon complained that ecclesiastical revenues in Béarn were being used to pay the wages of Protestant ministers and to support students of Protestant theology. Such a misuse of Catholic funds, he suggested, was like allowing concubines to drink from sacred chalices! He reminded his audience of St Rémy's testamentary prophecy that the kingdom would be doomed if the Catholic faith were destroyed or altered.[17] His message evidently struck home: on 25 June the king's council ordered Catholic worship and all church property in Béarn to be restored.

The estates of Béarn protested energetically against the royal decision, and for a time it seemed as if Louis XIII would temporise. This was because he was distracted by Marie de' Medici's latest revolt. As soon as he had signed the Treaty of Angers in August 1620, he led his army south. On 15 October, at Pau, the council of Béarn begged for Louis' pardon. Two days later he dismissed the Protestant governor and appointed a Catholic in his place. On 19 October he formally announced the union of Béarn and Navarre with

France. At the same time, he ordered the restoration of Catholic worship in both territories as well as the restitution of church property. Next day, half a century of Huguenot austerity came to an end at Pau as a solemn Te Deum was sung in the main churches.

The French annexation of Béarn was not the only calamity suffered by Protestantism at this time; another was the defeat by the Habsburgs of Frederick V, Elector Palatine and king of Bohemia, at the battle of the White Mountain. The two events, happening so close to each other, struck fear into the hearts of Huguenots, who had been feeling increasingly vulnerable since the death of Henry IV. In December 1620, at an illegal assembly at La Rochelle, they decided to resist the government, by force if necessary. Not all the Huguenot nobility shared in this decision. Lesdiguières, Sully and Bouillon stayed away from the assembly, leaving the responsibility for action to die-hards such as La Force, Soubise and La Trémoille. The assembly ordered troops to be raised whose wages were to be paid out of public funds wherever possible. Protestant France was divided into eight military regions or *cercles* under the supreme command of Henri de Rohan. The *places de sûreté* were put on a war footing and provincial assemblies were summoned to organise resistance.[18] In short, the 'United Provinces of the Midi', which had given such a headache to the monarchy in the final decades of the Wars of Religion, were revived. The chancellor, Brûlart de Sillery, who was old enough to remember these troubles, imparted his fears to the Venetian ambassadors:

> I tell you in confidence, Messieurs. I do not know what will become of us. The disease is in our blood and in our entrails. The Huguenots have set up a body which damages the king's authority and wrests the sceptre from his hand. At La Rochelle they hold an assembly without permission, they draw up statutes, they decide on taxes, they collect money, they arraign militias, they build fortifications as if the king did not exist and as if they were absolute masters[19]

Not all members of the government relished the prospect of renewed conflict with the Huguenots, but Louis XIII, who had a fanatical streak in him, did not hesitate for a moment. Indeed, he may be accused of having fired the first shot, for

his decision to march against the Huguenots of the south-
west was taken almost a month before the decisions reached
at the assembly of La Rochelle. Before leaving Saumur he
took communion and prayed as if he were setting off on a
crusade. Following the capitulation of St Jean d'Angély on
24 June, his confidence grew apace. 'He is so determined to
come to the end of his enterprise,' the Venetian ambassadors
reported, 'that he treats with contempt those who assure
him of the contrary. He says in effect that he is on the
way to becoming truly king of France and that anyone who
seeks to sidetrack him will never be his friend.'[20] In August
1621 the assembly of the clergy, meeting in Bordeaux, was
invited by the king's commissioner to grant Louis 1 million
livres towards the fulfilment of his sacred purpose. 'Since La
Rochelle is the capital of the schism and the revolt,' he said,
'its conquest will ensure the destruction of the monster [of
heresy]. All else being set aside, it must be attacked and its
loss made inescapable.'[21] While the clergy looked for ways
of raising so great a sum, the royal crusade gathered momentum. On 4 August Clairac surrendered to the king after
a ten-day siege. At Montauban, however, he encountered
stiff resistance. The siege dragged on from 21 August until
18 November and the royal army melted away under the
combined effect of desertion, treason and plague. Out of a
force of 20,000 men only 4,000 remained. Louis was forced
to retreat while Luynes negotiated with Rohan.

Following this humiliation, Louis returned to Paris and
ordered peace talks with the Huguenots, but winter passed
without a decision. In April 1622 the king gathered an army
at Nantes, whence he advanced westwards and confronted a
large Huguenot army led by Soubise that had been ravaging
Brittany and Poitou. On 15 April the royal forces defeated
Soubise on the Île de Riez. This victory was followed by
the construction of Fort-Louis, commanding the landward
approaches to La Rochelle, which was to become a large
bone of contention. The citizens claimed that it called their
loyalty to the king into question and disrupted their trade.[22]
By midsummer, 8,000 royal troops were encamped outside
the town. But instead of attacking La Rochelle immediately,
the king preferred to lay siege to Montpellier, another major
Huguenot stronghold further south. The defenders looked
to Rohan for help, but he had trouble raising troops and

money. When he advanced towards Montpellier in October, he found his way barred by the king's army and decided not to risk a battle. Louis XIII, for his part, was becoming anxious about the situation in Italy, where the Habsburgs had gained control of the Valtelline. Thus both sides in the civil war had good reasons for signing the peace of Montpellier (18 October 1622). While confirming the Edict of Nantes, this provided for the destruction of Huguenot fortifications except at La Rochelle and Montauban.

The Huguenots emerged seriously weakened from the war of 1622. Except for five towns and the Cévennes, they had lost control of lower Languedoc. La Rochelle was being systematically isolated, but the government knew that its capture would be difficult and expensive. It also needed to consolidate its position in the south as the peace of Montpellier was not easily enforced. The Huguenot cities were extremely reluctant to demolish their fortifications and offered all kinds of excuses to delay the process.[23] But the government, while attending to other problems, did not lose sight of its ultimate objective of conquering La Rochelle. It maintained a strong garrison at Fort-Louis, and set about weakening Rohan's position by encouraging Protestant nobles to become Catholics.

Richelieu by now had become the king's Chief Minister. He was much concerned with international affairs. French troops occupied the Grisons and in alliance with the duke of Savoy laid siege to Genoa. France also sent military help to the Dutch and subsidized Mansfeld. But, after a promising start, the French military effort slowed down, largely through lack of money. The cardinal's position in the government was also threatened.[24] This seemed a good moment for the Huguenots to try to regain lost ground. Soubise started a revolt and called on the people of La Rochelle to join him, but they were deeply divided. The oligarchy which governed the town assured the Crown of its loyalty, but it was overruled by the rest of the citizens. In May 1625 La Rochelle joined Soubise's rebellion.[25] With so many French troops committed elsewhere, Richelieu bided his time by playing on the divisions among the Rochelais. He was still negotiating with them on 14 September, when a large royal fleet under the duc de Montmorency approached La Rochelle, cutting off its communications with Soubise whose fleet lay off the Île de Ré. After a running battle that lasted two days, Soubise was defeated and fled to England. Protracted talks ensued between the government and La Rochelle, the main sticking point being the town's demand that Fort-Louis be dismantled. This could only be sustained as long as the Huguenots could hope for assistance from England, but ambassadors sent out by Charles I to the French court allowed themselves to be manipulated by Richelieu. They were made to understand that their national interests would best be served by persuading the Rochelais to accept peace terms.[26] On 5 February 1626 a peace treaty was duly signed: the Rochelais were forbidden to own any warships and required to demolish a fort. The king, for his part, was allowed to keep Fort-Louis and to garrison the offshore islands of Ré and Oléron.

The majority of Rochelais were understandably unhappy with the settlement. They found it hard to stomach the continued existence of Fort-Louis and feared the presence of royal troops and warships just outside their walls. They also resented the fact that they could no longer import wine from the Île de Ré and lived in dread of being subjected to the *gabelle*. Richelieu did his best to assuage their fears, but his words fell on deaf ears. The Rochelais continued to call themselves slaves. The Crown, they felt, was intent on destroying them as a first step towards ruining the Protestant religion in France as a whole. England seemed their only hope. 'Our hands are tied,' one of them declared,

> Our salvation can only come from the north, that is to say from the most serene monarch, who is the guarantor of the peace and its execution, which is not being done . . . . Whoever holds the islands holds the heart of the town, if not its arms. This maxim is infallible.[27]

King Charles I was seen by the Huguenots as their protector, and La Rochelle sent him envoys who added their voices to those of Soubise and other exiles.

In 1627 Charles I's favourite and minister, George Villiers, duke of Buckingham, mounted a naval expedition against France. It comprised 84 ships and carried about 10,000 men. On reaching the Île de Ré, on 20 July, Buckingham sent a deputation to La Rochelle with a request to enter the harbour. Much to his surprise, this was refused. The mayor explained that the citizens were loyal to the king of France. Even Soubise was only able to enter La Rochelle with difficulty. After further negotiations the Rochelais thanked the English for their help and wished their expedition success. But they refused to act until they had consulted the other Huguenot churches. Buckingham, in the meantime, landed on the Île de Ré and laid siege to the fortress of St Martin, which was defended by marshal Toiras. The duke believed that if only he could capture the fortress, the Huguenots would rise *en masse*. But supplies and reinforcements, which he had requested from England, failed to arrive. 'Our provisions grow low,' he wrote on 14 August, 'and our men decrease.'[28] Early in September, however, the Rochelais at last committed themselves openly to support the English and soon afterwards Buckingham received 2,000 Irish reinforcements.

The duc d'Angoulême, who commanded Louis XIII's army outside La Rochelle, sent an urgent appeal for help to Louis XIII. St Martin, he explained, would not be able to hold out much longer unless an army was sent to the Île de Ré at once. Meanwhile, Toiras explored the possibility of a negotiated settlement, but Richelieu would not consider this as long as any English troops remained on French soil. Louis XIII, he announced, would soon take charge of the army and no effort would be spared to relieve St Martin. Pending the king's arrival, his brother Gaston was placed in charge of military operations.[29] By late September Toiras's men were on the verge of mutiny. He approached Buckingham for surrender terms, but the duke, instead of drawing them up himself, invited Toiras to state his own terms. This gave the French on the mainland time to assemble a relief fleet. On the night of 7 October twenty-nine French boats, full of men and supplies, slipped past the English. Thus was the fortress of St Martin relieved just as it was about to surrender. Next morning, the English besieging the fortress were greeted with the sight of chickens, turkeys, hams and tongues stuck on pikes above the parapets by the triumphant French garrison.[30] A last attempt by the English to storm the fortress on 6 November ended disastrously. The French captured forty-four standards, which were carried in triumph to Paris and displayed in Notre-Dame. On 8 November, Buckingham sailed for home.

The departure of the English enabled Louis XIII to concentrate his efforts on reducing La Rochelle. Having taken over command of his army on 12 October, he planned to blockade the town. On the landward side a semicircular line of fortifications was constructed, linking each extremity of the bay of La Rochelle. This was manned by a large and well-paid army. As Richelieu remarked: 'a soldier's pay is his soul and sustains his courage.' But La Rochelle, being a port, needed to be sealed off from the sea as well. The French navy was not seen as a sufficient safeguard against a possible relief operation by the English. A dry-stone dyke with a gap in the middle to relieve the pressure of the ocean was accordingly built across the entrance to La Rochelle's harbour. It was designed by two French engineers, Clément Metezeau and Jean Thiriot, and built by volunteers from the army. Even Louis XIII lent a hand from time to time. As an additional safeguard against small vessels slipping through, wooden staves linked by cross-beams were driven into the sea-bed beyond the gap. Close to Fort-Louis, an alternative harbour, called Port Neuf, was created to provide shelter for the king's fleet, which arrived in January.[31]

The Rochelais could not hope to free themselves from the blockade without outside help. They rested their hopes mainly on England, but also looked to their co-religionists in southern France. On 11 September 1627 a Protestant assembly at Uzès confirmed Rohan as commander in chief of all the Huguenot churches and accepted an alliance with England. Many Huguenot towns, however, refused to join his revolt. This made it difficult for him to raise enough money to support an army. He fought quite well against Condé and Montmorency, the royal commanders in the south, but was gradually cornered in the Cévennes.[32] Thus he was unable to answer La Rochelle's cry for help. English assistance was the only hope left to the Rochelais. But an English relief fleet commanded by the Earl of Denbigh made no serious attempt to break through the French king's blockade.

On 10 February 1628 Louis XIII returned to Paris, leaving Richelieu as his lieutenant-general in charge of military operations. That same night he wrote to him: 'You may rest assured always of my affection and believe that I shall keep my promise to you until death! I feel lost when I think that you are no longer with me.'[33] With the help of

Father Joseph, the cardinal dedicated himself to the task in hand. He was afraid that noblemen commanding the regiments would not readily obey a clergyman, but they were too jealous of each other to worry about him. Thus he met no serious obstruction as he pressed on with preparations against La Rochelle. At the same time he kept the king informed of all that was going on, including an unsuccessful attempt on 11 March to take La Rochelle by surprise. About mid-April, Louis returned to the camp outside the town, and Richelieu reverted to being his principal lieutenant. After inspecting the army and the dyke, Louis wrote to his mother expressing his confidence in the cardinal. 'You are more than ever in his mind,' Marie wrote to Richelieu, 'he says that without you everything would be going badly!'[34]

By mid-August, however, Louis began to feel that the siege had lasted long enough. The cost of keeping a huge army in the field and of keeping the dyke under constant repair was mounting fast. The king was also anxious about events in Italy. So peace-feelers were extended to the Rochelais, but their new mayor, Jean Guiton, was keen to fight on. He allegedly struck a table with his dagger saying: 'Thus will I strike the first person to talk of surrender.'[35] However, opinion among the Rochelais was far from unanimous, and Richelieu contrived to widen their disagreements by using propaganda. A government pamphlet which found its way into the town blamed the unjust tyranny of a few for its misfortunes. They kept all the available corn for themselves, watched the poor die of hunger, and would eventually monopolize the benefits of a treaty with the king.[36]

On 23 August Buckingham was murdered in Portsmouth as he was supervising preparations for another expedition to assist La Rochelle. Despite the loss of its commander, the expedition sailed on 7 September under the Earl of Lindsey. It arrived off La Rochelle at the end of the month, but failed to break through the royal blockade, thereby proving that Charles I could not fulfil his promise of aid. On 26 October La Rochelle decided to ask for the king's pardon. His councillors were divided as to how to respond: some advocated the harshest punishment; others wanted only the leaders of the revolt to be punished. Richelieu spoke out for clemency. The Rochelais, he argued, had never renounced their allegiance to the king. Clemency would bring him renown, facilitate the final capitulation of the Huguenots in the Midi and forestall any move by the English to enhance their prestige by mediating between the two sides. In the end, this was the course adopted by the king. The Rochelais were allowed to keep their lives, property and faith, but not their fortifications or their privileges. They had no choice other than capitulation. A deputation was accordingly sent to offer the town's submission to Louis and to receive his pardon. Next day his army entered the town under strict orders to avoid molesting the inhabitants. They were followed that afternoon by Richelieu and the papal nuncio. Guiton came forward with his halberdiers to welcome them, but Richelieu sent them packing. He told Guiton that he was no longer mayor and forbade the town magistrates to meet as a body until the *présidial* had been restored.

On 31 October hundreds of carts filled with victuals, along with herds of cattle and flocks of sheep, entered La Rochelle to feed the starving population. Sappers from the king's army set about burying the dead lying in the streets or houses. On All Saints' Day, Richelieu celebrated mass at the church of St Margaret. In the afternoon, Louis XIII, wearing armour beneath a scarlet cloak, made his entry into the town amidst his troops. Two days later he took part in a religious procession. The windows overlooking the route were crowded with people anxious to see him. Having once feared him so much, they now regarded him as an angel who had rescued them from the arms of death. On 18 November Louis left the city after formulating rules for its administration. Four regiments of troops stayed behind to supervise the destruction of the fortifications.[37]

In certain respects the Rochelais had been treated leniently by the Crown, but they had lost all those features which had given them a unique degree of independence among French towns. Their administration was now handed over to royal officials and their revenues were taken over by the Crown. The legal powers formally vested in the municipality were now transferred to the *présidial*, acting under the local *sénéchal*. The loss of La Rochelle's privileges, which dated back to the twelfth century, exposed it to the full rigour of royal fiscality. It was now subject to import and export duties while its revenues from shipping were diverted to Richelieu as *Grand maître et surintendant général de la navigation*. Henceforth, the Rochelais had to pay an annual subsidy to keep their exemption from the *taille*. In 1638 various duties on commodities ranging from wine to soap were introduced or increased 'to meet the cost of the war'. The Crown also gained direct access to the salt pans near La Rochelle from which it drew high duties.[38]

As far as religion was concerned, the Rochelais had to accept a revival of Catholicism in their midst. Provision was made by the Crown for the reorganisation of parishes, the maintenance of priests and Catholic control of hospitals. The Protestant *temple* in the city centre was turned into a Catholic church, though Huguenots were promised a new church on a site to be chosen by the king. Permission was sought from Rome to turn La Rochelle into a bishopric. Between 1628 and 1637 a large number of religious orders set up houses in the town. This movement coincided with a sharp rise in the Catholic population. This was largely the result of a rule which forbade Huguenots to settle in the town if they had not resided there before 1629. Catholics had no such restriction. Thus by the mid-1630s Catholics numbered 10,000 and Huguenots only 8,000. By 1676 the imbalance was even worse: 23,000 Catholics as against 5,000 Huguenots. Yet the latter continued to dominate La Rochelle's commercial and maritime life till the revocation of the Edict of Nantes in 1685.[39]

The fall of La Rochelle in 1628 led almost inevitably to the surrender of the Huguenots in the Midi. This did not happen immediately, however, as the king's army was moved to Italy for a time. Rohan was also encouraged to continue his resistance by promises of aid from England, which never materialised. Eventually, Richelieu brought the army back to Languedoc. In May 1629 Privas was mercilessly sacked after a ten-day siege. The cardinal expressed dismay at the carnage, which took place without his knowledge, but he consoled himself with the thought that it might persuade other Huguenot towns to submit without a struggle.[40] This, in fact, is what happened and, on 28 June, Louis XIII issued the Edict of Alès. Though often called a peace, it was not a treaty but an act of remission or pardon. It confirmed the Edict of Nantes, but only in respect of the basic text. The additional clauses guaranteeing the Huguenots' political and military rights were now cancelled. All their fortifications and fortresses were to be demolished. After the king's return to northern France, Richelieu stayed in Languedoc and personally supervised the destruction of twenty town walls. When a deputation from Montauban asked for theirs to be reprieved, he threatened them with a siege. They promptly gave way. Even so, Richelieu exacted twelve hostages chosen from Montauban's notables before he would lift a threat of reprisals. He then entered the town under arms and, after a Te Deum at the church of St Jacques, watched the removal of the first stone from the town's ramparts.

The Huguenots were no longer a political force, but they remained a significant religious minority. Their right of worship was recognised in theory by the state, but the period from 1629 till 1685 was marked by much intolerance towards them. In May 1634 the king's council, availing itself of a clause in the Edict of Nantes, banned all Protestant worship on Richelieu's estates. A year later a new decree, instigated by Richelieu, forbade all Protestant preaching on ecclesiastical lordships. In January 1642 the council ordered the Huguenots of Vitré to abandon their church because it stood too close to the Catholic one. On several occasions pastors were forbidden to preach outside their place of residence. Official harassment of the Huguenots was backed up by the *Compagnie du Saint-Sacrement*, a secret society of lay and clerical members dedicated to the glory of God. One of its prime activities was the conversion of heretics, another was keeping them out of professions and trades. Yet in spite of all this persecution, the total number of Huguenots did not fall between 1630 and 1656; it may even have increased.[41] So the 'peace' of Alès did not destroy them; it merely destroyed the so-called Huguenot republic. After 1628 La Rochelle was an ordinary seaport and the towns of the south-west were ordinary French cities. To this extent Richelieu struck an important blow for the political and economic unity of France. He did not, however, solve the religious problem handed down from the sixteenth century.

Richelieu was preoccupied by the religious division of France till the end of his life. In 1640, Mazarin disclosed that the cardinal spent his leisure moments writing about important matters. This testimony was confirmed by the posthumous publication in 1651 of Richelieu's *Traité qui contient la méthode la plus facile et la plus assurée pour convertir ceux qui se sont séparés de l'Église* (Treatise containing the easiest and surest method of converting those who have left the Church). In this work Richelieu focuses on the basic tenets of the Catholic faith and tries to win over the Calvinists by pointing to their doctrinal differences with the Lutherans and to their own inconsistencies. The cardinal had long wanted to organise a grand debate between theologians from both sides, believing that truth would prevail and bring the Huguenots back into the Catholic church. But his plan received no support from Rome, which distrusted such debates with heretics. Richelieu, however, continued to hope. In September 1641 the nuncio Grimaldi reported that

> once peace is concluded the principal thought of His Eminence will be to bring the French heretics into the Catholic faith, and that is why he is now trying to facilitate it, wishing it to be realised not only by fear of force, but also to persuade by arguments and win over the ministers following whom the people will easily be converted.

But peace with the Habsburgs was not concluded within Richelieu's lifetime, so that he was never able to give the signal for the decisive drive towards religious unity.[42]

.   .   .

NOTES AND REFERENCES

1. Garrisson Janine 1985 *L'Édit de Nantes et sa révocation: histoire d'une intolérance*. Paris, Seuil, pp. 28–33.
2. Neale J E 1943 *The Age of Catherine de Medici*. London, Cape, p. 101.
3. Mousnier R 1973 *The Assassination of Henry IV*. London, Faber & Faber, pp. 316–63.
4. Greengrass M 1984 *France in the age of Henry IV*. London, Longman, pp. 76–7.
5. Sutherland, N M 1980 *The Huguenot Struggle for Recognition*. New Haven, CT, Yale University Press, p. 371.
6. Buisseret D 1984 *Henry IV*. London, Allen & Unwin, p. 72.
7. Greengrass *France in the age of Henry IV*, p. 79.

8. Garrisson *L'Édit de Nantes*, p. 44.

9. Avenel D L M (ed.) 1853 *Lettres, instructions diplomatiques et papiers d'état du Cardinal de Richelieu*, Paris, 1.15.

10. Lacroix L 1890 *Richelieu à Luçon: sa jeunesse – son épiscopat*. Paris, Letouzey; reprint J Prim, 1986, pp. 119–23.

11. Ibid., pp. 125–27; Richelieu *Mémoires* xxi *bis*, p. 105.

12. Ibid.

13. Ibid., p. 107.

14. Hayden J Michael 1974 *France and the Estates General of 1614*. Cambridge, Cambridge University Press, pp. 15–16; Richelieu, *Mémoires* i, pp. 340–65.

15. Lacroix *Richelieu à Luçon*, pp. 302–9.

16. Hayden *France and the Estates General of 1614*, p. 181.

17. Garrisson, *L'Édit de Nantes*, p. 60.

18. Ibid., p. 64.

19. Ibid., p. 65.

20. Ibid., p. 66.

21. Ibid.

22. Grillon P 1975 *Les papiers de Richelieu*. vol. 1, Paris, Pedone, p. 106.

23. Lublinskaya A D 1968 *French Absolutism: the crucial phase, 1620–1629*. Cambridge, Cambridge University Press, pp. 211–12.

24. See above, pp. 20–21.

25. Parker, D 1980 *La Rochelle and the French Monarchy*. London, Royal Historical Society, pp. 42–3.

26. de Vaux de Foletier F 1931 *Le Siège de La Rochelle*. Paris, Firmin-Didot, pp. 33–4.

27. Ibid., p. 44.

28. Lockyer R 1981 *Buckingham*. London, Longman, p. 389.

29. Ibid., pp. 393–94.

30. de Vaux de Foletier, *Le Siège de La Rochelle*, pp. 115–16.

31. Ibid., pp. 152–54.

32. Lublinskaya *French Absolutism*, p. 218.

33. Chevallier P 1979 *Louis XIII*. Paris, Fayard, p. 337.

34. Ibid.

35. Ibid., pp. 337–38.

36. de Vaux de Foletier *Le Siège de La Rochelle*, p. 248.

37. Ibid., pp. 276–82.

38. Parker *La Rochelle and the French Monarchy*, pp. 52–3, 69–70.

39. Ibid., pp. 146–47.

40. Hanotaux G 1933 *Histoire du cardinal de Richelieu*, vol. 3, Paris, Plon, p. 222.
41. Garrison *L'Édit de Nantes*, pp. 88–90, 92–9, 108.
42. Blet P 1972 'La religion du cardinal' in A Adam *et al.* *Richelieu*, Paris, Hachette, pp. 172–73.

Chapter 6

RICHELIEU'S FOREIGN POLICY (1624–35)

Foreign affairs occupied much of Richelieu's ministerial attention. One of his aims, as stated in the most famous passage of the *Testament politique*, was to raise the king's reputation among foreign nations to its rightful level. Later in the same work, Richelieu underlined the need for continuous diplomatic activity: 'it is absolutely necessary,' he writes, 'for the well-being of the state to negotiate ceaselessly, either openly or secretly, and in all places, even in those from which no future prospects as yet seem likely.'[1]

Richelieu's pursuit of objectives abroad was necessarily conditioned by the situation within France: the financial resources of the government did not allow initiatives in too many areas at once, especially if they involved military support. For a long time the cardinal's freedom of action abroad was cramped by the Huguenot rebellion at La Rochelle.[2] Only after this had been crushed could he feel free in his dealings with foreign powers. Joy at his emancipation was expressed in a memorandum to the king of January 1629: 'Now that La Rochelle is taken,' he wrote, 'if the king wishes to become the most powerful monarch in the world . . .' At this stage, however, Richelieu was more concerned to check Spanish activities in Italy than worried about any increase of the Emperor's power in Germany. 'One's constant aim,' Richelieu wrote, 'must be to check the advance of Spain.' He was aware, however, of the need to act on a wider front as well: 'France must only think of fortifying herself at home and of opening gates into all the neighbouring states so as to defend them against Spanish oppression as the occasion arises. . . . We must think of fortifying Metz and, if possible, of reaching out to Strasbourg so as to gain entry into Germany' But, he added, 'this must be done in the long term, very discreetly and in a manner that is moderate and secret'.[3]

In outline there was nothing new about Richelieu's anti-Habsburg foreign policy: its roots stretched back at least to 1521, when King Francis I of France declared war on the Emperor Charles V who ruled the Netherlands, Franche Comté, the Holy Roman Empire, Spain, parts of Italy and of the New World. Never since Roman times had there been such a hegemony, and France felt hemmed in by it. The conflict between the royal houses of Valois and Habsburg was fought mainly in Italy and continued intermittently till 1559, when mutual exhaustion and a common desire to fight the threat of heresy brought both sides to the peace table. During the second half of the sixteenth century France was too preoccupied with her civil wars to resume the struggle. By then Charles V had abdicated and divided his empire into two parts: the Holy Roman Empire went to his brother Ferdinand I and all the rest to his son, Philip II. Thus by the time Richelieu came to power there were two branches of the Habsburg dynasty: one in Vienna headed by Ferdinand II; the other in Madrid headed by Philip IV. They had many interests in common, notably the defence of the Catholic faith against Protestantism. It is a mistake, however, to imagine that they were always able or even willing to assist each other.[4]

International relations in the early seventeenth century were largely determined by events of the previous century. Two were especially momentous: the Protestant Reformation and the Dutch Revolt. The Reformation broke the unity of Christendom. Whereas various states, like England and Sweden, became officially Protestant, others, like France, Spain and the Holy Roman Empire remained loyal to the Catholic faith. The choice, however, was seldom achieved peacefully. In France a significant minority of the king's subjects, as we have seen, adopted Calvinism as their religion, and the Crown's refusal to tolerate them was one of the causes of the so-called Wars of Religion which tore the nation apart between 1562 and 1598. In the Empire the situation was complicated by the political fragmentation of the state. Although the Emperor was the nominal head of government, power was effectively vested in some fifty ecclesiastical and thirty secular princes. The most important of them were the seven Electors: the duke of Saxony, the margrave of

Brandenburg, the king of Bohemia, the count Palatine and the archbishops of Mainz, Trier and Cologne. Below them were non-electoral princes, the Imperial Free Cities and a host of lesser authorities. Many of them adopted Protestantism, while others stayed Catholic. Under the Peace of Augsburg (1555) each prince was allowed to impose his own faith on his subjects.

The Dutch Revolt, which began in 1566, was an attempt by the people of the Netherlands to throw off the Spanish yoke that a dynastic accident had imposed on them.[5] Their struggle was mainly political at first, but as it developed it assumed a strongly religious aspect. Calvinism became closely linked to the cause of Dutch independence. In 1579 the seven northern provinces consecrated their independence from Spain by forming themselves into the United Provinces, one of the few republics in sixteenth-century Europe. The others remained under Spanish rule. The Dutch Revolt was not only a bipartisan conflict; other countries intervened on the side of the Dutch, principally England and France. Spain was naturally angered by this foreign interference in what she regarded as her domestic affairs. Her reply to England was the ill-fated Armada of 1588, and to France, her support for the Catholic League against the Huguenots, led by Henry of Navarre. Part of the price which the latter had to pay for the kingdom of France, apart from his conversion to Catholicism, was a war with Spain which was ended by the peace of Vervins in 1598. The help given by Spain to the League was long remembered in France and frequently cited as evidence of her desire to keep her subjects divided and weak.[6]

The Dutch Revolt imposed on Spain a gigantic military effort which taxed her resources severely. Transporting armies from Spain and Italy to the Low Countries was no easy task. As the sea route across the Bay of Biscay and up the Channel was too hazardous, Spanish troops travelled to the Netherlands overland from Genoa using a series of semi-parallel routes collectively known as 'the Spanish Road.'[7] This passed through Savoy, Franche-Comté, Lorraine and Luxemburg. Blocking 'the Spanish Road' was obviously a tempting prospect to the French government, which had always resented the encircling presence of the Habsburgs. Thus in 1601 Henry IV gained control of part of Savoy by the Treaty of Lyons, forcing Spain to find an alternative route for her armies further east. This was the Valtelline, a valley linking Lombardy and the Tyrol. It became crucially important to Spain when the truce which had brought the Dutch revolt to an end in 1609 expired twelve years later, in April 1621.

Richelieu's rise to power took place only a few years after the outbreak of the Thirty Years War. This began with a revolt in Bohemia. In 1617 the Archduke Ferdinand of Habsburg had become king of that country. Though a die-hard Catholic, he was accepted by the Bohemian Protestants on condition that he would observe the Letter of Majesty that had granted them toleration. But he soon disregarded this commitment. In March 1619 the Emperor Matthias died and Ferdinand was elected in his place. This triggered off a revolt in Bohemia. After deposing Ferdinand, the rebels offered his throne to Frederick V, the Elector Palatine, who was a Calvinist. This development carried important implications for Spain, which was soon to resume her war with the Dutch. As a precautionary measure, Spinola, commander of the Spanish army of Flanders, invaded the Palatinate, while in Bohemia Ferdinand staged a comeback, winning the battle of the White Mountain (1620). Frederick V went into exile at the Hague. He was placed under an imperial ban and, in 1623, lost his title and lands to Maximilian of Bavaria, leader of the Catholic League. The latter naturally resented Spinola's occupation of the Palatinate and by his intransigence prevented the general from launching a massive assault on the United Provinces in 1621. This gave the Dutch an opportunity to negotiate the Treaty of Compiègne with England and France in 1624. A year later Spain began a major offensive against the Dutch, which culminated in Spinola's capture of Breda, an event immortalised by Velázquez in one of his most famous paintings. In desperate need of foreign help, the Dutch turned to Christian IV of Denmark. A coalition was formed at the Hague in December 1625, which planned a three-pronged attack on the Habsburgs. But Christian had difficulty in organizing his allies. In August 1626 his army was routed by the imperial commander, Tilly, at Lutter. By late 1627 Christian had been driven back to his kingdom. Ferdinand, in the meantime, completed the subjugation of Bohemia, while his general, Wallenstein, overran Mecklenburg, pushing Habsburg power to the southern shore of the

Baltic. This offered Spain a chance to disrupt the Dutch economy, but it antagonised Sweden. Thus did the Thirty Years War spread like an oil stain across the map of Europe. At first, France tried to avoid any direct involvement, but, given her traditional hostility to the Habsburgs, it seemed only a matter of time before she too would be drawn into the conflict.

Historians have traditionally assumed that Richelieu imposed a decisive new stamp on French foreign policy from the moment he entered the king's council in April 1624. In fact, his opening moves were tentative and his successes limited.[8] He could not afford to take risks as long as he had not won the full confidence of Louis XIII and replenished the royal treasury. For a time Richelieu had to be cautious. His opening moves were aimed at securing as long a period of external peace as he needed to subdue La Rochelle. He merely continued where his predecessor, La Vieuville, had left off. Two matters, in particular, occupied his attention: the Anglo-French marriage and the Valtelline question.

La Vieuville had begun talks for the marriage of the Prince of Wales with Louis XIII's sister, Henrietta Maria. Politically, this match was intended to prevent an Anglo-Spanish *rapprochement* which had been frequently mooted in recent years. It was also seen as an obstruction to any collusion between the English Crown and the Huguenots. The *dévots* welcomed the marriage, hoping that it might lead to an improvement in the religious status of English Catholics. Before the negotiations were concluded, James I of England died, so that it was the new king, Charles I, to whom Henrietta Maria was married by proxy on 11 May 1625. Charles sent his favourite, Buckingham, to fetch his bride, and the duke used the occasion to propose secretly to Louis XIII an offensive alliance against Spain. But such a move appeared premature to Richelieu. His reticence upset Buckingham, who went on to scandalise French opinion by paying court to the young queen, Anne of Austria.[9]

. . .

THE VALTELLINE CRISIS

The first major international problem that Richelieu had to deal with on becoming Chief Minister was the Valtelline.[10] In 1620 Spain took advantage of a revolt by the Catholic inhabitants against their Protestant overlords, the Grisons or Grey Leagues, to set up a chain of forts along the valley. But the Valtelline was also used by France as a military corridor through which to reach Venice, her only reliable ally in Italy.[11] In 1622 France, Savoy and Venice agreed to expel the Spaniards from the Valtelline by force, whereupon Spain arranged for her forts to be manned by papal troops. Pope Gregory XV agreed to this arrangement, and Louis XIII was persuaded to let the matter rest. It was at this juncture that Richelieu came to power.

The cardinal's first move regarding the Valtelline was to seek the help of the new pope, Urban VIII. Though generally favourable to France, he was not inclined to give up the forts in the Valtelline without compensation. This obliged Richelieu to use force. In November 1624, a Franco-Swiss army expelled the papal garrisons. Urban sent a legate to Paris with a request that the Catholic inhabitants should not be handed back to the brutal rule of the Grisons. But the legate returned empty-handed after Richelieu had refused to do anything that might prejudice the Grisons' rights.

In March 1625 France and Savoy launched a joint attack on Genoa designed to interrupt Spanish traffic to the Valtelline. This led to a call in Madrid for an invasion of France from three directions. But the Spanish chief minister, the Count-Duke of Olivares, did not want a war that would undermine his position at home and ruin his exchequer. He temporised, therefore, even after Spinola's victory over the Dutch at Breda had increased pressure on him to mount a pre-emptive strike against France.[12]

By the spring of 1626 Richelieu was anxiously looking for a peaceful settlement in Italy. During the winter he had faced simultaneously a Huguenot revolt and the possibility of war with Spain. The state of the French royal treasury did not allow the taking of risks. The cardinal was also being harshly criticised by the *dévots* for his anti-papal policy in the Valtelline. He consequently began to draw back from his excessively exposed position: he negotiated a peace with the Huguenots (5 February) and instructed Du Fargis, the French ambassador in Madrid, to find a settlement of the Valtelline dispute. The result was the Treaty of Monzón (5 March), in which Spain agreed conditionally to the sovereignty of the Grisons over the Catholic inhabitants of the valley while France undertook to withdraw her troops. News of the treaty outraged opinion in France and abroad. France's allies (Venice, Savoy and the Dutch) felt that they had been abandoned. Richelieu disowned Du Fargis, saying that he had exceeded his powers, but, once the uproar had subsided, he ratified the treaty. There followed an improvement in Franco-Spanish relations which enabled the cardinal to concentrate on the war against La Rochelle.

The almost inevitable corollary of improved relations between France and Spain was a deterioration of those between France and England. This happened almost as soon as Henrietta Maria had married Charles I. When Bassompierre visited London with a view to settling disputes between the two countries, Charles I asked if he had come to declare war. Buckingham, who had personal reasons for disliking France, was also anxious to frustrate Richelieu's aim of building up France's naval strength. Meanwhile, both the duke and his master were being urged by Soubise, who had fled to England, to go to the aid of his beleaguered coreligionists in La Rochelle. Alarmed by these developments, Richelieu took steps to defend France's Atlantic coast against a possible English attack and prevent a *rapprochement* between England and Spain. In July 1626 Du Fargis proposed a Franco-Spanish alliance to Olivares. This delighted the *dévots*, who wanted French policy to rest on the 'natural' alliance of the two great Catholic powers. In Madrid, however, distrust of France ran deep. The Infanta echoed this general feeling by reminding Olivares of Philip II's maxim that Spain and France were fundamentally irreconcilable.[13] However, an accord suited both chief ministers at this moment, so that on 20 March 1627 a Franco-Spanish alliance against England was signed. Three months later Buckingham launched his ill-fated expedition to the Île de Ré.[14] In accordance with the treaty, Spain sent a fleet to help France repel the English attack, but it arrived after Buckingham's defeat.

. . .

THE MANTUAN WAR

Late in 1627, while Richelieu was still fighting the Rochelais, an event occurred in Italy calculated to upset the Franco-Spanish alliance. On 26 December Duke Vincenzo II of Mantua, the last of the male line of the Gonzagas, died, leaving a succession fraught with problems.[15] It comprised not only the duchy of Mantua but also the marquisate of Montferrat. Both were imperial fiefs, but whereas a female could succeed to the marquisate, only a male could inherit the duchy. Strategically, the duchy was important: it bordered on the Milanese which the king of Spain held as hereditary duke, while Montferrat contained the citadel of Casale, commanding the upper Po valley. This had long been coveted by Charles Emmanuel of Savoy. Shortly before his death, Vincenzo had appointed his cousin Charles duke of Nevers, who belonged to the French branch of the Gonzagas, as his heir. Pending Charles's arrival, his son, the duke of Rethelois, who was already in Mantua, acted in his name. He was also hastily married to Vincenzo's niece, Maria. The Emperor's permission was not sought, nor was Madrid informed. On arrival in Mantua, in January 1628, Nevers sent an envoy to plead his case with the Emperor.

Nevers's claim to Mantua was strong, but Spain resented his precipitate conduct. She was most anxious to prevent Milan from being exposed and outflanked by an alliance of Nevers, Louis XIII and Charles Emmanuel.[16] But the army of Milan under Gonzalo de Córdoba was short of money and men. What is more, the king of Spain in his capacity of duke of Milan was legally bound to act only as directed by the Emperor, and Ferdinand was not prepared at this stage to intervene militarily. So Gonzalo had to act on the authority of the Spanish king alone. In May 1628 he laid siege to Casale, but his forces were inadequate and he was still camped outside the fortress in October, when La Rochelle fell to Louis XIII. Richelieu was now able to give more attention to Italy. He urged his master not to jeopardise his prestige by failing to rescue his ally, Nevers. By acting speedily, he said, Louis would raise the siege of Casale and restore peace to Italy in May 1629. He would pacify the Languedoc in July and return to Paris victorious in August.

On 15 January 1629 Louis XIII left Paris, accompanied by Richelieu. To reach Casale the French army had to go through Savoy, but its passage was barred by the duke. On 6 March, however, the French forced their way through the Pass of Susa and a few days later Charles Emmanuel sued for peace. France offered him part of Montferrat in return for the right of passage to the marquisate and for help in driving out the Spaniards. Gonzalo who, as always, was short of money, lifted the siege of

Casale. The impact of these events on Spain was devastating. Philip IV went down with a fever; Olivares declared himself struck to the heart at seeing his nation overtaken by such ignominy.[17] Throughout April Louis XIII remained at Susa, where he received envoys from Florence, Genoa and Venice. Their liberties, he claimed, had been saved by his timely intervention. Leaving a garrison in Casale, he returned to France to deal with the Huguenot rebellion in Languedoc.

The situation in Italy, however, was far from settled. For years the Spanish government had looked to the Emperor Ferdinand for help, but troubles at home had prevented him from responding. In the spring of 1629, however, the German situation was sufficiently calm for him to attend to Italy. He had still not agreed to Nevers's investiture as duke of Mantua. By the end of May an imperial army was on its way to Milan and, in June, Ferdinand appealed to Madrid for joint action south of the Alps. Philip IV told Olivares: 'I am determined to do something against the French, who deserve what is coming to them.' Since Nevers showed no sign of accepting a peaceful settlement, the imperial army ravaged his duchy, while Spinola reluctantly laid siege to Casale again. As for the duke of Savoy, he showed no willingness to implement the Treaty of Susa. By July Richelieu had come to see that France would need to intervene in Italy again, but he did not command the full support of the king's council. A faction headed by Marillac and Bérulle disapproved of policies that threatened to cause a breach between France and Spain. They attached far less importance to upholding French prestige abroad than to solving the problem of heresy at home.

By November 1629 Richelieu had asserted his authority in the council sufficiently to secure a decision that the war in Italy should be resumed. But the need to bring Monsieur back from his self-inflicted exile kept Louis XIII in Paris. So Richelieu was given command of the new Italian expedition with the title of lieutenant-general. He crossed the Alps in mid-winter, and at Susa found his passage barred by the duke of Savoy. Hearing that part of the garrison at Pinerolo had been removed, he ordered marshal Créqui to take the town by surprise. It surrendered on 29 March, giving the French an important strategic base on the edge of Piedmont.

The fall of Pinerolo was an event of capital importance, for it obliged Louis XIII to choose between the policies of Richelieu

and Marillac.[18] It posed once and for all the question of peace
or war with Spain, since the Spaniards were unlikely to allow
the French to hold on to such an important base for future
military operations in Italy. The duke of Savoy demanded the
return of Pinerolo; otherwise he threatened to ally openly with
Spain. On 13 April Richelieu set out the choice facing the king
in a famous memorandum: 'It is not for me,' he wrote, 'to say
whether Pinerolo should be handed back or not, for I am too
far to know. All I can say is that if it is kept and refurbished,
the king . . . will be arbiter and master of Italy. If, on the other
hand, it is returned, he must forget about Italy for ever.' An
honourable peace, Richelieu continued, was feasible but would
endanger Italy's future. The alternative would be a long and
costly war. Before adopting this course one should find out if
the Crown's finances were capable of sustaining such an effort
and if the domestic peace of the kingdom could be assured.
While leaving the final choice to the king, Richelieu pressed
him to make up his mind: if he chose peace, then he should
do so at once while his prestige abroad was high; if he chose
war, then he must attack Savoy immediately and give up all
thoughts of repose, retrenchment and reform at home.[19]

The cardinal's dispatch reached Louis in Dijon shortly after
he had become reconciled to his brother. He did not reply
directly, but Richelieu was informed that the king would attack
Savoy. From Dijon, the king went to Lyons, where he took
leave of the two queens and his council. On 10 May he was at
Grenoble, where he was joined by Richelieu. They discussed
the Italian situation and rejected peace terms that Spain had
offered. Louis confirmed his decision to keep Pinerolo and
sent Richelieu to Lyons where it seems that he managed to
win the queen mother's assent to continuing the war. Soon
afterwards, the French attack on Savoy was unleashed. By
June the whole duchy had fallen into French hands except for
one fortress. Meanwhile, Spinola was besieging Casale for the
king of Spain, and Collalto was besieging Mantua for the emperor. Negotiations between all these parties now took place
under papal auspices. The go-between was Giulio Mazarini,
the future Cardinal Mazarin, who first attracted Richelieu's
notice at this time.[20]

In Lyons, meanwhile, Marie de' Medici and her followers
continued to snipe at the cardinal's policies. Hoping to restore
unity to the government, he arranged a meeting between the

queen mother and her son, but she refused to come on health grounds. So Louis went to Lyons himself. Richelieu feared that this might give the impression that the king did not intend to go to Italy after all. He was proved right when 6,000 French troops deserted. Nor did the king achieve anything in Lyons: the opposition continued to undermine Richelieu's efforts. In July Louis XIII rejoined the army and invaded Savoy, sweeping all before him, but illness forced him to return to Lyons, while Richelieu remained in Maurienne where news reached him that Mantua had fallen to the imperialists.

> If your wish could come true [he wrote to Marillac] that ears of corn might be changed into good soldiers, we would do wonders, especially if the plague could also be changed into good health, necessity into plenty, the inconstancy of Frenchmen into firmness, and if we had not spent three months demonstrating our desire for peace so that our enemies think us incapable of fighting.[21]

Early in September, after Richelieu had returned to Lyons, a truce was arranged at Casale. But, as prospects for peace in Italy brightened, gloom and uncertainty descended on the French court. Louis XIII was so gravely ill that his death seemed imminent. The heir to the throne, Gaston d'Orléans, and his party, began to look forward to Richelieu's overthrow. The king, however, suddenly recovered. The threat to Richelieu's position was consequently removed and his control of policy maintained. The recent truce having expired, a new French army marched to the relief of Casale. As it came within sight of its objective, a horseman waving a white sash appeared. 'Halt! Halt!' he cried, 'Peace! Peace!' It was Mazarin, who had managed to negotiate peace terms acceptable to everyone. Under the Treaty of Cherasco Spain agreed to withdraw from Montferrat, if the French would evacuate Casale and restore the duke of Savoy to his territories. Pending Nevers's investiture by the Emperor, his son, the duc du Maine, was to be given charge of strong points in the duchy of Mantua to be evacuated by French and Spanish troops.

. . .

THE SWEDISH ALLIANCE

Although Richelieu had so far focused his anti-Habsburg strategy on Italy, he had not underestimated the importance of events in Germany. But it was only in January 1630 that his policy in that area began to take significant shape. His aims were clearly stated in instructions given to Marcheville, an envoy sent to Germany at that time. He was to tell the German Electors that Louis XIII was 'driven by a very sincere desire to free Italy and Germany from the oppression to which they had been reduced by the manifest violence and ambition of the House of Austria'. He was ready to help them regain their liberty. They were to ask the Emperor to dismiss Wallenstein, restore peace in Italy or at least remove his troops from there, persuade Spain to evacuate the Palatinate, and to disarm and thus make possible the calling of a general diet. If Ferdinand refused, then Louis was willing at his own cost 'to bring a powerful army into some part of Germany that would not arouse their suspicion'. These instructions show clearly that Richelieu did not think of the Thirty Years War as a religious conflict. He believed that all the Electors, both Catholic and Protestant, had a common interest in resisting the Habsburgs. They also show how closely linked in the cardinal's mind were the German situation and the defence of French interests in Italy.[22]

The Emperor Ferdinand had recently aroused much discontent among the German Protestant princes by issuing the Edict of Restitution calling for the return of all property taken from the Catholic church since 1552. At the same time he wanted to get his son elected as King of the Romans. With this object in mind he called a meeting of Electors to Regensburg in the summer of 1630. Among the foreign diplomats present were two Frenchmen: Brûlart de Léon and Father Joseph.[23] Only the former carried official credentials; the latter was a sort of unofficial adviser, but the trust placed in him by Richelieu made him effectively the leader of the mission. His talks with the Electors have left few traces in his correspondence and a remark ascribed to the Emperor may be apocryphal. He allegedly complained 'that a poor Capuchin had disarmed him with his rosary and had managed, in spite of the narrowness of his cowl, to stuff six electoral bonnets into it.'[24] Father Joseph's instructions, however, are known. His main task was to prevent the Emperor's son from becoming King of the Romans. He was also to work for the creation of a third party in Germany, comprising Maximilian of Bavaria and the Catholic League whose neutrality could be guaranteed by France. The Electors, however, were only interested in getting Wallenstein dismissed and his army disbanded. Ferdinand conceded both demands, hoping to secure in return his son's election as King of the Romans, but this was refused by the Electors. The Emperor's authority was accordingly weakened and Richelieu was given cause to rejoice. But he had failed to detach Maximilian and the Catholic League from the Emperor.

In another respect the French mission to Regensburg was a failure. Brûlart de Léon and Father Joseph had not been expected to raise the Italian situation, but, in the course of their mission, Richelieu thought of bringing pressure to bear on Spain for an Italian peace through the Emperor. Ferdinand, however, cunningly made peace in Italy conditional on France undertaking not to assist his enemies within the Empire. The French envoys tried to obtain some mitigation of this condition, but failed. Consequently, the Treaty of Regensburg which they signed in October was never ratified by Louis.[25] The war in Italy continued till June 1631.

Richelieu's German policy was two-fold. On the one hand, he wanted to bring about a defensive alliance between Louis XIII and Maximilian of Bavaria which would deprive the Emperor of Bavarian support; on the other, he wished to conclude a treaty of financial aid with the king of Sweden which would enable the latter to invade Germany and attack the Habsburgs' hereditary lands. Maximilian and Louis XIII had a common interest in defending the Catholic faith as long as this did not play into Spanish hands; the Elector was also attached to those Germanic liberties which Louis claimed to have so much at heart. Yet the French and Bavarian positions were basically incompatible: France wanted to detach Bavaria from the Emperor and form a third party within the Empire which would prove a docile instrument of French policy. Maximilian, for his part, wanted to detach Louis XIII from his Protestant allies and with France's help liberate Germany from Habsburg domination without, however, compromising the success of the Counter-Reformation.[26] Because of this basic divergence of aims, the negotiations at Regensburg between Father Joseph and Maximilian were complex and tortuous. Eventually, however, a Franco-Bavarian alliance was formed at Munich (8 May 1631) and at Fontainebleau (30 May). The two parties promised not to assist each other's enemies directly or indirectly. Louis XIII promised to defend Maxmilian's electoral title. They guaranteed each other's possessions. But the Elector reserved his right in all circumstances to satisfy his obligations to the Emperor.

French historians used to think that the intervention of the Swedish monarch, Gustavus Adolphus, in the Thirty Years War had been engineered by Richelieu in order to gain time before France was herself prepared to enter the conflict. But Gustavus intervened for excellent reasons of his own.[27] He wanted to ensure Sweden's security by evicting imperialist forces from the Baltic shore. At the same time he wanted to galvanize the north German Protestant states into a union capable of resisting resurgent Catholicism. But, being short of money, he was not averse to receiving financial aid from abroad. Thanks largely to the tenacity of the French envoy, the baron de Charnacé, long-drawn-out negotiations between France and Sweden culminated in the Treaty of Bärwalde (23 January 1631).[28] Gustavus agreed to maintain in Germany an army of 30,000 men and 6,000 horse in return for a subsidy of 1 million *livres* per annum over five years. He promised to respect Catholic worship where it was being practised and to respect the neutrality of Bavaria and the League as long as they declared themselves neutral. This treaty was not an alliance but a subsidy agreement: France did not undertake to enter the war; nor did she guarantee any of Gustavus's conquests. Richelieu's view of the treaty was well summed up by Father Joseph: 'these things have to be used like poison; a little can serve as an antidote; too much kills.'[29] If the Treaty of Bärwalde looked at first like a triumph for French diplomacy, that was simply because the risks it contained did not surface for some time.[30]

French policy in Germany in the spring of 1631 rested, therefore, on two treaties negotiated independently of each other: the first with a Catholic prince, head of the German Catholic League; the other with a Protestant monarch who saw himself as the protector of the Protestant churches. Richelieu's problem was to run these allies in double harness: they needed to be brought into line, yet neither was interested in friendship with the other; hence the difficulties encountered by Richelieu in Germany during the following months. He may have hoped that dependence on the French subsidy would restrain Gustavus, but it is more likely that he misjudged the king's character and aims. The subsidy, while it helped to tide Gustavus over his immediate difficulties, ceased to be of major importance as his conquest of Germany got under way.[31]

In April 1631 the Protestant princes of Germany, led by John George of Saxony and George William of Brandenburg, gathered at Leipzig. They offered to assist Ferdinand against the Swedish invasion if he would annul the Edict of Restitution, but he refused, the edict being for him a matter of conscience. Soon afterwards the sack of Magdeburg by the imperial army under Tilly caused a wave of revulsion among the Protestant princes, leaving them no alternative but to join the Swedes. Meanwhile, Gustavus's army swept across Germany. On 17 September it crushed the imperial army at Breitenfeld.

Although officially Sweden's friend, Richelieu viewed Gustavus's astounding success with alarm. For it dashed all those hopes he and Father Joseph had entertained of arbitrating between the Protestant and Catholic princes. Gustavus, not Louis XIII, was now the champion of German liberties. His triumph, moreover, was bound to drive the Catholics into the Emperor's arms, particularly as Gustavus showed no inclination to treat them as neutrals. Much now depended on his next move. Would he put his troops into winter quarters, leaving the diplomats time to achieve some sort of pacification, or would he keep up the pressure on the Habsburgs by invading Bohemia and attacking their hereditary lands? Actually, Gustavus did neither: he sent the Saxon army to liberate Bohemia, while he himself swept through Franconia and Thuringia, capturing Erfurt, Würzburg, Frankfurt-on-Main and, on 20 December, Mainz. Soon Swedish detachments were infiltrating Alsace.

The westward drive of the Swedish army, as rapid as it was destructive, forced Richelieu to attend to the security of France's eastern border as a matter of urgency. A weakness in that area was the duchy of Lorraine, which, in the early seventeenth century, was still independent. But it was also a tangle of rival jurisdictions.[32] In the west the *Barrois mouvant* was a French fief, while the duchy proper, though theoretically independent of the Empire, formed part of the Upper Rhine Circle and contained many imperial fiefs. To complicate matters, the king of France claimed sovereignty over the towns of Metz, Toul and Verdun. In 1629, following a dispute over the see of Metz, imperial troops occupied the towns of Vic and Moyenvic. As for the duke Charles IV, he was on bad terms with Louis XIII, who had refused to recognise him as duke of Bar. He consequently gravitated towards the Habsburgs and gave refuge to Gaston d'Orléans at his court in Nancy after the Day of Dupes.[33] Richelieu feared that Lorraine might be used to mount an offensive designed to reverse the verdict of that fateful day. When the duke raised troops, ostensibly for service against the Swedes, Richelieu asked him to withdraw them from the French border. In December 1631 a French army recaptured Moyenvic from the Emperor and, on 6 January, Charles IV signed the treaty of Vic with France. He promised to observe good relations with her, handed over the fortress of Marsal for three years and promised free passage to French troops. This allowed Louis XIII to send troops into Alsace, should this be necessary, without their having to fight their way there. An invasion of Alsace was, it seems, considered at a French council meeting on 6 January, but dropped after Father Joseph had spoken against it.[34]

Early in January an embassy led by de Brézé, Richelieu's brother-in-law, called on Gustavus at Mainz with a view to persuading him to withdraw from the Rhineland and to respect the neutrality of Maximilian of Bavaria and the Catholic League. But the ambassadors were given a very rough ride. Gustavus, who expected immediate assistance from Louis XIII, resented the suggestion that he should evacuate the Rhineland and refused to consider the Catholic princes as neutral. When told of an impending visit by their representatives, he called them 'rogues and traitors' and threatened to string them up. 'He was so bitter,' wrote de Brézé, 'that it would have been easy for us to break off relations and declare war on him.' In the end, the envoys were bludgeoned by Gustavus into signing an agreement committing Richelieu to restore the status quo ante bellum in Germany and to break his engagements to Maximilian.[35] But the latter did not really care. On 28 February his army drove the Swedes out of Bamberg, thereby effectively dashing Richelieu's hope of averting a conflict between France's two allies. Early in March 1632 Gustavus left Mainz for central Germany.

After crossing the Lech, he swept across Bavaria, entering Munich in triumph. From here Gustavus marched north towards Saxony. On the way he ran into the imperial army at Lützen. In the ensuing battle (16 November) the imperialists were crushed, but Gustavus was killed leading his cavalry.

The year 1632 was a traumatic one for Richelieu. Although he never ceased to keep a close watch on events abroad, Montmorency's revolt in Languedoc absorbed most of his attention. Even after the duke's execution, restlessness among the high nobility kept the cardinal occupied. These events were evidently still fresh in his mind when news reached him of the death of Gustavus. 'If the king of Sweden had postponed his death by six months,' he wrote to Louis XIII, 'it seems likely that Your Majesty's affairs would have been more secure.'[36]

A mixture of relief and apprehension was the cardinal's reaction to the death of Gustavus. He had been too wilful for comfort, but his disappearance threatened a power vacuum in Germany which the Habsburgs might fill. As France was not as yet prepared for military intervention beyond the Rhine, she was most anxious that pressure on the Emperor should not be relaxed, for this might allow him to assist his Spanish cousin more effectively in Italy or the Netherlands. Thus the French ambassador, Feuquières, encouraged the Protestant Electors meeting at Heilbronn to continue the war.[37] But French diplomacy failed to prevent Maximilian of Bavaria and the Catholic League from joining forces against the Swedes and the League of Heilbronn, now led by Axel Oxenstierna, the regent of the young Swedish queen, Christina.

Richelieu, meanwhile, used every opportunity of tightening France's hold on Lorraine. Its duke, Charles IV, had violated the Treaty of Vic by secretly marrying his daughter, Marguerite, to Louis XIII's rebellious brother, Gaston. This gave Louis a pretext to invade Lorraine and impose a more demanding treaty on Charles at Liverdun (26 June). In addition to Marsal, France now gained the county of Clermont-en-Argonne, and French garrisons were planted at Stenay and Jametz. But, even now, Charles IV continued to favour the Emperor by taking Haguenau and Saverne under his protection against the Swedes. Although Richelieu wanted to avoid giving the impression that France aimed at territorial aggrandisement in Lorraine for fear of antagonising his German allies, Louis occupied part of Nancy in September 1633. Early in the following year Richelieu started a process in the Parlement of Paris for the annulment of Gaston's marriage to Marguerite, and charged the duke in the same court of Gaston's abduction and sequestration. Rather than face the charge, Charles IV abdicated in favour of his brother, Nicolas François, and entered the Emperor's service. Soon afterwards, Nicolas François fled to Italy, opening the way to the French annexation of the duchy.[38]

The French occupation of Lorraine facilitated the movement of French troops into Alsace, a highly sensitive area in which imperialists, Swedes and Spaniards competed for control. As far as Richelieu was concerned, the Swedes were as great a danger in the area as were the Spaniards. Ideally, he wanted to exclude both and replace them by French garrisons wherever possible. Feuquières was instructed to reassure Oxenstierna that Louis XIII had no long-term designs on the area: he simply wanted to set up 'barriers against eventualities in order to protect his friends'. By the autumn of 1633 the Swedes had overrun almost the whole of Alsace, except for the Sundgau and Breisach, which the Spaniards still held. But France did manage to secure some useful footholds. In July 1632 the Elector of Trier accepted French protection and allowed French troops to garrison Philippsburg. In October 1633 the duke of Württemberg placed under French protection his duchy of Montbéliard which partly covered the eastern approach to Burgundy, and, in December, the count of Hanau allowed French garrisons into three towns of lower Alsace. In January 1634 Haguenau, Saverne and the bishopric of Basel also came under French protection.[39]

Meanwhile, Richelieu had to advise Louis XIII on two major diplomatic approaches: one from the United Provinces and the other from Sweden. In the wake of a defensive alliance concluded in April 1634 between France and the United Provinces, the Stadtholder Frederick Henry tried to commit Louis XIII to military intervention in the Netherlands. Dutch envoys sent to Paris to ratify the alliance proposed another that envisaged the joint conquest and partition of the Spanish Netherlands. France would be given the Flemish coast as far as Bruges, and the United Provinces would receive the rest. The offer was tempting, and Richelieu carefully weighed its pros and cons. It had the advantage of pushing France's frontier well to the north of Artois, thereby reducing the vulnerability of Paris to invasion from that direction. But a war on three fronts at once – in the Netherlands, Germany and Italy – was extremely risky. France might also find herself drawn into the old war between the Dutch and the Spaniards. The cardinal, therefore, advised Louis to turn down the offer.

The Swedish initiative was, it seems, quite independent of the Dutch one. Fearing a break-up of the Heilbronn League, Oxenstierna looked to France to revive its flagging spirits. He decided in August to hand Philippsburg to the French, then proposed to Louis XIII an offensive alliance. Sweden would attack the Habsburgs in Bohemia and Silesia, leaving the French to defend the Empire further west. This too was a tempting proposal. If accepted, it would give Louis freedom of movement in the Rhineland. But here again there was a risk: namely, that the German princes would rally to the Emperor against the foreign invaders. Were this to happen, France would be involved in a war without end. It was a frightening prospect, and Richelieu, once again, advised his master to reject the offer. Even at this late stage he aimed to postpone France's entry into the Thirty Years War for as long as possible.[40] His hand, however, was soon forced by an unexpected turn of events.

In 1634 Philip IV's brother, the Cardinal-Infante Ferdinand, assembled a great army in Milan for service in the Netherlands. Because 'the Spanish Road' was blocked by the French in Alsace-Lorraine, he was advised that he would have to march through Germany, join the Emperor's forces and fight his way through the Protestant states in his path. On 6 September the joint Habsburg army inflicted a crushing defeat on the Swedish and Protestant forces at Nördlingen. Shattered by this disaster, the League of Heilbronn turned to France for help. It offered extensive concessions in return for an immediate declaration of war by France on Spain and the Emperor. In December, Oxenstierna left the League, and even Sweden's old ally, William of Hesse Kassel saw that only France could now save the Protestant cause. 'The House of Austria,' he wrote, 'wishes to subjugate all Germany

extirpating liberty and the Reformed religion. So in this
extremity we must look to France.'[41]

. . .

NOTES AND REFERENCES

1. Richelieu. André, L (ed.) 1947 *Testament politique*. Paris,
   Laffont, pp. 95, 347.
2. See above, pp. 73–8.
3. Pagès, G 1949 *La Guerre de Trente Ans, 1618–1648*. Paris,
   Payot, pp. 118–19.
4. Elliott J H 1986 *The Count-Duke of Olivares: the Statesman in
   an Age of Decline*. New Haven, CT and London, Yale University Press, pp. 217–19, 224–25; Stradling, R A 1986
   'Olivares and the Origins of the Franco-Spanish War,
   1627–35' *English Historical Review*, 101: 81.
5. Parker G 1977 *The Dutch Revolt*. London, Allen Lane,
   passim.
6. Thuau E 1966 *Raison d'état et pensée politique à l'époque de
   Richelieu*. Paris, A Colin, pp. 195, 197, 200–1.
7. Parker G 1972 *The Army of Flanders and the Spanish Road,
   1576–1659*. Cambridge, Cambridge University Press, pp.
   50–101.
8. Lublinskaya A D 1968 *French Absolutism: the Crucial
   Phase, 1620–29*. Cambridge, Cambridge University Press,
   pp. 262–71; Pithon, R 1960 'Les débuts difficiles du
   ministère de Richelieu et la crise de Valteline (1621–27)'
   Revue d'histoire diplomatique 74: 289–322.
9. Lockyer R 1981 *Buckingham: The Life and Political Career
   of George Villiers, First Duke of Buckingham, 1592–1628*.
   London, pp. 236–41.
10. See above p. 87.
11. Parker *The Army of Flanders*, pp. 74–6.
12. Elliott *Olivares*, pp. 229–33.
13. Ibid., p. 326.
14. See above, pp. 74–5.
15. Elliott *Olivares*, pp. 336–38.
16. Ibid., p. 368; Stradling, R A 'Olivares and the Origins
    of the Franco-Spanish War' *English Historical Review* 101:
    68–94; Stradling, R A 'Prelude to Disaster: the Precipita-
    tion of the War of Mantuan Succession, 1627–29' *Histori-
    cal Journal* (forthcoming).
17. Elliott *Olivares*, p. 377.

18. Pagès G 1937 'Autour du "Grand Orage": Richelieu et Marillac: Deux politiques' *Revue historique* 172: 82.

19. Ibid., pp. 82–5.

20. Dethan G 1977 *The Young Mazarin*. London, Thames & Hudson, pp. 41, 89, 91–2; Tapié, V-L 1984 *France in the Age of Louis XIII and Richelieu*, Lockie, D McN (ed.) Cambridge, Cambridge University Press p. 230.

21. Pagès 'Autour du "Grand Orage"', p. 93.

22. Pagès *La Guerre de Trente Ans*, pp. 121-22.

23. On Father Joseph's diplomatic role, see Fagniez, G 1891–94 *Le Père Joseph et Richelieu*, 2 vols, Paris; Church, W F 1972 *Richelieu and Reason of State*, Princeton, NJ, Princeton University Press, pp. 290–94.

24. Pagès *La Guerre de Trente Ans*, p. 123.

25. Ibid., p. 124.

26. Ibid., p. 126.

27. Roberts M 1967 'The Political Objectives of Gustav Adolf in Germany, 1630–2' in *Essays in Swedish History*. London, Weidenfeld & Nicolson, pp. 82–110.

28. Roberts M 1958 *Gustavus Adolphus: a History of Sweden 1611–1632*. London, Longmans, Green, vol. 2, pp. 466–67; Bonney R 1981 *The King's Debts*. Oxford, Clarendon, pp. 163–64.

29. Pagès *La Guerre de Trente Ans*, p. 129.

30. Roberts M (*Gustavus Adolphus* vol. 2, p. 467) describes it as 'a major reverse for Richelieu's foreign policy'.

31. Ibid., vol. 2, p. 469. But see also p. 594 for a seemingly contradictory statement.

32. Pagès *La Guerre de Trente Ans*, pp. 136–38.

33. Tapié *France in the Age of Louis XIII and Richelieu*, p. 204.

34. Roberts, *Gustavus Adolphus* vol. 2, p. 586.

35. Ibid., vol. 2, pp. 586–89; Pagès *La Guerre de Trente Ans*, pp 146–47.

36. Tapié *France in the Age of Louis XIII and Richelieu* pp. 311.

37. Ibid., pp. 316–21; Pagès *La Guerre de Trente Ans*, pp. 165–66.

38. Ibid., pp. 174–77; Tapié *France in the Age of Louis XIII and Richelieu*, pp. 323–25.

39. Pagès *La Guerre de Trente Ans*, pp. 174–75.

40. Ibid., pp. 177–79.

41. Parker, G 1984 *The Thirty Years' War*. London, Routledge and Kegan Paul, p. 141.

Chapter 7

RICHELIEU AND WAR
(1635–42)

News of the Swedish defeat at Nördlingen, on 6 September 1634 reached Paris on the 11th. Six hours after receiving it Richelieu addressed a memorandum to Louis XIII. This time he did not discuss the pros and cons of the situation: only one course of action seemed possible. If the League of Heilbronn was not helped promptly, it would dissolve, leaving France to bear the full brunt of Habsburg power. The cardinal had long believed that sooner or later France would have to substitute 'open war' for 'covert war'. The time for this transition had arrived. The most foolish course for France would be to act in such a way as to be left facing the combined forces of Spain and the Empire alone. Having said that, Richelieu still advised caution. He knew that France's finances were in poor shape, as was her army. She needed a few months to prepare for open war.[1]

Two important treaties were signed by France in the interval between Nördlingen and her entry into the Thirty Years War: one with the United Provinces; the other with Sweden. On 8 February 1635 a Franco-Dutch alliance was concluded, providing for a joint invasion of the Spanish Netherlands and their eventual partition. This was followed on 28 April by a new treaty, signed at Compiègne with Sweden, which was to come into force only after France had broken with Spain *and* the Empire. Neither treaty was wholly satisfactory to France. Provision for the partitioning of the Spanish Netherlands was left vague in the Dutch treaty. As for the other treaty, it left Sweden free to desert France at any time. By allowing Sweden to retain possession of the sees of Mainz and Worms, the treaty effectively condoned a serious infringement of the German Counter-Reformation. The two treaties marked the final defeat of Richelieu's attempt to reconcile the two religious camps in Germany.[2]

Meanwhile, the Emperor drew closer to the Protestant princes. The 'Preliminaries of Pirna' (November 1634) offered various concessions to the Saxon Elector. Above all, the date for the handing back of church lands under the Edict of Restitution was moved to November 1627. This allowed the Catholic princes to keep their gains in south and south-west Germany, while guaranteeing the secularised lands of the Protestants in the north. While diplomats on both sides were busily adjusting to the consequences of the Swedish débâcle at Nördlingen, fighting continued within the Empire. Bernard of Saxe-Weimar, one of the best commanders on the Protestant side, tried to check the westward advance of the imperial armies. After abandoning his duchy of Franconia, he managed for a time to hold the Rhine between Mannheim and Mainz. But, in January 1635, the imperialists captured Philippsburg and the Spaniards overran the Electorate of Trier. Although Louis XIII, in his role as protector of the Alsatian towns, kept to the left bank of the Rhine, to all intents and purposes he and the Emperor were already at war, though no declaration had yet been made.

On 26 March 1635 Spanish troops entered Trier and carried off the Elector as their prisoner. He was officially the protégé of France and the Spanish action was treated by Louis XIII as a serious provocation. A meeting of the French council of state on 1 April concluded that 'the king cannot avoid taking up arms to avenge the affront which he has received by the imprisonment of a prince who has been placed under his protection'.[3] On 19 May a French herald carried his master's defiance to the King of Spain and the Cardinal-Infante in Brussels. The declaration, however, was addressed only to Spain. This was in accordance with Richelieu's view of Spain as France's chief enemy. He was prepared to implement his side of the recent treaty with the Dutch, but had no intention at this stage of embarking on a conflict in Germany. He hoped that the French garrisons in Alsace would stand in the way of any Habsburg attempt to invade Lorraine or Burgundy.

A council meeting held at Compiègne on 28 April showed how ill-prepared France was for a major war. The councillors revealed themselves incapable of formulating any sort of overall strategy. All that Richelieu and his colleagues could do was to try to estimate the numbers of enemy troops ranged against them and to guess the aims of their commanders with a view to raising enough French troops to block their advance wherever this might be. They made no distinction between Spaniards and Imperialists in spite of Richelieu's determination that war should only be declared on the former. The main preoccupation of the councillors was the cost of maintaining a large army. A possible solution, they felt, was to give the troops more freedom to live off the countryside, 'albeit without departing too much from discipline and obedience'. One way of ensuring that they behaved reasonably towards the local inhabitants was to hold down the price of food; another was to let village communities supply the troops with victuals and give them hope of reimbursement. 'In short,' writes Pagès, 'no unity of command, strategic ideas of a more than mediocre kind, a deplorable lack of financial resources; such were the conditions in which France began the war'.[4]

France made the opening moves, but only against Spain. On 20 May, the day after war was declared, marshals Châtillon and de Brézé defeated a Spanish force at Avein, near Liège, but the hostility of the local people was aroused by the barbaric behaviour of the French troops. Desertion and disease also took their toll and the army soon degenerated into a rabble which the Dutch had to repatriate by sea. It was an inglorious end to the campaign. Richelieu expressed his bitterness in a letter to the king:

> My heart bleeds knowing of the misery which has attended the complete extinction of the army of Flanders ... It is of more importance to the king's affairs than is easily imagined, for his authority is brought into contempt by the misery in which his troops are seen to die.[5]

Nor did the cardinal find much cheer in Italy. After the duc de Rohan had occupied most of the Valtelline, France signed a treaty on 11 July with the dukes of Savoy and Parma for the joint conquest of the Milanese, but Richelieu failed to enlist the co-operation of other Italian states, and the ensuing campaign petered out almost as soon as it began.

In Germany, too, the war began badly for France. On 30 May the Elector of Saxony abandoned Sweden for the

Emperor. The Elector of Brandenburg soon followed suit. Other princes and most of the imperial cities then accepted terms laid down at Pirna. All that survived of the League of Heilbronn was a handful of minor princes. Some were fugitives, others disposed of a few troops. Louis XIII agreed to subsidise William of Hesse-Kassel and his army of 10,000 men. Another Protestant survivor was Bernard of Saxe-Weimar. He had lost his duchy, but retained the loyalty of his troops. In October Louis XIII agreed to subsidise his army of 18,000 men provided he placed himself under his authority. In return, Bernard was given the Alsatian lands of the Habsburgs. This gave him an incentive to hold on to Alsace and, if possible, to capture Breisach, which the Spaniards and Imperialists still held.[6] Thus all that remained of the grand anti-Habsburg coalition over which Gustavus Adolphus had once presided were two armies, both in the pay of France. The rest of the Empire followed the Emperor's lead.

As for Sweden, her alliance with France had always been precarious. Oxenstierna's aims differed from Richelieu's: he was not at war with Spain and would have been prepared to make a separate peace with the Emperor provided that Sweden's conquests in north Germany were guaranteed. Richelieu, on the other hand, believed that France's interests would best be served by a general peace involving both the Empire and Spain. Throughout 1635 the Swedes fought for themselves alone. Their principal army under Baner tried unsuccessfully to reach Bohemia, while further west the imperial army under Gallas forced Saxe-Weimar to retreat to Lorraine.

The year 1636 was for long remembered in France as 'the year of Corbie'. It was even worse than 1635. Believing that France would not be able to resist a concerted attack by Spanish and Imperial forces, the Cardinal-Infante arranged for Gallas to invade Burgundy, while he himself planned to march into Picardy from Artois. Neither commander met with significant resistance. While Gallas laid siege to St Jean-de-Losne, the Cardinal-Infante captured La Capelle, then Corbie, guarding the approach to Paris from the north. The Bavarian cavalry under von Werth, after taking Roye and Montdidier, foraged as far as the walls of Compiègne and Pontoise.

During the nine days' siege of Corbie, panic had spread to the French capital whose fortifications were not up to scratch. Many Parisians fled south; but Louis XIII stood firm. He appealed to the municipal government, the sovereign courts, the merchants and artisans for funds to raise and maintain troops. All unemployed men who were capable of bearing arms were urged to volunteer for service under marshal de la Force. Eventually, an army of 30,000 men was assembled to defend the capital. Louis XIII, meanwhile, rode through the streets without an armed escort, dispensing words of encouragement to passers-by. Richelieu showed less fortitude at first. Poor in health and overwhelmed by cares, he even offered to resign, but, egged on by the king, he too took to the streets, where people had only recently been clamouring for his blood. His apparent calm had the desired effect: the people were assuaged; some even prayed God to bring the cardinal success. Yet Richelieu was pessimistic. He advised a retreat to the Loire, but the king dismissed the idea.[7] On 1 September Louis set out to reconquer the towns of northern France that had fallen to the enemy. His task proved easier than expected, for the Cardinal-Infante, disappointed in his hopes of help from Gallas's Germans, prudently decided to withdraw in the face of the French counter-offensive. On 14 November Corbie was recaptured by the French. Meanwhile, in Burgundy little save devastation was achieved by the Imperialists. The little town of St Jean-de-Losne covered itself with glory by holding up Gallas's advance, thereby earning the nickname of St Jean-Belle-Défense. In the autumn Gallas was recalled to Germany.

France had weathered the storm of 1636. She had survived the Cardinal-Infante's invasion and a wave of anti-fiscal revolts in south-west France. But Richelieu had little to rejoice about, particularly as a new plot to overthrow him was being laid by Gaston d'Orléans and the comte de Soissons. Understandably, he looked for a respite. In March 1637, the baron de Pujols informed Olivares of Richelieu's willingness to engage in talks. Tortuous negotiations followed, but they merely underlined the differences between France and Spain. Richelieu wanted a truce; Olivares, a general peace based on the reciprocal restitution of conquests. Each side wanted to detach the other's allies; neither was prepared to make serious concessions.[8]

In 1637, as the war in northern France came virtually to a standstill, some important developments took place in Italy. Following the death of Charles of Nevers in September 1636, the duchy of Mantua had passed into the hands of his widow, who was wholly devoted to Spain. A year later, on 8 October 1637 Victor-Amadeus of Savoy died. His widow, Christine, who became regent, was Louis XIII's sister, but she had to reckon with her two brothers-in-law, Cardinal Maurice and Prince Thomas, who were pro-Spanish. Piedmont soon went over to their side and the duchess found herself relegated to the citadel of Turin. Eventually, she escaped to France, but refused to allow her son to be brought up at Louis XIII's court. Another disappointment for Richelieu concerned the Valtelline. The duc de Rohan tried to reconcile the inhabitants to the Grisons, but he managed only to alienate the latter, who forced him to evacuate the valley. This made any French intervention in Italy impossible while reopening the road to the Tyrol for Spanish troops. Yet all did not prosper for Spain in 1637. An attempt to invade France from Catalonia ended in a humiliating Spanish defeat at Leucate on 27 September.

In Germany, Ferdinand II at last obtained what he had wanted for so long: on 22 December 1636 his son, Ferdinand, was elected King of the Romans. He succeeded to the Empire when his father died on 15 February 1637. He aimed at restoring peace and prosperity to the German lands that had been devastated by the recent campaigns and by terrible epidemics. By 1637 Oxenstierna had given up hope of securing Swedish control of Pomerania through a separate peace with the Emperor. He consequently drew closer to France, signing the Treaty of Hamburg (15 March 1638). This committed France to declare war on the Emperor, which she did soon afterwards. The allies were now expected to combine their offensives: Sweden in Saxony; France in upper Germany.

. . .

THE ARMY UNDER RICHELIEU

French historians have generally assumed that Richelieu's ministry was marked by a steady improvement in the military fortunes of France. They have ascribed this improvement to a reorganisation of the army undertaken by the cardinal as from 1635. This, according to Pagès, was not based on any systematic plan, but on the provision of urgent necessities. It had two main features: the preponderant role given to civilians and a huge increase in the number of troops. The civilians included the minister in charge (Servien in 1635; Sublet de Noyers as from February 1636), royal muster commissioners, and an *intendant* of justice attached to each army, who not only supervised the payment of the troops and the distribution of supplies, but also tried offences committed by soldiers. In July 1635 there were not less than nine armies in the field comprising a total of 160,000 men (134,000 infantry; 26,000 cavalry). Richelieu tried to add to it by calling the feudal levy (*ban et arrière ban*), but dropped the experiment after it had proved unsuccessful. He also tried to improve deliveries of bread and forage to the army.[9]

If Richelieu achieved so much, why was he unable to defeat the Habsburgs decisively within his lifetime? Spain in the 1640s was reaching the limits of her resources, yet managed to continue fighting till 1659. This was because the war did not proceed so consistently in favour of France as historians have led us to believe. Ironically, it was in the opening stages of the war that the only victories in battle of Richelieu's ministry were won. Thereafter, France became committed to a war of sieges. These were a normal feature of seventeenth-century warfare, but they absorbed a share of available resources not always justified by the results. Throughout Richelieu's ministry victories were offset by defeats. Yet France had many advantages over Spain: good material resources, powerful allies (Sweden and the Dutch), a resilient economy and relatively short communications. So what went wrong? The answer, according to David Parrott, may be found in a chronically deficient military administration.[10]

The figures commonly given for the strength of the French army in the 1630s are misleading. They emanate from the *Bureau des Finances* and are pre-campaign estimates. More realistic figures are provided by the musters carried out by the *commissaires des guerres*. These suggest that in the first half of 1635 the army comprised some 60,000 infantry and 8,000 to 9,000 cavalry. In the course of the campaign some 50,000 to 60,000 additional troops were raised to fill the gaps caused by death, wounds, sickness and desertion. Thus the original totals remained broadly the same. In subsequent years the scale of campaign recruitment was greater, yet again this did not produce significantly larger armies in the field.

The army, then, was probably smaller than is commonly assumed. 70,000 to 80,000 men would seem a reasonable estimate. Yet it was still too large to be adequately supplied and regularly paid by the government. One reason for this was the Crown's burden of debt. Long before 1635 it had become entangled in a network of loans and *traités* negotiated on each year's revenues. Even in peacetime the Crown borrowed so as to keep its creditors at bay without losing too much income. The finance minister spent much of his time raising new loans to meet the interest on debts or to repay old ones. A high proportion of the Crown's revenues was spent on debt or interest repayments to financiers. What was left was for military expenses and it was not enough. Only the main army in a particular campaign could expect its costs to be met in cash, albeit subject to delays and shortfalls. Other units were likely to be disappointed. In 1638 Richelieu blamed Bullion's abuse of assignations for the poor war effort without, however, offering a solution to the problem.

Financing the war effort was, of course, a general problem in seventeenth-century Europe: all governments had to cope with armies that had expanded faster than their traditional income. France, however, was unique in one respect. Other countries made use of the entrepreneurial system. A military entrepreneur would raise and maintain an army at his own expense against subsequent reimbursement by the government concerned. In the 1620s and 1630s the system developed in conjunction with taxation, called 'contributions', levied upon enemy or neutral territory. This was used to cover the army's subsistence and to repay part of the entrepreneur's investment. The entrepreneurial system, being to some extent self-financing, made possible the growth of much larger armies than in the past. It also made for military efficiency, since commanders had a financial stake in their armies. But France, for political reasons, would not accept entrepreneurship.[11] The experience of her civil wars explains her government's reluctance to delegate military authority to her subjects. It did not, however, object to having foreign entrepreneurs in its service, like Bernard of Saxe-Weimar.

While generally rejecting military entrepreneurship, the French government made use of a system that was arguably more dangerous. The military profession enjoyed the highest social status in France, and the scramble for military offices was even more intense than that for their civilian counterparts. In allocating such offices the government tended to favour petitioners who were prepared to take upon themselves the costs of levying and maintaining their own troops. In effect, such men were making loans to the Crown without expectation of reimbursement. A military office-holder, however, was not allowed any proprietary right over his unit. He could not sell or transfer it without royal permission; nor was he compensated if his unit was disbanded. Thus many officers found themselves heavily burdened financially. Since they were volunteers, not salaried employees, they did not feel bound by military discipline or by any obligation to remain at their post. Thus officer absenteeism became rife – more so than in any other contemporary army. Even if an officer was present, he would commonly engage in corrupt practices of all sorts in an effort to recoup his losses.

An efficient administration might have curbed the worst abuses in the French army, but Richelieu failed to bring this about. The army *intendants* do not seem to have been as effective as their civilian counterparts, several becoming the clients of aristocratic commanders. This may be why, in the 1630s, the government enlarged the responsibilities of the *commissaires des guerres*. Some of them were authorised in 1637–38 to levy and distribute a new tax (*subsistances*) designed to meet the cost of quartering troops in the winter. But the expedient was abandoned as it gave the commissioners scope for corruption and maladministration. By the 1640s the *intendants* had become the key figures in military administration.

Faced by the government's consistent failure to cope with the problems of financial distribution, supply and discipline, Richelieu drew upon the services of clients, who used their own personal resources to remedy the failures of military suppliers. But there was a limit to what they could do. Bonds of clientage offered no permanent solution to the basic inadequacies of the military administration. In 1650 Le Tellier described the French army as a 'republic, whose cantons are made up of the forces of the corps commanders'. This has

usually been taken to reflect the breakdown of royal authority during the Fronde, but Dr Parrott takes it 'as a verdict
upon the comprehensive failure of Richelieu's ministry to
tackle the problems created by a significantly larger military
establishment than France had deployed hitherto'.[12]

. . .

THE TURN OF THE TIDE

In October 1637 the Stadtholder Frederick Henry captured
Breda, thereby forcing Spain to move some of her troops out
of Germany. Taking advantage of their departure, Bernard
of Saxe-Weimar advanced along the Rhine from Basel. After
capturing Rheinfelden, he laid siege to the important fortress of Breisach. Meanwhile, in the Netherlands, marshal
Châtillon laid siege to St Omer and, in the south-west, the
prince of Condé advanced to the Franco-Spanish border and
laid siege to Fuenterrabía. A fleet under Sourdis, archbishop
of Bordeaux, supported his operations by sea. Fortified by
these achievements, Richelieu offered the Spaniards a truce,
based essentially on the status quo. He and Don Miguel de
Salamanca met secretly at Compiègne but failed to agree.
Richelieu was clearly hoping for more military successes. But
more disappointments lay in store for him. In the north,
Châtillon retreated from St Omer after foolishly ignoring
a canal by which supplies had been reaching the enemy. In
Italy, Créqui was killed and his successor, Cardinal de La
Valette, was defeated at Vercelli. But the worst news came
from Fuenterrabía. Richelieu was expecting to hear that the
town had fallen to the French, when he learned that they
had made no attempt to take it by storm after breaching its
defences. Instead, they had been routed by a much smaller
force. 'I am so grieved about Fuenterrabía,' wrote Richelieu,
'that it will kill me'. However, he could take some consolation
from French successes at sea, including an action by his
nephew Pont Courlay off Genoa. 'I am overjoyed by these
victories of His Majesty,' he wrote, 'and it gives me great
content to see that his fleet which is my especial charge is
doing its duty.'[13]

On 17 December Breisach fell to Bernard of Saxe-Weimar:
its loss deprived Spain of two vital military corridors: one to
the heart of the Empire, the other to Flanders. This was

particularly serious at a time when a shortage of seasoned veterans obliged Spain to move troops frequently from one theatre of war to another. But the capture of Breisach was not without risk to France. Bernard of Saxe-Weimar wished to become duke of Alsace, and it was possible that he would seek an understanding with the Emperor. However, he died at the end of the year, and his heir proved loyal to France. With Breisach out of her control, Spain had to fall back on the sea to keep her life-lines open. In 1639 a powerful armada was assembled at Corunna laden with troop reinforcements and bullion for Flanders. It was not quite as large as the Invincible Armada of 1588, but its fire-power was greater. In mid-September, after a running battle with the Dutch fleet under Tromp, the armada took refuge in the Downs. On 21 October the Spaniards were heavily defeated by the Dutch as they tried to slip past them. This was a disaster of the first magnitude for Spain. With control of the northern waters lost to the Dutch, she was forced back on the defensive everywhere.[14] The main concern of Olivares, as 1640 opened, was to avoid another spring campaign. 'The sign that God wishes for peace to be made,' he wrote, 'is that He is visibly depriving us of the means of waging war.'[15] The Spanish council of state shared this view and wanted to reach an understanding with France. Richelieu's spirits, however, had been lifted by Tromp's victory. He was planning naval operations off the Spanish coast and in mid-Atlantic and did not want his Dutch and Swedish allies to misinterpret his motives if they should learn of his secret talks with Spain. When a Spanish emissary called on the cardinal at Compiègne in June 1640, he haughtily dismissed the terms that were offered him.

Historians have sometimes suggested that Richelieu was better able to concentrate on winning the war after 1638 once France's domestic affairs had become more settled. But he continued to have serious problems at home in the form of tax revolts and aristocratic plots. In 1639 a revolt broke out in Normandy. It was 'a movement of such dimensions that it all but threw the realm into confusion and made it difficult to continue the war abroad'.[16] Yet France's domestic problems were relatively minor compared with those of Spain. In 1640 two major revolts broke out in the Iberian peninsula: one in Catalonia, the other in Portugal. The Catalan revolt, centred on Barcelona, was fuelled by a long tradition of regional autonomy and hatred of Castilian rule. It culminated in the assassination of the Viceroy in June. Catalonia's proximity to France made the revolt doubly dangerous. Even before its outbreak, Richelieu had indicated his willingness to assist the rebels. On 16 January, their leader, Pau Claris, announced that Catalonia had become an independent republic under French protection. A few days later, he declared Catalonia's allegiance to Louis XIII 'as in the time of Charlemagne'. The French gave the rebels full military support: on 26 January a combined French and Catalan army defeated a Spanish army at Montjuic, near Barcelona. Meanwhile, in Portugal, another revolt erupted. Plans for a rising had been made, probably with Richelieu's connivance, in the autumn of 1640. On 1 December they were put into effect, the duke of Braganza being proclaimed King John IV. 'This year,' Olivares wrote, 'can undoubtedly be considered the most unfortunate that this Monarchy has ever experienced.'[17]

The disasters that befell Philip IV and his ministers in 1640 inevitably sapped their war effort. 'There is only one resort left to us,' wrote the Cardinal-Infante; 'it is to build up a following in France and try with its help to induce the government in Paris to show itself amenable.'[18] This was a feasible option, given Richelieu's unpopularity at home. In the spring of 1641 a plot to overthrow the cardinal was laid by the comte de Soissons, the duc de Guise and the duc de Bouillon. With Spanish backing and subsidies they raised an army and invaded France from Sedan in the summer. Marshal Châtillon tried to bar its way but was routed at La Marfée. Soissons, however, was killed in the action and the plot collapsed. Early in 1642 it was revived by Louis XIII's favourite, Cinq-Mars, in favour of Gaston d'Orléans. He sent an agent to Spain, who made an agreement with Olivares, but a copy fell into the hands of Richelieu, sealing Cinq-Mars' fate.[19]

Louis XIII and Richelieu were at that time engaged in a new campaign aimed at capturing Perpignan, capital of Roussillon. Its surrender on 10 September was a devastating blow to Spanish morale. Olivares allegedly begged Philip IV for permission to throw himself out of a window.[20] Another Spanish defeat soon followed at Lerida. Meanwhile, in Germany, the army of the late Bernard of Saxe-Weimar, now under the command of marshal Guébriant, and the Swedish army under Torstensson carried out a series of rapid operations which began to throw the imperial army into disarray. Early in the winter of 1641–42 France and Sweden offered the Emperor two simultaneous conferences – one at Münster, the other at Osnabrück – with a view to working out a peace settlement. Thus, if there was as yet no end in sight to the war with Spain, by the time Richelieu died on 4 December 1642 there was at least a prospect of peace beyond the Rhine. In fact, the Thirty Years War continued until the Peace of Westphalia of 1648, and the Franco-Spanish war till the Peace of the Pyrenees of 1659.

What had the war achieved for France by 1642? Certainly she had become a stronger, more respected nation than she had been twenty years earlier, when Richelieu had become Chief Minister. Territorially too, she was a larger country. Her northern border extended as far as Artois. Further east, she dominated Lorraine and Alsace. She had a foothold in Italy and, in the south, occupied Roussillon. Diplomatically, her alliance with Portugal drove a wedge in the Iberian peninsula. At sea, too, she was a power to be reckoned with. But all these gains were achieved at the price of untold misery for the French people, and the question must be asked: was it all worth while? The cost of the war would have been less had it been shorter. Spain would certainly have liked to reach a settlement sooner. Richelieu, we are told, never ceased to look for peace, but the fact remains that it was his intransigence in the early 1640s that kept the war going.

. . .

NOTES AND REFERENCES

1. Pagès G 1949 *La Guerre de Trente Ans, 1618–1648*. Paris, Payot, pp. 181–82.
2. Ibid., p. 192.
3. Bonney R 1981 *The King's Debts: Finance and Politics in France, 1589–1661*. Oxford, Clarendon, p. 169.
4. Pagès *La Guerre de Trente Ans*, p. 201.
5. Ibid.
6. Ibid., pp. 202–3.

7. Carmona M 1983 *Richelieu: l'ambition et le pouvoir*. Paris, Fayard, pp. 582–84.
8. Elliott J H 1986 *The Count-Duke of Olivares: the statesman in an Age of Decline*. New Haven, CT. and London, Yale University Press, p. 523.
9. Pagès *La Guerre de Trente Ans*, pp. 206–7.
10. Parrott D 1987 'French Military Organization in the 1630s: The Failure of Richelieu's Ministry' *Seventeenth-Century French Studies* IX: 151–67.
11. Ibid., p. 161.
12. Ibid., p. 165.
13. Tapié V-L 1984 *France in the Age of Louis XIII and Richelieu*. D McN Lockie (ed.) Cambridge, Cambridge University Press, p. 385.
14. Elliott *The Count-Duke of Olivares*, pp. 548–52.
15. Tapié *France in the Age of Louis XIII and Richelieu*, p. 408.
16. Ibid., p. 399.
17. Elliott *The Count-Duke of Olivares*, p. 591.
18. Tapié *France in the Age of Louis XIII and Richelieu*, p. 415.
19. See above, pp. 59–61.
20. Elliott *The Count-Duke of Olivares*, p. 637.

Chapter 8

RICHELIEU, TAXATION AND POPULAR UNREST

Richelieu's foreign policy proved very expensive. Even before 1635, France had to disburse large sums in the form of subsidies to her allies. Once she had actually entered the Thirty Years War, her military expenditure rose by leaps and bounds: from an average of less than 16 million *livres* a year in the 1620s to over 33 million after 1635 and over 38 million after 1640. In theory, the Crown should have been able to meet these expenses since its revenue in 1636 was estimated at 108 million. But the amount actually received by the monarchy was less than this official total.[1] As the war dragged on, Richelieu and his fellow-ministers were drawn into highly unpopular fiscal policies which occasioned domestic unrest serious enough to threaten their war effort.

.   .   .

THE SINEWS OF WAR

The responsibility for funding France's war effort fell on two ministers, Claude de Bullion and Claude Bouthillier, who were appointed in August 1632. In 1635 Richelieu wrote to Bullion:

> I fully admit my ignorance of financial matters and realise that you are so well-versed in the subject that the only advice I can give you is to make use of those whom you find most useful to the king's service, and to rest assured that I will second you in every way I can.[2]

Bullion's task was far from easy. Although the king's revenues had increased since 1630 from 43 million *livres* to nearly 57.5

million, the amounts of cash actually received by the Treasury were far less.[3] The main reason for this appears to have been the rapid alienation of royal taxes in the period 1632–33.

The French Crown in the early seventeenth century relied on three main types of revenue: direct and indirect taxes and extraordinary revenues (*finances extraordinaires*). The main direct tax was the *taille*, which was levied annually, the amount being fixed by the council of finance.[4] There were two kinds of *taille*: the *taille réelle*, a land tax payable by everyone irrespective of social rank, and the *taille personnelle*, which fell mainly on non-privileged commoners. The former, though fairer, was found in only a few areas, including Languedoc and Provence. The *taille personnelle* was the more common form, but even among the non-privileged there were many exemptions. Several professional groups were exempt, as were the inhabitants of many towns, including Paris. The government also levied occasional supplements to the *taille* called *crues*. There was also a military tax, called the *taillon*.

Indirect taxes included the *gabelle* or salt-tax, which was levied mainly in the northern and central provinces (*pays de grandes gabelles*).[5] Here the salt was taken to royal warehouses (*greniers*) where it was taxed before it could be sold. Every household was required by the state to buy enough salt for its needs from a royal *grenier*. Some parts of France (such as Normandy) did not have to pay the *gabelle*. Other indirect taxes included the *aides*, which were duties on consumption and the movement of certain drinks and food, especially wine, and the *traites*, which were customs dues levied not only along the borders of the kingdom, but even within it at certain provincial borders.

Direct and indirect taxes were administered differently. The former were the responsibility of two groups of office-holders: the *trésoriers* and the *élus*, whose respective fiscal areas were called *généralités* and *élections*. Each autumn a *trésorier* was supposed to carry out an inspection of his *généralité* to assure himself of its capacity to pay the next year's *taille*. He was to take note of any disaster, such as a bad harvest, which might affect the fiscal capacity of a given area. Once the *trésorier* had been informed of the total amount of tax required by the government, he divided it among the *élections*, and the *élus* then carried out parish assessments in their areas. Though fairly simple in theory, the system suffered from serious defects. The office-holders responsible, having purchased their offices from the state, were not always punctilious in discharging their responsibilities. Some *trésoriers* did not carry out their tours of inspection or they favoured one area at the expense of another. The worst offenders were the *élus*, who made up for the fall in the value of their offices by cheating the state. They were repeatedly accused of tampering with the tax-rolls to oblige their friends and relatives.

Collectors of the *taille* were elected from the local community. They were responsible for the total amount of the tax they were due to collect; if this turned out to be less than anticipated, they had to supply the deficit themselves or face imprisonment. Many such imprisonments took place between 1636 and 1648: they might last a few days or months. A rich prisoner could expect an early release; a poor man without influence had little to hope for. French prisons were allegedly full of tax-collectors, who were left to die of hunger. Not surprisingly, few parishioners volunteered to serve in that capacity.[6] Payment of the *taille* was a responsibility shared by an entire community. Even a tax-payer who had paid his share might be held accountable for his neighbours.

Among the various kinds of revenue available to the crown, the *taille* was especially important during the war with Spain. It was also extremely unpopular among the peasantry, which bore the heaviest burden, and there was widespread resistance to its collection. As a result, the yield from the *taille* fell seriously into arrears from the 1630s onwards. To give only a few examples, in 1641 the *élection* of Loches owed more than 1 million *livres* from 1632 and subsequent years; by 1643 the *généralité* of Bourges was 2.25 million in arrears over a six-year period; in September 1642 five *élections* in the *généralité* of Montauban owed 1,175,073 *livres* from the years 1639–41. The situation was made worse by receivers of the *taille* using peasant resistance as an excuse for defaulting on their duties. Throughout 1642 Bouthillier warned Richelieu of the need to improve the collection of the *taille*.[7]

In 1634 the government set up a commission to look into the administration of the *taille*, which foreshadowed the financial responsibilities soon to be placed on the shoulders of the *intendants*. In August 1642 they were given responsibility for assessing the *taille*. Each *intendant* was to be assisted by one *trésorier* and three *élus* of his own choice. He was to ensure that assessments were fair and that collectors were appointed in every parish. The *intendant* was also to investigate cases of fraud and peculation and ensure that the *élus* behaved responsibly. Inevitably, the application of the new regime was not universally endorsed. In many places the *intendants* were opposed by the existing office-holders, but they pressed on regardless. They investigated arrears of the *taille* from 1636 to 1640. In general, they tried to favour those parishes which had at least attempted to pay their arrears.[8] But, however well-meaning, their activities were widely seen as a more effective, and consequently more unpopular, intrusion of the central government into village affairs.

Such was the resistance to taxation encountered by the government that it had to use force to bring in the *taille*. This took several forms: confiscation of property, imprisonment, the billeting of troops and the establishment of special military units. It was customary for the Crown to seize the movables and animals of a defaulting tax-payer. They would be auctioned outside the parish church and kept in store for a few days to give the owner a chance to buy them back and pay the costs of the seizure. The officials who carried out such confiscations would sometimes wait for a few years before descending on a village and virtually putting it to the sack. The inhabitants, finding their homes and stables empty, would be driven from their lands. The task of forcing tax-payers could not be shouldered by minor local officials alone. The Crown also used troops. These would be billeted on obstructive parishes at their own cost and not removed until the taxes had been paid. The troops, of course, behaved badly, thereby provoking enormous popular resentment. In November 1638 representatives of the communities of Guyenne, meeting at Bordeaux, begged the government to levy taxes in accordance with ancient custom and not to use troops 'on account of the ruin and great expense inflicted by them on the people'. By resorting to force, the state abandoned the age-old principle of 'no taxation without consultation'.[9] This was one of the most sinister manifestations of absolute monarchy.

Under Richelieu, troops specially assigned to aid the fiscal administrators were posted in most provinces. They were light cavalry formed into companies of between fifty and 100 men, each under officers. Their duty was to escort government officials on their tax-collecting rounds and arrange the billeting of troops on reluctant communities. Recruited and paid by the *traitants* and controlled by a local *intendant*, they were handsomely paid to ensure their loyalty. The first company of *fusiliers pour les tailles* was established in Angoumois in May 1636, but was soon disbanded on account of its misdeeds. Between 1640 and 1644, however, many such companies were attached to the service of the *intendants*. Oddly enough, fiscal garrisons were not abolished in France till February 1877![10]

Indirect taxes were farmed out: that is to say, financiers undertook to administer them and in return to pay the Crown a fixed sum each year.[11] But the taxes, being essentially on consumption, became increasingly difficult to administer in wartime. The interruption of trade between France and Spain and the devastation of the frontier provinces led to a fall in consumption which in turn reduced the profitability of the tax farms. Another difficulty encountered by contractors was the refusal of the sovereign courts to register some fiscal legislation. As a result, the farmers were unable to levy certain taxes. Even where these obstacles did not arise, the revenues accruing to the state from indirect taxation were far less than anticipated.

Thus, for a variety of reasons, the yield from taxation, both direct and indirect, was insufficient to cover all the government's heavy wartime expenses. It was consequently obliged to turn to extraordinary revenues, such as the sale of *rentes* and offices.[12] These were administered by separate contracts or *traités*. The contractor (*traitant* or *partisan*) was either an individual financier or a financial consortium. In either case, a fixed interest payment or *remise* was specified in the contract. Public *rentes* had grown enormously since they had been launched in 1522. Each *rentier* in return for a capital sum was assured by the state of an annual payment of interest or *rente*. The sale of such *rentes* was evidently an easy way for the government to acquire large sums of cash quickly, but at the same time it added to its long-term expenditure. This was assigned on taxation from which the government could expect correspondingly less for other purposes, however urgent. It attempted to avert disaster by creating new *rentes* to pay the interest on old ones, but this only compounded its long-term difficulty. Under Louis XIII the whole system got seriously out of hand: in February 1634 *rentes* worth 11 million *livres* were created. But the market was soon flooded and the value of the *rentes* collapsed. By January 1639 *rentes* worth 600,000 *livres* remained unsold.[13]

Rentes were exploited for private speculative gain by the financiers who undertook to sell them for the government. The majority of such men were Frenchmen based in Paris. They were usually office-holders and, therefore, noblemen. Richelieu described them as 'a separate part, prejudicial to the state, yet necessary'.[14] They were 'necessary' as money-lenders to the state, yet 'prejudicial' because they were out to benefit themselves. Profiteering was their stock in trade. How to stop them was a constant preoccupation of the government; it was not easy to devise controls which would not destroy their confidence. Ministers too were guilty of private speculation and, therefore, afraid of any investigation which might spill over into their own dubious activities. As one historian has written: 'the interrelationship of public and private finance at the centre of government meant that there were matters which needed to be hidden from the public eye'.[15]

Contracts were most productive in respect of the sale of offices. Richelieu saw the disadvantages attached to the practice, but offices had become too deeply entrenched to be easily removed. In any case, the government did not have the means to indemnify office-holders for the abolition of their offices. It could have desisted from creating yet more, but, as always, it needed the profits accruing from their sale. It was a vicious circle from which there seemed to be no escape. As in the case of the *rentes*, the sale of offices was lucrative in the short term, but entailed long-term expenditure. For the office-holders were paid a salary by the state. In 1639 Richelieu estimated the bill at 34 million *livres*. This too had to be funded from taxation. By 1640 payments to *rentiers* and office-holders amounted to about 48.8 million *livres*, and Bullion was obliged to cut back on them. This inevitably increased the government's unpopularity. When Bullion died, he had to be buried in secret to avoid an outburst of public rejoicing.[16]

Bullion's management of the finances was on the whole disastrous. Almost the only good thing he did was to devalue the currency in 1636. This strengthened France's monetary position: Spanish coin flooded into the kingdom to be reissued as French coin. The devaluation also made French trade more competitive by stimulating exports; it encouraged private investment in royal financial transactions and reduced the real cost of the subsidies paid to France's allies. But in all other respects, Bullion did untold damage to the state's finances. His excessive use of *rentes* played into the hands of the private financiers. Bullion, writes Bonney, created 'the worst of all worlds: an illogical and unpopular system that worked to the advantage of few at the expense of many without any real gain to the crown'.[17] His death, unfortunately, did not lead to any change of course. His successor, Bouthillier, presided over an escalation of royal borrowing. Loan contracts were negotiated totalling 15.9 million *livres* in 1639 and 37.6 million in 1640. At the same time receipts from all forms of taxation were being anticipated at least one year ahead by means of loan contracts with financiers. By the time Louis XIII died, the revenues of the following two years were being anticipated to the tune of 12 million *livres*.[18] That way lay bankruptcy.

Richelieu died without achieving the peace settlement which would have reduced the tax burden on the people of France. He had also failed to secure sufficient revenues to continue the war indefinitely.

.   .   .

OPPOSITION

Taxation was the principal grievance of the peasantry in the 1630s. It was all the more burdensome in that it coincided with an economic recession: after rising slowly, prices generally stagnated after 1630 and fell sharply after 1640. Peasants and artisans consequently made small profits and were less able to pay their taxes. Their lot was further aggravated by exceptionally bad weather. A series of harsh winters and wet summers ruined several harvests, causing famine, sickness and death. There was a heavy death toll between 1630 and 1632. Plague struck Burgundy in 1636 and spread westward across the southern half of France, reaching its climax in the summer of 1637. Productive manpower was seriously reduced because farm-workers and artisans for various reasons suffered heavier losses relatively than other social groups. Trade, too, was disrupted as markets and fairs were suspended and strangers denied access to towns. Bad harvests also encouraged vagabondage. Impoverished peasants joined large bands of migrants drifting from the poorest regions to the less poor and from the countryside to the towns. This in turn created difficulties for the towns: feeding the hungry and treating the sick caused municipal authorities to run into debt.

One of the main results of a royal fiscality which weighed more heavily each day on people hard-pressed by worsening economic conditions was popular revolt. From the spring of 1630 till the end of Louis XIII's reign 'revolt was endemic within the nation'. Three major uprisings took place during Richelieu's ministry: in Quercy (1626), in the south-west (1636–37) and in Normandy (1639). The largest uprisings were those of the *Croquants* (1636) and of the *Nu-pieds* (1639). The revolt of the *Croquants*, which started in May 1636 in different parts of the south-west, eventually covered an area larger than that affected by the *Jacquerie* in the fourteenth century. It may fairly be described as the most important peasant revolt in French history. It was directed from the start against tax officials, some of whom were cruelly put to death. '*Vive le Roi sans la gabelle! Vive le Roi sans la taille!*' were the rebels' favourite slogans. In 1637 they placed themselves under a nobleman from Périgord, called La Mothe La Forêt, who organised them into a well-disciplined army. In a manifesto he called on the king to abolish the new taxes, remove tax officials and restore the provincial Estates. Resentment of arbitrary taxation by 'these gentlemen of Paris' figured prominently among the *Croquants*' motives.[19]

Normandy was the most heavily taxed province in France. In fact, the *taille* had increased so much since the last meeting of the provincial Estates in 1635 that people could no longer pay it. In 1639 out of 139 parishes, 82 failed to contribute to the tax. Towns which were exempt had to pay forced loans. On top of all this the province was hit by plague between 1619 and 1639 and overrun by troops in 1636. By 1639 it was seething with discontent. The revolt of the *Nu-pieds* was only the most serious of several Norman revolts in that year. It was triggered off by a rumour that the *gabelle* was about to be introduced into Lower Normandy. After lynching an official who had come to Avranches on quite different business, the rebels organised themselves into 'an army of suffering' under a 'general' nicknamed Jean Nu-Pieds, who has not been identified for certain. Their chief aim, it seems, was to free the 'fatherland' (that is, Normandy) from tax officials (*gabeleurs*) and return to the period before 1635 when the provincial Estates used to meet.[20]

Though known to French historians for a long time, the popular revolts of early seventeenth-century France were not given the attention they deserved until the Russian historian B F Porchnev published an important work on them in 1948.[21] In his view, the revolts, though sometimes led by noblemen, were essentially spontaneous risings of the peasantry and urban poor. If the rebels invariably began by attacking tax officials, they soon turned against the rich in general, setting fire to châteaux and town houses without discrimination, for their enemy was not the Crown so much as the whole feudal order. They complained not merely of royal taxes but of the whole range of feudal dues and services. France, according to Porchnev, was still a feudal state in the seventeenth century: economic power remained in the hands of the landed aristocracy, and royal absolutism was the political means by which it tried to perpetuate its dominance over the rest of society. The monarchy, in other words, was part of the feudal order, and royal taxation was simply a centralised form of feudal revenue.

Porchnev's Marxist interpretation has not generally found favour with French historians. Roland Mousnier has argued against the spontaneity of the revolts.[22] All the most important ones, he claims, were instigated, if not led, by noblemen and office-holders. A few *seigneurs* may have antagonised their tenants by harshness and rapacity, but the majority tried to protect them from the Crown's fiscal demands. In acting thus, the *seigneurs* were defending their own interests, for the increase in royal taxation inevitably made it more difficult for the peasants to pay their feudal dues. Seventeenth-century France, according to Mousnier, was no longer a feudal state: her economy had been significantly permeated by capitalism, and absolutism, far from being the tool of the aristocracy, had grown at its expense. The aim of the nobility was not to strengthen absolutism, but to destroy it by reverting to the feudal past. What is more, a class war was impossible in seventeenth-century France, for her society was stratified, not horizontally into 'classes' but vertically into 'orders' based on social esteem, rank and honour unconnected with the production of material goods.[23]

In recent years much new light has been thrown on the popular revolts of seventeenth-century France. Y-M Bercé, working on the risings in south-west France, has ruled out any correlation between them and times of bad harvest, famine or plague.[24] Far more significant, it seems, was the relatively sudden development of a royal fiscality which rode roughshod over many local institutions and privileges. Bercé aptly describes as 'fiscal terrorism' the methods used by the government from the time of Richelieu onwards. They affected all sections of a given community, including the nobles, so that a revolt commonly took the form of an uprising by a whole town or village against a royal tax-collector. A broadly similar view emerges from Pillorget's work on the revolts in Provence.[25] These were on a smaller scale and far less destructive than those in Aquitaine. The majority took place within a single community, and there is no evidence of the proletariat of several towns or villages ganging up against the rich. Madeleine Foisil, focusing on the revolt of the *Nu-pieds*, likewise finds no evidence of class conflict. The revolt was strictly localised: it comprised several independent risings which never tried to join forces. The rebels lacked any programme of social reform: they were only concerned to defend their traditional rights and privileges against the inroads of the central government.[26]

Aristocratic instigation or encouragement of peasant unrest suggests that the nobility was less immune to contemporary fiscal pressures than is commonly assumed. In fact, during the first half of the century, the government tried systematically to curb fiscal privilege. In areas of *taille personnelle* it conducted enquiries into the credentials of people claiming exemption from taxation and, where this exemption could be vindicated, it tried to restrict it to a single estate per person. In areas of *taille réelle* the government tried to compel nobles to pay tax for non-noble land in their possession. Another means of tapping aristocratic wealth was to manipulate the feudal levy (*ban et arrière-ban*): it would be summoned only to be disbanded in return for a composition which could be as much as 15 to 20 per cent of the estimated annual revenue of a fief. This was taxation in disguise.

The government could not have picked a worse time to put pressure on the nobility whose income was being reduced as a result of war and economic recession. A memorandum sent to the king after the Assembly of Notables of 1626–27 refers to the financial distress of the entire estate. The muster rolls of the *bailliage* of Amiens for the years after 1639 show nobles being exempted from the feudal levy on grounds of poverty. In 1651 nobles complained that taxes had become so heavy that their tenants could no longer pay them their rents. They also complained of armed searches by officials of the *gabelle* and of damage caused by troops billeted on them. In view of such evidence, it comes as no surprise that nobles felt restless and were tempted at times to come to the aid of other social groups resisting the government.[27]

.   .   .

SUPPRESSION

Richelieu's reaction to the revolt in Normandy was less than helpful. He rounded on the financial officials who had been trying to raise cash for the war. 'I have to admit,' he wrote to Bouthillier, 'that I do not know why you do not give more thought to the decisions you take in your *Conseil des finances*. Diseases [*les maux*], even the most incurable, are easily avoided; but, once they have struck, they cannot be remedied.'[28] The cardinal thought that a serious error had been committed by introducing the *gabelle* into Normandy, thereby infringing one of its most cherished privileges and damaging its economic life. The profit to be gained by so doing was not worth the price. But if Richelieu was being wise after the event, he also stood fast by the principles enunciated in his *Testament politique*. A revolt against the authority of the state, however justified, must be put down with exemplary severity. 'Harshness towards individuals who flout the laws and commands of the state,' he wrote, 'is for the public good; no greater crime against the public interest is possible than to show leniency to those who violate it.' 'In the matter of state crime,' Richelieu also wrote, 'one must close the door on pity, ignore the complaints of the parties concerned and the speeches of the ignorant populace which sometimes condemns that which is most useful and necessary.'[29] On 26 December 1629 the cardinal expressed his approval of steps taken to crush the rebels in Normandy. 'You have started so well,' he wrote to the chancellor, 'that I do not doubt that you will bring your journey to a happy conclusion which will impose such a settlement on Normandy that there will be nothing to fear from this province or the others who will assuredly follow their duty out of fear.'[30] A deputy from Normandy who called on the cardinal reported 'that he had become well aware that the aim of the king's council was to treat the affair of Rouen as a matter of state of the first importance and to serve as an example'.[31]

Louis XIII was deeply disturbed by the unrest among his subjects at a time when he was defending the borders of the kingdom against the foreign enemy. 'These popular uprisings . . .,' he wrote, 'are of such consequence and upset me so much that no one can serve me better than by helping to put them down'.[32] At first the king's council looked to the local authorities to do this. But, in Saintonge, the *vice-sénéchal* did not have enough troops to restore order. An attempt on his part to enlist the services of the local nobility proved unavailing. So 'old troops' had to be brought in, but they were soon recalled to north-east France to face the foreign threat. The only option left to the government was to temporise: commissioners were instructed to reassure the rebels. They were to be told that the king had been misled by his ministers and intended to punish those speculators who had enriched themselves at his subjects' expense. He waived his demand for arrears of the *taille* and merely asked that this year's tax should be paid promptly and in full.[33] But the government's attitude encouraged other areas to resist taxation. By the autumn of 1636 the fiscal administration in south-west France had almost collapsed.

The revolt of the *Croquants* in Périgord was even more serious; it posed a major problem to the government at a time when France was threatened by foreign invasion. The duc d'Épernon, governor of Guyenne, was old and sick. On 12 May he wrote to Richelieu: 'All, especially the well-to-do, are so bewildered as not to know what will become of them.' Fortunately for the duke, he was able to call his son, the duc de La Valette, who hurried northward from the Spanish front with an army of 3,000 foot and 400 horse. About 3,000

Croquants shut themselves up in the village of La Sauvetat. After they had refused to surrender, La Valette launched an assault. Two hours of bitter hand-to-hand fighting ended in a bloodbath. About 1,500 *Croquants* and between 200 and 800 royal troops were killed. The *Croquants* who survived joined another rebel force under La Mothe la Forêt at Bergerac.

La Valette was most anxious to avoid another slaughter. He negotiated with La Mothe, who agreed to disband his force on certain conditions. But the spirit of revolt lived on and La Valette urged the Parlement of Bordeaux to be severe. Repression, he argued, would be all the more effective if it were directed mainly against 'persons of condition and professionals who foment and support the revolts with public effrontery'. He suggested that their homes should be destroyed and their confiscated property distributed to loyal captains who had distinguished themselves at La Sauvetat. From mid-June till mid-July leaders of the *Croquants* were tried and sentenced by judges of the Parlement of Bordeaux. About ten were executed. On 23 June the government granted an amnesty to the other rebels in return for prompt payment of the *taille*, but it did not imply any softening of the Crown's attitude to future tax revolts. The *élus* who had fled at the first sign of trouble were now replaced and the south-west occupied by troops sent to enforce collection of the *taille*.[34]

A distinction may be drawn between the Crown's response to the revolt of the *Croquants* and that of the *Nu-pieds*. Regarding the former, it looked to the local authorities – the governor of Guyenne and the Parlement of Bordeaux – to restore order. It was content that an example should be made of the rebel leaders, particularly if they had social influence, and was even ready to make fiscal concessions. In Normandy, the government played a much more direct role, partly, no doubt, because of the province's nearness to the capital. Three extraordinary missions were sent out, led respectively by the *intendant* Charles Le Roy de La Potherie, colonel Jean de Gassion and the chancellor Pierre Séguier.[35] On 5 December 1639 Louis XIII sanctioned the execution of thirty prisoners. All the others, he explained, were to be sent to the galleys. The commissioners were also to destroy the homes of rebels in Avranches before moving on to Vire and demolishing its ramparts. At Caen, Gassion billeted troops on the inhabitants without regard for their privileges. But the most spectacular aspect of his mission was a pitched battle fought with the 'army of suffering' near Avranches in which more than 300 rebels were killed. Richelieu congratulated Gassion on 26 December: 'You cannot give the king greater satisfaction,' he wrote, 'than by putting down the Norman rebels. You will not find the task easy, but you should be satisfied even if it only gains you the king's esteem.'[36]

Of the three missions sent to Normandy the most important was Séguier's, which lasted more than three months (from 19 December 1639 to 27 March 1640). He was accompanied by a large team of councillors, masters of requests and chancery officials. Wherever he passed in Normandy, existing municipal officials and office-holders were suspended. The chancellor also sentenced several leaders of the rebellion to death without trial. At Rouen, however, his assistants were surprisingly lenient. Believing that disturbances in the town had been misrepresented by certain local financiers, they allowed many prisoners to go free.

If the royal repression of the Norman revolt was less violent than might have been expected, the towns of the province were not let off lightly. In addition to losing their *échevins* and privileges, huge sums were extracted from them by way of compensation to the victims of the rebellion. For example, Coutances had to pay 31,200 *livres*, Bayeux 22,000 *livres* and Vire 26,820 *livres*. At Caen, all the inhabitants had to surrender their arms. The town also lost its privileges while its revenue was annexed to the king's domain. At the same time, it was ordered to pay 159,215 *livres*. In order to raise such a sum the townspeople were allowed to tax goods entering the town. A few months later they were asked for another 10,000 *livres* to help pay for troops sent to maintain order in the province. At Rouen, the *échevins* were suspended, the bourgeoisie disarmed, crushing fiscal charges levied and the town's revenue alienated. The fiscal charges amounted to 1,085,000 *livres*. On 17 December 1639 the Parlement of Rouen was suspended, its judicial functions being temporarily transferred to the officials, who had accompanied Séguier on his mission. The suspension lasted till October 1641, when the court was restored in a much weakened form. It was divided into two sixth-monthly sessions, forty-four new councillors being created to fill the new posts thus created.[37]

Richelieu had warned the king that war would mean the indefinite postponement of domestic reform. What he had not anticipated, it seems, was a serious outbreak of domestic unrest capable of compromising the success of the war effort, even of endangering the kingdom's security. Having originally advocated a reduction of the tax burden weighing on the king's subjects, Richelieu was driven into a policy that entailed a complete reversal of that recommendation. In the words of V-L Tapié: 'by clinging to various disastrous practices imposed on him by the realm's military and financial requirements, he thrust her [France] back into the rut from which he sought to pull her'.[38]

· · ·

NOTES AND REFERENCES

1. Bonney R 1981 *The King's Debts*. Oxford, Clarendon, p. 173.
2. Tapié V-L 1984 *France in the Age of Louis XIII and Richelieu*. Lockie D McN (trans. and ed.) Cambridge, Cambridge University Press, p. 247.
3. Bonney *The King's Debts*, p. 164.
4. Dent J 1973 *Crisis in Finance: Crown, Financiers and Society in Seventeenth-Century France*. Newton Abbot, David and Charles, pp. 34–5.
5. Ibid., pp. 36–7.
6. Bercé Y-M 1974 *Histoire des Croquants*. Geneva, Droz, vol. I, pp. 96–102.
7. Bonney R 1978 *Political Change in France under Richelieu and Mazarin, 1624–1661*. Oxford, Oxford University Press, pp. 174–76; Bonney *The King's Debts*, p. 186.
8. Bonney *Political Change*, pp. 184–85. See also below, p. 144.
9. Bercé *Histoire des Croquants* vol. I, p. 107.
10. Ibid., pp. 108–12.
11. Bonney *The King's Debts*, p. 13; Bonney *Political Change*, pp. 171–72.
12. Dent *Crisis in Finance* pp. 44–64.
13. Bonney *The King's Debts*, pp. 165–66.
14. Richelieu 1947 *Testament politique*. André L (ed.) Paris, Laffont, p. 250.
15. Bonney *The King's Debts*, p. 19.

16. Ibid., pp. 179, 185.
17. Ibid., p. 168.
18. Ibid., p. 186.
19. Bercé *Histoire des Croquants*, vol. 1, pp. 402–62.
20. Foisil Madeleine 1970 *La révolte des nu-pieds et les révoltes normandes de 1639*. Paris, PUF, pp. 171–228.
21. Porchnev B F 1963 *Les soulèvements populaires en France de 1623 à 1648*. Paris, SEVPEN. For a translation of the preface, see *France in Crisis, 1620–1675* Coveney P J (ed.), London, Macmillan, pp. 78–102.
22. Mousnier R 1958 'Recherches sur les soulèvements populaires avant la Fronde' *Revue d'histoire moderne et contemporaine* V: 81–113. For an English translation, see *France in Crisis* Coveney P J (ed.) pp. 136–68.
23. Mousnier R 1973 *Social Hierarchies*. London, Croom Helm, pp. 23–7.
24. Bercé *Histoire des Croquants* vol. I, pp. 24, 42–3.
25. Pillorget R 1975 *Les mouvements insurrectionnels de Provence entre 1596 et 1715*. Paris, Pedone, pp. 987–1009.
26. Foisil *La révolte des nu-pieds et les révoltes normandes*, pp. 339–42.
27. Deyon P 1964 'A propos des rapports entre la noblesse française et la monarchie absolue pendant la première moitié du XVIIe siècle' *Revue historique* CCXXXI: 341–56. For an English translation, see *France in Crisis* Coveney P J (ed.), pp. 231–46.
28. Avenel D L M (ed.) 1867 *Lettres, instructions diplomatiques et papiers d'état du Cardinal de Richelieu*. vi. 500.
29. Richelieu *Testament politique*, pp. 339–40, 342.
30. Foisil *La révolte des nu-pieds et les révoltes normandes*, p. 285.
31. Ibid.
32. Bercé *Histoire des Croquants* vol. I, p. 396.
33. Ibid., vol. I, pp. 396–97.
34. Ibid., vol. I, pp. 425–32, 443–51.
35. Foisil *La révolte des nu-pieds et les révoltes normandes*, pp. 287–301.
36. Ibid., pp. 292–93.
37. Ibid., pp. 312–26.
38. Tapié *France in the Age of Louis XIII and Richelieu*, p. 261.

Chapter 9

RICHELIEU AND ABSOLUTISM

Cardinal Richelieu has traditionally been hailed as the architect of French absolutism. But 'absolutism' as a form of
government is much older. Its theory can be traced back at
least to Roman times: it was in the third century that Ulpian
coined the saying: *quod principi placuit legis habet vigorem*
(what pleases the prince has the force of law). The idea of the
king as emperor within his own kingdom was given currency in
fifteenth-century France. Although the term 'absolutism' dates
only from the French Revolution, the phrase 'absolute power'
is medieval.[1] As for the practice of absolutism, it is more difficult to date with precision. It is essentially a regime wherein
the ruler's power is subject to no institutional limitation other
than divine law. Such a regime existed in France long before
Richelieu. Royal authority in early sixteenth-century France
was already absolute inasmuch as the king was deemed to be
divinely appointed and answerable to no one save God. Yet
his power was also limited in the sense that he was expected
to rule in accordance with the precepts of divine and natural
justice.[2] By the seventeenth century, however, royal power
was conceived differently by some of its servants. Thus for
Richelieu the normal processes of the law were applicable to
the king's subjects in their dealings with each other, yet could
be lawfully disregarded where the interests of the state were
concerned. To this extent he may be said to have contributed
to a more extreme, and arguably a more secular, definition of
'absolutism'.

. . .

PARLEMENTS AND ESTATES

The greatest obstacle to the unrestricted exercise of royal

power was the authority vested in the 'sovereign courts'. Though 'sovereign' in the sense that they had once formed part of the *Curia Regis* and still exercised the king's authority, they had become sufficiently independent in the course of time to develop interests and attitudes of their own which did not necessarily coincide with those of the king or his ministers. Thus the parlements, especially the Parlement of Paris, which was the most important of them, were critical of certain royal policies. In addition to being the highest lawcourts in the realm beneath the king, they had the duty of registering edicts and of protesting against legislative proposals which seemed objectionable to them. The Parlement's right of remonstrance could seriously impede government action, particularly in wartime, though the king could enforce his will by means of a special session, called *Lit-de-justice*, in which he personally supervised registration by resuming temporarily the authority he had delegated to the Parlement.[3]

A deep-seated grievance repeatedly voiced by the Parlement under Louis XIII was the government's use of special judicial commissions. This, however, was not an innovation: such commissions had a long history stretching back to the fifteenth century, when they had often been used for political purposes. Even so, they were regarded by many as detractions from the legitimacy of monarchy which was deemed to rest on the proper administration of justice. The circumstances in which the Crown might intervene in the procedures of the sovereign courts had been limited by laws of 1562 and 1579, but they were disregarded by Louis XIII and Richelieu. In the words of one *parlementaire*: 'There are more affairs in petty justice decided by commissions than by ordinary judges.' Towards the close of the reign the presidents of the Parlement complained that the king could have anyone tried by anyone he designated as a judge.

Special commissions to try crimes of *lèse-majesté* were used by Luynes early in Louis XIII's reign to eliminate his political enemies. His example was closely followed by Richelieu, who used hand-picked judges to try Puylaurens, marshal de Marillac, the duc de Montmorency and Cinq-Mars. Similar commissions were set up to deal with other crimes as well. The most famous was the *Chambre de l'Arsenal*, which was used to mete out summary justice to political offenders. Its creation in 1631 was resisted by the Parlement for several months, but eventually it had to give way, and the new tribunal was able to function without hindrance. It became notorious on account of its cloak-and-dagger operations and nocturnal executions. Sometimes, Richelieu dispensed with legal formalities altogether. Thus the *abbé* of St Cyran, who was suspected of Jansenist sympathies, was imprisoned at the château of Vincennes for four years without trial. After the Norman revolt of 1639, chancellor Séguier sentenced people to death without trial on his word alone. In the eyes of Louis XIII and his chief minister such judicial excesses were perfectly in order. One of Richelieu's propagandists declared that 'the justice, virtue and integrity of the sovereign function entirely otherwise than those of individuals'.[4]

Richelieu not only helped to circumscribe the Parlement's judicial powers; he also opposed its political pretensions. Here again he was conforming to tradition. Crown and Parlement had been in conflict over politics for a century at least. In 1527 Francis I had forbidden the court to meddle in state affairs. Under Louis XIII the same prohibition was expressed by the Keeper of the Seals, Michel de Marillac; he reminded the magistrates that their duty was to dispense justice, not to attend to matters of state. In 1629 the *Code Michau* laid down that the registration of proposed royal legislation should be automatic unless remonstrances were presented within two months of its being received by the Parlement. In January 1632, after the Parlement's refusal to register the edict setting up the *Chambre de l'Arsenal*, a deputation of magistrates appeared before the king at Metz. 'You are here,' he told them, 'only to judge master Peter and master John, and I intend to keep you in your place; if you continue your machinations, I will cut your nails to the quick.'[5]

Friction between Crown and Parlement reached a climax in 1635 following the outbreak of war with Spain. Louis held a *Lit-de-justice* in December to register a number of edicts creating new offices, twenty-four in the Parlement itself. The edicts were registered, but certain members of the *Enquêtes* tried to get them discussed by a plenary session of the court. The most outspoken were arrested in January 1636 and banished from the capital, whereupon their colleagues staged a judicial strike that lasted till March. Peace was restored when the king agreed to reinstate the exiled magistrates and reduce the number of new offices to seventeen. In 1638 there was another clash when the Parlement protested at the government's failure to honour certain *rentes*. Five magistrates were banished and there was another judicial strike. This time, however, the Parlement capitulated without exacting concessions from the king. Early in 1640 two more magistrates were exiled after opposing the creation of more offices. In February 1641 the Parlement was forced to register an edict reducing its capacity to comment on state affairs. Henceforth edicts of a political rather than a financial or judicial kind were to be registered without prior discussion.[6]

Popular representation had no role to play in absolute government. No meeting of the Estates-General – the only body that was both representative and national in France – took place during Richelieu's administration. But representative estates survived in several provinces (Dauphiné, Burgundy, Languedoc, Provence and Brittany). These were the *pays d'états*, which were subject to a different fiscal regime from that operating in the *pays d'élections*. Whereas in the latter taxes were imposed by the king's council and levied by royal officials (*trésoriers de France* and *élus*), in the *pays d'états* they were voted upon, assessed and collected by the estates themselves. However, during the reign of Louis XIII, the central government tried to extend the system of *élections* to the *pays d'états*.

In March 1628 Louis XIII issued an edict creating ten *élections* in Dauphiné, each with twenty-seven officials. He explained that he wanted to ensure an even distribution of taxes and that no levies should be made without his consent. But the move was evidently designed to raise money for the government by creating more offices for sale. The cost of the new system to the people of Dauphiné was likely to be much higher than that of the existing one; they resisted the reform, but were overruled. The *élus* were imposed upon them and their estates ceased to function. In Burgundy, a comparable move by the Crown was opposed more effectively. In February 1630 resistance in Dijon turned violent. The king threatened to strip the town of its privileges and to raze its walls. The chancellor lectured the municipality on the need for obedience: 'It is not for inferiors,' he said, 'to examine the reasons for an order . . . . If they obey only when they find it reasonable, they no longer have a superior. The key to public tranquillity and order lies in the reverence which is due to the superior powers.' Although Dijon submitted, it lost its privileges, as did the province. In Provence too there was violence when the Crown set up ten *élections* with a total of 350 officials. The Crown's representative, Dreux d'Aubray, who had been sent to Aix to oversee registration of the edict by the local Parlement, had his carriage burnt, while he himself escaped over the rooftops. The royal edict was denounced by the estates as 'the most prejudicial thing not only in regard to the goods, but also to the liberties, even the very lives of the inhabitants of this *pays*'. By November 1629 Aix was up in arms, and the province was still without *élus*. In Languedoc it was the same story. An edict setting up twenty-two *élections* with a staff of 700 officials was bitterly resisted by the Parlement of Toulouse. Among the *pays d'états* only Brittany was spared the government's campaign to achieve fiscal uniformity. Why this should have been so is a matter for conjecture. The Bretons were renowned for their fiercely independent spirit. They may also have been protected by Richelieu, who needed their co-operation in developing his maritime and trading interests.[7]

In September 1629 the English ambassador to France, Sir Thomas Edmondes, ascribed to Richelieu the responsibility for the Crown's attack on the provincial estates:

> Hee hath abolished that custome of callinge the states by the gouvernor and hath appointed that upon the issuinge of any Commissions from hence for the leavyinge of any Monnies in any of the provinces the same shale be executed only by the Esleus of the Countri, who are the persons that are accustomed to make the severale taxations throughout the Countrie, and by this meanes, of making their authority more absolute, they doe sell the places of the saide Esleus att a much dearer rate, and doe cleane cutt of the profitt of the gouvernors. This hee hath already (as is saide) putt in execution in the provinces of Provence, Dauphine, and Languedoc, and if hee can establish the like in Bretaigne, which will bee of greater difficulty because they are more strongly founded in their privileges, hee will then bee able to make the same to bee afterwards more easily received in the other Countries.[8]

But the accuracy of this contemporary report has been challenged by the historian John Russell Major. He points out that the ambassador was new, inexperienced and inclined to attribute all policy decisions to Richelieu. In Major's opinion, the minister responsible for extending the system of *élections* to the *pays d'états* was the Keeper of the Seals, Marillac, not Richelieu. Except in the case of Languedoc, he claims, Richelieu had little to do with the estates. He never mentioned them in his various reform proposals, and almost never in his correspondence.[9] It is dangerous, however, for the historian to read too much into silence. Moreover, another historian, Orest Ranum, has pointed to the futility of trying to determine who was responsible for a given act or decision in the government of Louis XIII. 'The central principle of monarchy,' he writes, 'that the king was the source of political power in the state, did not permit ministers to acknowledge, to their credit or detriment, political decisions.'[10]

But what happened to the provincial estates after the Day of Dupes, when Richelieu triumphed over Marillac? The policy hitherto pursued by the government was reversed. Absolutism, according to Major, was abandoned. The factual evidence, on the surface at least, seems to bear out this conclusion. In Burgundy talks between the Crown and the estates were soon resumed. During a visit to Dijon Louis XIII declared himself prepared to revoke the edict on the *élections* because of his need for money. The estates offered him 1.6 million *livres*, which he accepted. Burgundy thus kept its estates and Dijon regained its privileges. In Provence, the new governor, Condé, offered to revoke the edict on the *élections* for a substantial payment. After a certain amount of haggling, the estates agreed to pay 375,000 *livres* a year for four years. By the autumn of 1631 the province was almost back to normal. In Languedoc, no immediate change took place: taxes continued to be levied without the consent of the estates. But in September 1631 the *élections* were suppressed by the Crown. Louis XIII asked for 3,886,000 *livres* to compensate the *élus*. This was accepted by the estates, and the *élus* were abolished. Only in Dauphiné was the system of *élections* maintained. This was probably due mainly to the failure of the estates to settle their long-standing quarrel over the nature of the *taille*.[11]

All this, according to Major, suggests a drift away from absolutism after Richelieu had triumphed over Marillac. But the change of policy could well have been due to a change of circumstances rather than of personalities. The creation of *élections* in the *pays d'états* had met with much opposition. Resistance had frequently turned to violence. As France prepared to enter the Thirty Years War, her government could not allow domestic turmoil to get out of hand. It also needed money, and the policy of revoking unpopular legislation in return for substantial cash payments must have seemed more sensible than persisting in a course that merely provoked trouble at home. Can we be certain that even Marillac would have wanted fiscal uniformity at any price? Major believes that Richelieu was in favour of introducing *élections* into Languedoc. Why then did he agree to their abolition in 1631? He evidently saw that new circumstances called for new policies. The evolution of the absolutist state, as David Parker has shown, 'was not the result of the consistent application of a new view of government or society, but a pragmatic, frequently *ad hoc* and contradictory attempt to *restore* royal authority in the context of a rapidly changing world'.[12] It is, in any case, a mistake to equate the system of *élections* with absolutism. For 'there were very good and well-understood reasons for not regarding the creation of *élections* as a panacea for the government's financial problems or as the best method for developing fiscal uniformity'.[13] The policy involved a huge increase of administrative costs. What is more, the *élus* were renowned for their inefficiency and corruption. A far more effective way of solving the government's problems was not to add to the already excessive number of venal office-holders, but to send out commissioners whose powers could be easily revoked by the Crown.

. . .

OFFICE-HOLDERS AND *INTENDANTS*

The sale of offices was an expedient much used by the French Crown since the Middle Ages to increase its revenues. An office was more than a post in the royal civil service. As defined by the seventeenth-century jurist Loyseau, it was 'an ordinary dignity with public authority'.[14] By 'ordinary' he meant 'permanent' as distinct from a temporary or 'extra-ordinary' commission; by 'dignity' he meant social status, for offices conferred nobility. The highest offices of state (for example, the chancellorship) conferred hereditary nobility, while lesser ones conferred nobility for the lifetime of the holder only. But a family could be permanently ennobled if it retained an office for three successive generations over a period of twenty years. This was made possible by the fact that an office-holder could buy the right to hand over his office to someone else. For an office was also treated as a piece of private property which could be bought, sold and transferred. Thus a nobility of office-holders (*noblesse de robe*) grew up alongside the old nobility (*noblesse d'épée*). The salaries attached to offices were not usually high; but many perquisites were attached to them. They were, therefore, desirable, and the Crown created more than was necessary functionally to satisfy an ever-growing demand on the part of people who wanted to rise socially or improve their income.

Politically, the sale of offices was dangerous because it caused the king to lose control of part of his authority. For office-holders developed a group consciousness and collective interests which did not necessarily coincide with what the king wanted or needed. Thus offices tended to be held by relatively few families which became a sort of fourth estate in the kingdom. The mere fact that offices were sold meant that they could easily pass into the hands of people who lacked the training or ability required to carry out their functions. In short, by the early seventeenth century a situation had developed in which the king could no longer be sure that the office-holders, whom he had originally created, would carry out his will. Venal offices, in other words, had become an obstacle in the path of strong government. As fiscal necessity remained a constant feature of government, particularly after the outbreak of the Thirty Years War, it became necessary to bypass the office-holders by means of officials more directly under the king's control. These were the *intendants*.

The *intendant* was not a sudden creation. His appearance in the early seventeenth century marked the culmination of a long process whereby the central government had sent out commissioners to the provinces to carry out certain specific tasks. This happened in the sixteenth century. Under Henry III, for example, the *maîtres des requêtes* were sent on tours of inspection, called *chevauchées*. Under Henry IV commissioners were sent out by the central government on several occasions, as for example in 1598–99 to regulate the *taille*. They received constant guidance and support from Paris and their powers were gradually extended to cover all kinds of provincial affairs. But if the origins of the *intendants* of Louis XIII can be traced back to a variety of commissioners, called by different names, as far back as the sixteenth century, it was in the 1630s that the *intendant* came into his own. It was then that he ceased simply to supervise existing fiscal officials – the *trésoriers de France* and the *élus* – and actually took over their functions.[15]

As we have seen, Richelieu's foreign policy proved extremely expensive. By various means the government sought to increase its revenues. But it had to overcome the inadequacies of its fiscal officials. In May 1635 Louis XIII complained bitterly that they had obstructed the implementation of royal edicts and commissions. In 1630, for example, the *trésoriers de France* in Bordeaux objected to a tax levy before the relevant royal edicts had been registered by the local Parlement. They were not acting improperly, but in wartime the king could not tolerate such obstructionism. The office-holders were also largely to blame for other troubles faced by the government. Taxes, as we have seen, were a major cause of popular unrest, but even more unpopular were the unfairness of their distribution and abuses in their collection. Thus, an *intendant* sent to Bordeaux in 1634 found *trésoriers* who had no idea of the tax-paying capacity of certain parishes and had not altered the distribution of taxes for sixty years. The financial exploitation of office-holders by the government in the early seventeenth century had had a disastrous effect on their reliability as fiscal administrators. By 1635 the *élus* claimed that successive creations of offices had halved the value of existing ones. They tried to make up the loss by engaging in peculation, thereby reducing the Crown's income from taxation.[16] Peasant resistance to taxation was used as an excuse by royal receivers for non-cooperation with the government. This was bad enough in peacetime; in wartime it threatened disaster. The Crown needed to eradicate such abuses in order to receive its due, relieve the weak and helpless and avoid the risk of revolt.

In December 1633 the Crown decided to send out commissioners to the provinces in order to ensure that the *taille* was fairly distributed among the parishes and tax-payers. The commissioners were sent to all the *pays d'élections*, but the government did not yet intend to replace the office-holders, even temporarily. It simply wanted a better service from them. This was made clear by an edict of May 1635 which created four *intendants présidents et généraux* in each *bureau des finances*. Their task was to ensure that royal edicts were implemented in full and without delay. The *trésoriers* were not deprived of their functions. But this move proved inadequate: one year later there were more disturbances which were blamed for abuses of the office-holders. In 1637 the government decided to levy a forced loan on towns. Anticipating resistance, it entrusted the levy to commissioners; again they were only temporary. For in November 1641 the king again complained about the failure of the *trésoriers de France* and *élus* to distribute and collect taxes fairly. This time, however, he threatened to replace them by commissioners unless they gave satisfaction in respect of the *taille* for 1642. On 22 August 1642 the government formally entrusted the distribution and collection of the *taille* and other taxes to the *intendants*, thereby effectively demoting the existing office-holders. They lost all their authority in respect of taxation unless the *intendants* chose to use them as auxiliaries. This was a truly momentous step: it turned the *intendant*, who was directly responsible to the Crown and could be easily dismissed, into a provincial tax administrator.[17]

A typical *intendant* was a member of the Parisian *noblesse de robe*. Trained in the law, he would practise it for a few years before entering the sovereign courts in his early or mid-twenties. He would buy an office of *maître des requêtes* for a considerable sum (usually 150,000 *livres*) which would entitle him to preside in various courts and on royal judicial commissions. Traditionally, the *maîtres des requêtes* received petitions sent to the king by his subjects. By 1610 they had acquired a monopoly of presenting business to the *Conseil privé*. But their responsibilities were subseqently enlarged. Becoming an *intendant* was not an end in itself; it was usually the preparation for a lengthy career in the king's council.

The *intendants* shared certain ideas and attitudes. They adhered to the principle enunciated by Le Bret in his *De la souveraineté du roy* that 'necessity knows no law'. This was used in wartime to justify tax increases and various arbitrary measures.

An *intendant* was both judge and administrator. His powers were defined in a commission which could be either general or specific. Local circumstances might cause one *intendant* to receive wider powers than another. The first commission that specified the three powers of justice, *police* and finance was issued in 1621. Thereafter they became common. The powers of *intendants* were a flexible instrument of government, and they did not constitute a threat to the Crown, for an *intendant*'s decisions were always subject to cancellation by the king's council. Only in certain criminal cases could he issue definitive sentences not subject to appeal to the council.[18]

A historian has claimed that in 1624 *intendants* 'were almost everywhere . . . and in charge of almost everything'.[19] This is a gross exaggeration. Only about 120 were appointed between 1560 and 1630. Their number rose to between 120 and 150 between 1630 and 1648. As Bonney writes: 'War, above all the fiscal demands of war, was to prove the decisive factor in the establishment of the intendants.'[20] They were to be found in all the *pays d'élections* by November 1641. A relatively firm three-year rule operated, after which an *intendant* would be re-appointed, sent to a new province or recalled. On average *intendants* remained at their posts less than three years between 1634 and 1648.

The increased use of *intendants* by the Crown inevitably had an impact on the provincial governors, who in the past had been all-powerful in local affairs and subject only to the competing influence of the local parlements. During Richelieu's administration an extraordinary number of governors were removed, disgraced, exiled or imprisoned. But this was due to their participation in various aristocratic plots, not to any deliberate plan by the cardinal to destroy the governorships as such. In fact, he was keen to acquire them for himself and for his relatives and clients. The earliest *intendants* were expected to assist the governors. Such co-operation was potentially most useful in securing the registration of royal decrees by the sovereign courts, in military affairs, in controlling towns and levying taxes. For a governor commanded a vast network of patronage locally which lay outside the *intendant*'s control. But the co-operation did not always materialise. For provincial governors generally failed to take up arms against nobles who supported peasants resisting the government's tax demands. The *intendants* were thus left to act alone. From 1629 onwards they policed the activities of lesser nobles as a matter of course. In August 1642 they were empowered to prosecute anyone – even a *seigneur* – who delayed the king's tax returns.[21]

Another duty which befell the *intendants* was to fight municipal autonomy. Most towns were controlled by oligarchies which jealously guarded their privileges, including fiscal immunities. They also preferred to resist or oppose royal commands rather than provoke unrest by the urban mob. Even so, there were many urban riots, mostly provoked by taxation, during Richelieu's administration. The forced loan on towns (December 1636), the *taxe des aisés* (1639–40) and the *sol pour livre* (1640) helped to fuel unrest. After each disturbance an *intendant* investigated its causes and prosecuted the ringleaders. Most urban riots under Richelieu were limited in scope, yet they were sufficiently serious to warrant tighter royal controls on municipal affairs. After 1642 the *intendants* were used to impose a kind of administrative tutelage on the towns.[22]

It was under Richelieu that the *intendants* first came into their own as agents of royal absolutism. In the long term they helped to make the monarchy far stronger than it had been in 1624. From the absolutist standpoint the *intendant* had great advantages over the office-holder: his powers could be modified according to circumstances; they could also be revoked if he failed in his duty. Unlike the sovereign courts, the provincial governors and the estates, the *intendants* could not become an alternative source of power to the Crown. At the same time, their social and professional background ensured a common approach to their work and served to guarantee their loyalty to the state. Their prime purpose was to remove obstacles in the path of France's war effort. This they achieved with considerable success. Without their efforts, it is hard to see how France could have emerged victorious from the Thirty Years War. Richelieu did not live long enough to see this happen. The biggest test faced by the *intendants* – the Fronde – had still to come when he died. But by making them instead of the office-holders the principal agents of royal power in the provinces, Richelieu contributed decisively to the growth of absolutism in France.

. . .

NOTES AND REFERENCES

1. Bonney R 1987 'Absolutism: What's in a name?' *French History*, vol. 1, pp. 93–117. See also his *L'Absolutisme*. Paris, PUF, 1989. Also Mousnier R 1982 *La monarchie absolue en Europe du Ve siècle à nos jours*. Paris, PUF.
2. Parker D 1983 *The Making of French Absolutism*. London, Arnold, p. 1.
3. Hanley S 1983 *The 'Lit de Justice' of the Kings of France*. Princeton, NJ, Princeton University Press, pp. 282–95.
4. Kitchens J H 1982 'Judicial commissions and the parlement of Paris' *French Historical Studies* XII.
5. Champollion-Figeac A (ed.) 1855–57 *Mémoires de Mathieu Molé*. Paris, Société de l'Histoire de France, vol. 2, pp. 143–44.
6. Shennan J H 1968 *The Parlement of Paris*. London, Eyre & Spottiswoode, pp. 249–54.
7. Major J Russell 1980 *Representative Government in Early Modern France*. New Haven, CT and London, Yale University Press, pp. 524–67.
8. Ibid., p. 570.
9. Ibid., pp. 570 n3, 572, 580.
10. Ranum O 1963 *Richelieu and the Councillors of Louis XIII*. Oxford, Clarendon, p. 3.
11. Major *Representative Government in Early Modern France*, pp. 581–607.
12. Parker *The Making of French Absolutism*, p. 90; see also Briggs R 1989 *Communities of Belief*. Oxford, p. 129.
13. Ibid., p. 72.
14. Mousnier R 1971 *La vénalité des offices sous Henri IV et Louis XIII*. Paris, PUF, p. 7.
15. Mousnier R 1970 *La Plume, la fauçille et le marteau*. Paris, PUF, pp. 179–99; Bonney R 1978 *Political Change in France under Richelieu and Mazarin 1624–1661*. Oxford, Oxford University Press, pp. 29–50.
16. Ibid., pp. 168–69.
17. Mousnier *La Plume, la fauçille et le marteau*, pp. 181–91.

18. Bonney *Political Change*, pp. 76–159.
19. Lublinskaya A D 1968 *French Absolutism: the Crucial Phase, 1620–1629*. Cambridge, Cambridge University Press, p. 319.
20. Bonney *Political Change*, p. 36.
21. Ibid., pp. 284–317.
22. Ibid., pp. 318–43.

Chapter 10

RICHELIEU AND THE ECONOMY

Richelieu was always interested in the sea. Some historians have tried to explain this interest in ancestral terms. True, his great-grandfather had been a vice-admiral, his grand-father a sea captain and his father a privateer. But the cardinal's interest probably owed less to his ancestors than to his own keen awareness of economic realities.[1] As an intelligent observer, Richelieu listened to the lively debate that was going on around him about the state of France's economy. In particular, he was aware of the crucial role played by overseas trade in the life of the nation.

By the seventeenth century the main focus of international trade had shifted from the Mediterranean to the Atlantic. France with coasts on both seas was inevitably caught up in this shift, but during her religious wars she had allowed much of her overseas trade to fall into the hands of the English and the Dutch. They had larger ships and operated highly successful trading companies, such as the Dutch East India Company. The activities of their merchants received active encouragement from their governments in the form of protectionist legislation. English and Dutch merchants were to be seen everywhere in France's Atlantic ports. The Baltic trade in French salt had become a Dutch monopoly. Much the same was true of the wine trade. The Dutch were not content merely to carry wine from the Bordeaux region to northern Europe; they moved into the vineyards themselves and set about producing *eau-de-vie*. Even in the Mediterranean, English and Dutch merchants were much in evidence, seriously threatening the privileged place occupied by French merchants in the Ottoman empire since the early sixteenth century.[2]

France should have been in the forefront of trading nations. As contemporary writers were at pains to point out, she had a long coastline with many excellent harbours, numerous forests capable of supplying timber for ship-building, and a large sea-faring population. Yet her merchant fleet was comparatively small and made up of ships of low tonnage. Many were built in the United Provinces, and a large number of French sailors (estimated by one writer at 200,000) served on foreign ships because there was no employment for them at home. As for France's war fleet, it was almost non-existent at the start of Louis XIII's reign. As a result, French merchants were an easy prey to corsairs and pirates. The Dutch, though officially allied to France, did not hesitate to attack them. But the worst pirates of all were those from the Barbary coast. They captured not only ships and their cargoes, but also the sailors, whom they sold into slavery.

There were at least three reasons for France's weakness at sea. The first was the preoccupation of successive governments with continental issues. The French monarchy did not feel that it could defend itself on land and sea simultaneously; given the choice, it opted for land. A more important reason perhaps was the traditional prejudice felt by Frenchmen for trade. Whereas in England and the United Provinces trade was not regarded as socially downgrading, in France it was despised. A nobleman who dabbled in trade risked losing his privileges under the rules of *dérogeance*, while a merchant usually aspired to becoming a nobleman by investing his profits in land or buying an office.[3] He would also educate his son for one of the liberal professions rather than for business. As a result, France lacked mercantile dynasties of the kind that flourished in other countries.

Richelieu knew of these problems and also of the remedies being offered by contemporary economic theorists. Among the most famous of these was Antoine de Montchrétien, who published a *Traité d'économie politique* in 1615. This denounced foreigners as leeches who sucked the nation's lifeblood. 'The most royal task which Your Majesties can undertake,' he wrote, 'is to restore order where it has been destroyed, to regulate the mechanical arts which are in monstrous confusion, to re-establish trade and commerce which have been interrupted and troubled for so long.' To achieve these ends, the author argued, it was necessary to protect French trade and industry from competition by the English and the Dutch. They imposed harsh restrictions on French goods, and France should retaliate with simi-lar measures. Montchrétien noted with approval the strict regulations covering commercial transactions in London as compared with French ones that were 'full of licence and liberty'. He recommended tighter controls on foreign ships in French harbours, the building of more ports and the use of French ships in preference to foreign ones. He also urged his government to follow the example set by the Dutch East India Company. A war fleet was also essential to protect French interests on the high seas.[4]

Richelieu gave official expression to his maritime interests in a *réglement* of 1625.[5] It was essential, he explained, for the king always to have forty galleys with which to protect French merchants trading with the Levant from attacks by Barbary corsairs. He had consequently ordered the treasurer of the *épargne* to disburse 150,000 *écus* for the construction of thirty galleys. Deserted harbours along the coast also needed to be fortified and garrisoned so as to prevent them being used as convenient bases for corsairs. The Estates of Provence would pay for the forts, while he would pay the garrisons. The cost of maintaining the galleys would be met out of duties on tobacco and sugar. Richelieu also considered the political advantages of achieving control of the sea passage to Italy. Not only would it oblige Spanish troop-ships bound for Italy to face the hazards of keeping to the high seas; it might also encourage the oppressed people of Naples and Sicily to overthrow their Viceroys and the Italian princes to send military aid to Louis XIII.

In October 1626, by an edict issued at St Germain, Richelieu was confirmed as *Grand Maître et surintendant-général du commerce et de la navigation*.[6] This new office gave him control of merchant shipping and of the king's navy. But, before taking charge of maritime policy, he needed to get rid of the existing archaic naval administration. This consisted essentially of the Admiral of France and three admirals for Guyenne, Brittany and Provence respectively. An admiral at this time was not a seaman, but an administrator with jurisdiction over ports and shipping and with the right to levy a wide variety of tariffs on ships and merchandise. In 1612 Henri II duc de Montmorency took the first step towards unifying the administration by combining the admiralty of France with that of Brittany. A year later he secured that of Guyenne as well. In August 1626 Richelieu persuaded Montmorency to give up all three admiralties for the sum of 1,200,000 *livres*. The three offices were then abolished, and their powers transferred to the *Grand Maître*. But the edict of St Germain still needed registration by the parlements. Several complied, but the parlement of Rennes resisted, claiming that the admiralty of Brittany was traditionally exercised by the provincial governor. 'I am not planning to do anything new in Brittany or elsewhere,' Richelieu explained, 'but only to look meekly and agreeably for ways by which those who wish to trade may do so in safety'. The difficulty was overcome when the duc de Vendôme resigned as governor and Richelieu accepted an invitation from the Breton estates to succeed him. This left only the admiral of Provence outside the new administration. In June 1629 Louis XIII extended the powers of the *Grand Maître* to the Mediterranean. The duc de Guise, who was governor of Provence, complained bitterly about the loss of his admiralty, but soon afterwards he fell from favour and went into exile, leaving Richelieu in full control.[7]

In November 1626 a knight of Malta, called Isaac de Razilly, dedicated a memorandum to Richelieu outlining a vast programme of maritime development and overseas expansion. He dismissed as an 'old chestnut' the notion that France was self-sufficient in all the necessities of life and did not need to import anything from abroad. On the contrary, argued Razilly, she needed to exploit her natural advantages and develop her overseas trade. 'Whoever is master of the sea,' he wrote, 'also has great power on land.' One had but to look at the king of Spain to see the truth of this assertion: since he had armed at sea, he had conquered so many lands that the sun never set on his dominions. Even small nations, like the United Provinces, had acquired influence as a result of their sea-power. The king of France, by contrast, had not even been able to put down the rebellion of the duc de Rohan without calling on foreign help. Frenchmen, Razilly continued, needed to change their attitude to trade. Impoverished nobles should seek to redress their fortunes by going to sea. Companies should be founded like those of the English or the Dutch. If the right steps were taken, the king of France could become 'master of the sea' in ten years.[8]

In addition to Razilly's memorandum, Richelieu studied the reports of Capuchin missionaries in the Levant and elsewhere, which his friend, Father Joseph, passed on to him. Though mainly about religious matters, they also contained useful information about trade, for the missionaries often rubbed shoulders with French merchants and their rivals.[9] The cardinal also read the reports sent by French diplomats. They told him of the severe restrictions imposed on French merchants in Spain and England. While French cloth was banned in England, France was being flooded with cheap English cloth. In 1626 the French ambassador in England complained that the English had declared war on Spain, yet they were waging it only against the French. They had declared all French ships trading with Spain as lawful prize. As for the Dutch, they were officially allied to France, yet they showed no compunction about plundering her ships.[10]

On 18 November 1626 Richelieu addressed a memorandum to the Keeper of the Seals, Marillac, for use in preparing his speech to the Assembly of Notables due to open in Paris on 2 December.[11] It began with the following statement:

> It has been till now a great shame that the king who is the eldest son of the Church is inferior in his maritime power to the smallest prince in Christendom. His Majesty, seeing the harm that his realm and subjects have suffered therefrom, is resolved to remedy the same by making himself as powerful at sea as he is on land. But for this determination one might as well write off our trade. For the king's subjects have been cheated daily, not only of their goods but of their freedom. Our neighbours have assumed that they have the right to sell us their goods and to buy ours on their terms. But these miseries will now cease, His Majesty having decided to maintain thirty good warships with which to guard the coasts, keep his subjects in their obedience and teach his neighbours the respect due to so great a nation.

When the notables gathered in December, the king explained that they had been summoned to cure the state's disorders.[12] Later, Richelieu himself declared: 'The duration of this Assembly must be brief but the fruit of its deliberation must last for ever'. The navy and trade were only part of an extensive programme of domestic reform submitted to the notables. Marillac, as it turned out, did not use in his speech all the points in Richelieu's memorandum, which may explain why the cardinal felt impelled to address the notables himself.[13] He did not give a detailed account of the reforms he had in mind, confining himself to broad issues. On 11 January 1627, however, he presented a memorandum of thirteen articles outlining the government's plans for the reform of trade, the legal system, the army and the fiscal system.[14] Also included were proposals for educational reform. Too many people, it argued, were being educated for the liberal professions, not enough for technical pursuits. It was necessary, therefore,

> to reduce the number of colleges existing in small towns of the kingdom which cause merchants, even *laboureurs*, to remove their children from their own occupations in order to train them for another in which more often than not they will earn nothing and bring ruin to others.

The cardinal also believed that nobles had a contribution to make to the nation's prosperity and urged a relaxation of the rules of *dérogeance*.

The Notables were duly impressed by Richelieu's arguments and by the supporting evidence he put before them. They endorsed the need to restore to the kingdom 'the riches of the sea' and supported the creation of trading companies, the building of more ships and the introduction of regulations against the importation of foreign manufactured goods.[15] The cardinal could feel satisfied. His past efforts had met with approval and he was given virtually a free hand for the future. The famous *Code Michau*, which Marillac drafted after the Assembly, contained several commercial clauses.[16] Thus it allowed nobles to trade without derogating from their status, forbade French sailors to serve on foreign ships and banned the importation of foreign manufactured goods. The *Code Michau* was registered by the parlement in 1629, but it encountered so much opposition from office-holders that it became a dead letter, following Marillac's fall from power. Richelieu never tried to enforce it.

. . .

THE NAVY

France's weakness at sea in the early seventeenth century is well illustrated by an incident that happened to Sully, when he visited England as ambassador in 1603. He travelled from Calais on an English ship, but his companion, Dominique de Vic, travelled on one flying the French flag. The English captain, resenting this insult to James I's alleged sovereignty of the sea, demanded that the French flag be lowered. On being refused, he fired three cannon shots into the French ship and would surely have sunk her if Sully had not persuaded de Vic to comply with the Englishman's request. The humiliation, which was allowed to go unavenged, was recalled by Richelieu in his *Testament politique*. The shots, he writes, 'pierced the heart of the good Frenchman'. He determined to do all in his power to prevent any repetition of such a national insult.[17]

One of the first steps taken by the cardinal to improve France's standing as a sea power was to commission two enquiries into the state of her navy, one for the Atlantic or *Ponant*, the other for the Mediterranean or *Levant*. The former was entrusted in 1629 to Louis Le Roux, *sieur* d'Infreville, and the latter, in 1633, to Henri de Séguiran, *seigneur* de Bouc. Infreville's mission lasted almost two years, and resulted in a detailed report which painted a grim picture of the French Atlantic fleet. Along the entire coast from Calais to Bayonne he counted only 60 captains, 46 pilots, 820 shipwrights, 200 gunners, 500 masters and 5,300 sailors. Yet the seafaring population of the Atlantic provinces numbered 6,000 or 7,000. The reason for the low recruitment figures was the lack of interest in the sea so far shown by the Crown. This caused people to look to the land for a living or to service on foreign ships. The lack of manpower was directly related to the lack of ships. Only Normandy and Brittany had privately owned ships capable of conversion to wartime use. As for the ports along the Atlantic coast, they were decrepit and anarchical. At Boulogne, for example, the port was becoming more ruinous daily; at Caen, French pirates in Spanish pay were preying on French ships; at Nantes, the river channel was fast dwindling in size owing to neglect. The only reasonably cheerful part of Infreville's report concerned the king's navy, which was being enlarged as a direct result of Richelieu's encouragement of ship-building. But its stores and arsenals left much to be desired. At Brest, only four walls remained of the store built by Francis I. At Châteaulin, five out of twenty-four guns tested by the commissioner proved useless. At Nantes, the forge-master explained that he was under contract to make 500 gun barrels and a large quantity of cannon balls, but did not know the length of the barrels or the size of the balls. So far, he had made nothing, as he had received no payment.

Séguiran's mission lasted only two months and covered a much smaller area, the coast of Provence. But he was, if anything, more systematic than Infreville. Wherever he went, he called meetings of municipal officials and chief inhabitants to brief him on the past and present state of maritime trade. He also personally inspected ports, ships and arsenals. Assisting him was Jacques de Maretz, a mathematician, who drew plans that were subsequently incorporated into a large map (since lost) of the Provençal coast. It was on the basis of this map that Richelieu decided to fortify the coast in various places. This was urgently needed, for along its entire length people lived in dread of the Barbary pirates and lacked proper defences. For example, at Cassis, the fort was defended simply by its custodian with two falconets, one of which was wind-blown. At Toulon, the fortifications were quite inadequate. The garrison consisted of a 'bonhomme de gouverneur', who had not been paid for twenty years, his wife and a servant. Yet, unsafe as they were, the ports of Provence remained active and its seafaring population large. Excluding Marseilles and Toulon, Séguiran counted 7,000 sailors. The Provençal fleet, excluding the galleys, comprised forty-one long-distance vessels and 427 coastal ones. But only five of these ships were convertible to warships.[18]

Richelieu's reform of the navy consisted of four elements: a naval administration, a recruitment policy, the provision of ports, ship-building yards and arsenals and the building of warships. On 6 January 1624, Louis XIII had set up a Conseil de Marine to consider proposals from Admiral Montmorency and his staff, and to refer matters of substance to the king's council. Under Richelieu, its main function was to prepare administrative orders requiring his signature. A major document of this kind was the Réglement sur le fait de la marine of 1631.[19] This decreed that the king's ships would be concentrated in the ports of Brouage, Brest and Le Havre. Each port was given a *commissaire-général* with responsibility for maintaining ships and their crews, and a *chef d'escadre* responsible for defence. Each official had a staff, and the entire administration was placed under the cardinal's uncle, Amador de La Porte, *intendant-général de la navigation et du commerce*. Eight *lieutenants-généraux* were given charge of patrolling the coast.

The recruitment of sailors proved difficult. Whereas the army could be supplied with volunteers, the navy required men with experience of the sea. To fill this need Admiral Montmorency had suggested in 1624 that a register be kept of ship's captains and pilots. The idea was taken up by Richelieu and elaborated upon in the *Code Michau*, but it was never properly applied.

Richelieu was also anxious to set up powerful bases along the Atlantic and Mediterranean coasts, each provided with a fortress, a ship-building yard, an arsenal and a harbour fully provided with such necessities as rope, sailcloth and tar, and a team of skilled workmen capable of carrying out repairs. He eventually chose three ports on the Atlantic – Le Havre, Brest and Brouage – and one on the Mediterranean, Toulon. Richelieu had personal reasons for being interested in Le Havre, for his great-grandfather had helped to found it and his father had commanded a ship there. In 1635 the cardinal paid for important works that included a basin, a lock and various kinds of fortification. But he was even fonder of Brest, which acquired under his administration some imposing fortifications, numerous stores, a rope factory and ship-building yards. Such was the cardinal's pride in the port that he called it 'my Brest'. But Brouage, on which he lavished much attention and expense, proved disappointing: it silted up continually and was abandoned by Richelieu's successors. In the Mediterranean, the development of Toulon as a naval base only began in 1640, so that the fruits were not seen till after the cardinal's death.[20]

A few statistics may suffice to show how far Richelieu succeeded in giving Louis XIII 'mastery of the sea'. In 1625 there was no permanent fleet in the Atlantic and only a dozen galleys in the Mediterranean. Ten years later there were three squadrons of round ships in the Atlantic and one in the Mediterranean in addition to the galleys. From the start of his ministry Richelieu accepted the need for an increase of naval forces in both seas. Late in 1626 he ordered the building of eighteen ships and in February 1627 raised this number to twenty-four. As the admiralty had no yards of its own, private ones, mainly situated in Normandy and Brittany, were used.

To expedite matters Richelieu employed three captains: Razilly and du Mé in Normandy and A de Beaulieu in Brittany. The cardinal expected them to work fast. 'Although I know that there is no need to press you,' he wrote, 'I cannot but beg you to hasten the ships.' Richelieu imagined that France could provide all the necessary ship-building materials, but it was soon found necessary to import timber from Germany, iron from Biscay and Sweden and hemp from Riga. This required both time and money. France also suffered from a shortage of skilled labour. As a result, the ships, once completed, often proved unreliable. As de La Porte reported in 1634,

> many of the ships built by His Majesty in this kingdom have not been well fastened or built. Some have fallen apart under their own weight without sailing, while others have let in the sea with the loss of men and merchandise. . ... This is due to lack of knowledge and skill on the part of the builders.

In 1627 Richelieu thought up a scheme to recruit fifty master-carpenters to build ships and inspect them for seaworthiness, but nothing came of it. He, therefore, had to import foreign workers and order ships abroad.

Despite these shortcomings, Richelieu did succeed in giving France a sizeable war fleet. It comprised forty-one ships in 1633 and forty-six in 1635. The fleet which Sourdis took to the Mediterranean in 1636 was the largest ever assembled in the *Ponant*, but it lacked homogeneity. English and Dutch naval squadrons were made up mainly of ships of 500 tons and a larger flagship. Richelieu's Atlantic fleet consisted in the main of smaller vessels of around 300 tons. It was better adapted to lightning strikes than to set battles. A notable exception was the *Couronne*, a warship of 2,000 tons, armed with seventy-two guns and with a crew of 600. Built in France, she was much admired, even by foreigners. In the *Levant*, galleys continued to predominate. In 1635 Richelieu ordered eleven to be built so as to bring the total to twenty-four. He also created a squadron of round ships, which eventually numbered eighteen. Maritime novelties too interested the cardinal: he developed the use of fireships, commissioned a sort of barge intended 'to produce a notable effect at sea', and gave a twelve-year privilege to the inventor of a submarine.[21]

In his *Hydrographie* of 1643, Father Fournier claimed in the preface addressed to the king:

> The sea has never owed so much to any of our kings as it owes you; never has it been as rich and glorious as in your reign. Never has France less deserved the just reproach that used to be made that she neglected maritime affairs [*la navigation*] to the prejudice of her state.[22]

Although Fournier did not mention Richelieu in his panegyric, the cardinal deserved much of the credit for the rapid improvement in France's sea power.

· · ·

TRADE

With a better fleet at his disposal Richelieu could expect to improve France's standing as an international trading power. He was interested in developing her trade in the Mediterranean and the Atlantic. We know that he underwent a change of mind regarding the direction of French trade. Having at first been swayed by the argument that trade with the Levant was draining the kingdom of specie merely in order to bring back unnecessary luxury goods, he came to see that this was wrong. As an anonymous Marseillais explained in a report commissioned by the cardinal in 1628, France could not do without imports from the Levant. If Frenchmen did not fetch them, foreigners would and the goods would have to be purchased from them, giving them the profits that Frenchmen would have got. The Levant trade also offered employment to many French people and provided an outlet for their manufactured goods. It stimulated ship-building and brought a useful income to the royal treasury from customs duties.[23] Richelieu was won over by such arguments. Thus he wrote in his *Testament politique*:

> I admit that I was long mistaken about the trade of the Provençaux with the Levant. I believed along with many others that it was damaging to the state, sharing the common view that it drained the kingdom of money simply in order to import inessential luxuries. But, after acquiring a precise knowledge of that unpopular trade, I have changed my mind for reasons that are so well grounded that anyone who troubles to find them out will see that I am right.[24]

Richelieu was keen to develop direct links with Persia, which he valued as a potential supplier of raw silk to the Tours industry that he had taken under his patronage. In 1626 he sent Louis des Hayes de Courmenin to Turkey in the hope of reviving trade with that country. The cardinal was anxious to restore the good name of French merchants which they had compromised by various dishonest practices. Unhappily, one of the worst offenders was Harlay de Césy, the French ambassador in Constantinople, who had contracted huge debts with many foreign traders. He resented Courmenin's mission and placed obstacles in his path. Eventually, Courmenin had to abandon his intended journey to Persia, thereby dashing Richelieu's hopes of closer commercial ties with the Shah. But Turkey was not the only route by which French merchants might reach Persia. A possible alternative lay through Muscovy. In the sixteenth century the English had established a factory at Archangel from which they had travelled, with the tsar's permission, as far south as the Caspian Sea. Richelieu hoped that Frenchmen might be allowed to do likewise, using Narva as a staging post.

In 1626 Courmenin set off on a new mission, this time to Denmark and Muscovy. He was instructed to negotiate with the Danes a reduction of the dues charged on goods passing through the Sound, and, with Muscovy, for the right of overland transit to Persia. On 14 July 1629 a commercial agreement with Denmark reduced the duty on French goods passing through the Sound. But a serious rebuff awaited Courmenin in Muscovy. Tsar Michael Romanov was happy that Frenchmen should visit his country, but refused them transit to Persia. He promised to sell them silk so cheaply that they would not need to go there. Thus it was that Richelieu's 'grand design' of a direct Franco–Persian trade route by way of the Baltic and Muscovy never materialised. A useful by-product of Courmenin's mission, however, was the revival of French trade with the Baltic. In 1628 not a single French ship passed through the Sound. By 1630 the number had risen to twenty and by 1631 to seventy-two. But this revival was short-lived. Following France's entry into the Thirty Years War, her Baltic trade collapsed.[25]

By the early seventeenth century, the Atlantic had overtaken the Mediterranean as the main focus of international trade. Despite their increasing dependence on the Dutch, France's Atlantic ports maintained a high level of economic activity. Each, however, functioned on its own account without regard for the national interest. Any moves by the government to develop France's colonial and maritime assets on a collective basis ran into stubborn resistance from merchant groups. They had little interest in long-term projects, preferring quick returns from fishing or fur-trading. They were only prepared to take advantage of the government's plans if this helped them to compete with their French rivals.[26] It was against this background of local particularism and mercantile myopia that Richelieu tried to set up companies comparable to those of the English and the Dutch.

In July 1626 Louis XIII set up the *Compagnie du Morbihan*.[27] One hundred merchants with a joint capital of 1,600,000 *livres* were granted Morbihan as a 'free town' which they undertook to develop in various ways. They were assured of the same privileges as those enjoyed by noblemen. At the same time they were given a monopoly of trade with the East and West Indies, New France and the Levant and allowed to found colonies. But the realisation of this ambitious scheme was strongly resisted by the Parlement of Rennes backed by the merchants of Nantes and St Malo, who saw the company as harmful to their privileges. By the time the Estates of Brittany had accepted the scheme, so much time had been lost that it was abandoned. It was closely followed by another called the *Compagnie de la Nacelle de St Pierre Fleurdelysée*.[28] This planned to set up two 'free ports', one on the Atlantic, the other on the Mediterranean, as well as depots in all the main towns of France. It also intended to promote a wide range of industrial and agricultural activities, such as coal-mining, deep-sea fishing, and the growing of rice and sugar cane. Furthermore, it undertook to send twelve fully equipped vessels to New France and within six months 100 families. The company was exempted from *dérogeance* and its foreign members were to be regarded as Frenchmen. But for reasons that remain obscure the *Compagnie de la Nacelle* never left the drawing-board.

The commercial exploitation of North America loomed large among plans to develop French overseas trade in the early seventeenth century. By 1627 little remained of 'New France', the name given to the colonies which the French had established in Canada and Acadia (now Nova Scotia). Each winter the tiny population of 107 found itself cut off from Europe. It lived on whatever food was left in its stores and waited for new supplies to arrive in the spring. If the ship bringing them from France was delayed for any cause, famine ensued. Politically, the organisation of the colony was rudimentary. Its only notable achievement was the profitable fur-trade, which extended far inland and rested on good relations with the Indians. But this alone could not make up for the numerical insignificance of the French settlement or its precariousness.[29]

Richelieu tried to breathe new life into France's feeble north American colony. In April and May 1627 he signed the act of association of a new company, called *Compagnie de la Nouvelle France*.[30] Its headquarters was to be in Paris and it was to comprise at least 100 members (hence its other name: *Compagnie des Cent Associés*). The capital was fixed at 300,000 *livres*, each member contributing 3,000 *livres*. The profits were not to be distributed for three years, but added to each member's capital. Thereafter he would be allowed to withdraw a third of the profits. This was to ensure the permanence of the enterprise. Besides Quebec, two warships and four cannon, the associates were granted 'New France', which was defined as a huge territory stretching from Florida in the south to the Arctic circle in the north, and from Newfoundland in the east to the Great Lakes in the west. The members were also granted the monopoly of trade in New France for the first fifteen years, except the fisheries; after fifteen years, it was to cover only hides, skins and pelts. Five important concessions were made to boost the company: nobles and clergy who joined it were allowed to trade without losing their privileges. Twelve members of the company were to be ennobled. Any emigrant who wished to return to France after practising his craft in New France would be accorded the title of 'master craftsman' and might hold 'open shop'. The descendants of the settlers would be deemed French. Lastly, for the first fifteen years all goods shipped either way between France and New France would be tax-free. The 100 associates for their part undertook to settle 4,000 colonists – all French and Catholic – during the first fifteen years.

The new company was hastily launched, Richelieu becoming one of its members. Another was Samuel Champlain, who had founded the French settlement in Quebec in 1608. A list drawn up on 17 May 1627 totalled 107 members. Of these, twenty-six were merchants, the rest mainly office-holders. Whereas in the past the French colonization of North America had stemmed mainly from Brittany and Normandy, it now drew its strength from Paris. Unhappily, the launching of the project coincided with the outbreak of Anglo-French hostilities in 1627. Just as the Hundred Associates were about to launch their first expedition, a rival company was formed in England by Gervase Kirke with the specific object of occupying key regions of New France and monopolizing its trade. In 1628 a fleet sent out by Kirke destroyed two French settlements in and near the St Lawrence estuary. It also captured the fleet of the Hundred Associates with its precious cargo of food and goods for barter. In 1629 an Anglo-Scottish expedition captured Quebec. The French ambassador in England, aided by Champlain, began talks aimed at recovering the French settlements. Charles I was willing enough to hand back Quebec, but not Acadia, which had been granted to a Scotsman, William Alexander. For three years, while the talks dragged on, the St Lawrence remained closed to France, with consequential heavy losses for the Hundred Associates. On 29 March 1632, however, under the treaty of St Germain, England agreed to evacuate New France. The Hundred Associates could now resume their original programme. However, on returning to New France in July 1632 they found the buildings destroyed, the animals scattered and the land turned to waste. Only the fur trade remained intact. The sequel is a sad story. The company failed to recover from its losses during the war with England. By the time Richelieu died, it had lost all its original dynamism. Although the company continued to own New France, it conceded its trade monopoly with Canada in 1645 to the Community of Inhabitants; two years later it gave its monopoly in Acadia to Menou d'Aulnay.[31]

One has only to consider the state of New France in 1663 to see how far it had fallen short of the objectives the Company of the Hundred Associates had set itself in 1627. Instead of the 4,000 settlers originally envisaged, there were only about 2,500. As compared with other European colonies in North America, this was a pathetically small figure: New Holland had 10,000 and Virginia 30,000. The small French population was extremely vulnerable militarily and economically. By 1663 New France had no important fisheries or any industries. Its economy rested almost exclusively on the fur trade. If this failed, as it did during the war between the Iroquois and Huron Indians, it had nothing to fall back upon. The only redeeming feature of New France was the remarkable flowering of Catholic missions. The Jesuits, who set up a college at Quebec – the first in North America – led the field. They were followed in 1639 by the Ursulines, who founded a girls' school, and by the *Hospitalières de Dieppe*, who provided a hospital. Yet these foundations were premature, given the generally backward state of the colony. All in all, the colonization of New France under Richelieu was not a success.[32]

On paper, at least, Richelieu showed little interest in trade with the Caribbean, yet paradoxically it was here that his colonial ventures proved most successful. In 1626 two Frenchmen, Urbain de Roissy and Pierre Belain, *sieur* d'Esnambuc, formed a company with a view to settling the islands of St Kitts (called St Christophe), Barbados and others 'facing Peru', and on 12 February it was given the name of *Compagnie des Îles d'Amérique*. Richelieu became a member, contributing out of his own pocket 3,000 *livres* and a ship worth 8,000 *livres*. In addition to promoting French emigration to the West Indies, the company transported slaves from Sénégal to work on the tobacco and cotton plantations in Martinique, Guadeloupe and Santo Domingo. The company also encouraged the manufacture of sugar. By the time Richelieu died, there were 7,000 French settlers in the West Indies.[33]

How far did Richelieu succeed in revitalizing French overseas trade? The answer has to be qualified. While paving the way for Colbert's work later in the century, the cardinal was unable in the short time at his disposal to turn France into a first-rate commercial power. He had done little more than indicate the paths his compatriots should follow if they seriously meant to challenge the commercial pre-eminence of the Dutch. Nothing short of a miracle was required to alter some of their fundamental attitudes in regard to trade. Even under Louis XIV a huge gulf separated France and the United Provinces as commercial powers. By 1661 all the trading companies that had been dreamt of under Louis XIII were either dead or moribund. As for the French overseas empire, it barely existed. All that remained were a few hundred settlers in Canada and a larger number in the West Indies.[34]

. . .

INDUSTRY

Industry, as we know it today, did not exist in early seventeenth-century France. The word itself was not used. Instead, the phrase '*arts et manufactures*' was employed, implying a close union between artist and craftsman. Factories of the modern kind did not come into existence till the eighteenth century. Previously work was done by artisans working in many small workshops. The crafts to which they belonged were either free or subject to guild regulations (*métiers jurés*). But in the sixteenth century the Crown sponsored the creation of *manufactures*. These consisted of many small workshops employing hundreds, even thousands, of isolated artisans who worked for a single entrepreneur. He distributed to them the raw materials and undertook to sell their products.

The main reason for the interest shown by Francis I and his successors in industrial production was their concern to stop the exportation of specie from France in exchange for foreign luxury goods, such as Flemish tapestries or Venetian glassware. But it was not until the reign of Henry IV that royal *manufactures* became important. Out of forty-eight that existed in 1610, only eight antedated the reign. At first, the royal manufactures were concentrated in the Paris region or the Loire valley. Lyons, the second industrial centre after Paris, jealously guarded its economic independence. With the passing of time other *manufactures* were set up by private individuals with royal backing, which commonly took the form of a monopoly. According to one historian, 260 *manufactures* were created between 1589 and 1660, but many soon collapsed.[35]

Richelieu, it has been said, showed much less interest in industry than in trade. Yet he did not neglect it entirely. He was particularly interested in the silk manufacture of Tours which lay close to his ducal domain. He ordered furnishings from it for his residences in Paris and in the country, and he praised the quality of its products in his *Testament politique*.[36]

However, such encouragement as he gave to French industry needs to be measured against the damage inflicted by an excess of government regulation. From the late sixteenth century onwards the French Crown tried to regulate all existing crafts, with varying degrees of success. The reason behind this policy was purely fiscal. Whenever a guild (*communauté de métiers*) was set up, a tax was paid to the Crown. Similarly, no craftsman was allowed to practise as a master without a diploma of mastership (*lettres de maîtrise*), which again was subject to tax. Under Richelieu the government introduced more industrial controls. For example, in 1625, royal inspectors of beer were instituted, ostensibly because bad beer was thought to produce colds and other illnesses. In the following year, controllers were appointed in every *bailliage* to check the quality of iron.[37] As these offices were venal, the Crown stood to gain financially from their creation and multiplication. But the policy was widely resented in industrial circles. In 1639 the revolt of the *Nu-pieds* began in Rouen with the lynching of a government inspector of textiles.[38] In 1643 the people of Rouen complained that royal officials were prying into their workshops at all times and spoiling their merchandise.

However, Richelieu's foreign policy and wars needed to be paid for, and industrial regulation was one method of raising revenue. Hence Hauser's judgement that the cardinal's industrial achievement was 'eroded by fiscality'.[39] Another historian, John Nef, has argued that government regulation hampered technological change and was in part responsible for France's industrial backwardness by comparison with England in the time of Louis XIII. With three times the population of England, she had less than a third of England's mines and small factories; only in the making of luxury goods, such as silks and tapestries, was she ahead.[40] Richelieu must share some of the blame for this backwardness.

. . .

NOTES AND REFERENCES

1. Boiteux L-A 1955 *Richelieu 'grand maître de la navigation et du commerce de France'*. Paris, Editions Ozanne; Hauser, H. 1944 *La pensée et l'action économiques du Cardinal de Richelieu*. Paris, PUF, p. 16.

2. Chaunu P. and Gascon, R. 1977 *Histoire économique et sociale de la France*, vol. 1: *1450–1600: l'État et la ville*. Paris, PUF, pp. 336–43.

3. Ibid., pp. 357–68; Bitton, D. 1969 *The French Nobility in Crisis, 1560–1640*. Stanford, CA, Stanford University Press, p. 66; Zeller G. 1964 'Une notion de caractère historico-social: la dérogeance' in *Aspects de la politique française sous l'Ancien Régime*. Paris, PUF, pp. 336–74.

4. Parker D 1980 *La Rochelle and the French Monarchy*. London, Royal Historical Society, pp. 59–60.

5. Grillon P (ed.) 1975–85 *Les papiers de Richelieu* (6 vols). Paris, Pedone, i 242–44 (no. 85).

6. Ibid., i. 511–15 (no 280).

7. Boiteux *Richelieu*, pp. 65–76, 85, 99–103, 136–48.

8. Hauser *La pensée et l'action économiques*, pp. 38–42.

9. Ibid., pp. 36–8.

10. Ibid., pp. 54–63.

11. Grillon i. 531 (no. 300).

12. Tapié V-L 1984 *France in the Age of Louis XIII and Richelieu*. Cambridge, Cambridge University Press, p. 166; on the assembly in general, see Petit J 1937 *L'Assemblée des Notables de 1626–27*. Paris.

13. Hauser *La pensée et l'action économiques*, p. 50.

14. Carmona M 1983 *Richelieu*, Paris, Fayard, p. 455.

15. Hauser *La pensée et l'action économiques*, p. 71.

16. *Receuil général des anciennes lois françaises* Isambert, F.A. (ed.) Paris xvi, 223 *et seq.*

17. *Testament politique* p. 403. Cf. Avenel DLM (ed.) *Lettres, instructions diplomatiques etc.*, vol. iii, pp. 177–78.

18. Lacour-Gayet G 1911 *La marine militaire de la France sous les règnes de Louis XIII et de Louis XIV* vol. 1, Paris, Champion, pp. 34–44.

19. Ibid., p. 46.

20. Ibid., vol 1, pp. 52–6; Boiteux *Richelieu* pp. 158–62.

21. Ibid., pp. 153–55.

22. Lacour-Gayet *La marine militaire de la France*, pp. 59–61.

23. Hauser *La pensée et l'action économiques*, p. 96.

24. *Testament politique* p. 423.

25. Hauser *La pensée et l'action économiques*, pp. 84–91. 108–20.

26. Chaunu and Gascon *Histoire économique et sociale de la France*, p. 335; Parker *La Rochelle and the French Monarchy*, pp. 63, 71.

27. Grillon i. 303–13 (no. 47); *Mémoires de Richelieu*, Société de l'Histoire de France, vol. vi, p. 145; Hauser *La pensée et l'action économiques*, pp. 130–31.

28. Ibid., pp. 131–32; Grillon, i. 321–38 (no. 61).

29. Trudel M 1973 *The Beginnings of New France, 1524–1663*. Translated by Patricia Claxton, Toronto, pp. 169–80.

30. Trudel M 1971 *Initiation à la Nouvelle-France*. Montreal, Editions HRW Itee, pp. 49–50.

31. Ibid., pp. 50–3.

32. Ibid., pp. 61–5.

33. Hauser *La pensée et l'action économiques*, pp. 137–42; Grillon, i. 508–510 (no. 278).

34. Goubert P 1966 *Louis XIV et vingt millions de Français*. Paris, Fayard, p. 21.

35. Zeller G 1964 'L'industrie en France avant Colbert' in *Aspects de la politique française sous l'ancien régime*. Paris, pp. 319–35.

36. *Testament politique* pp. 419–20.

37. Nef J U 1957 *Industry and Government in France and England, 1540–1640*. Ithaca, NY, Cornell, pp. 20–1.

38. Foisil, M. 1970 *La révolte des nu-pieds et les révoltes normandes de 1639*, Paris, PUF, p. 160.

39. Hauser *La pensée et l'action économiques* p. 164.

40. Nef *Industry and Government* pp. 1–2.

Chapter 11

RICHELIEU AS A PROPAGANDIST

The political importance of public opinion was widely appreciated in early seventeenth-century France. It was a commonplace that princes should rule their subjects' minds as well as their bodies. As Colomby wrote in 1631, 'it is not enough for princes to be ordained by God, their subjects need to believe it'. To achieve this end the king needed to mobilise preachers and writers to defend their policies and serve his interests. In the opinion of another writer, Naudé, twelve preachers were worth more than two armies in securing the obedience of subjects to their prince. No one understood this better than Richelieu who probably attended more closely to propaganda than any other statesman of his day.

From the start of his career Richelieu tried to find out as much as possible about what people were saying and thinking about matters of state. In 1614 he collected pamphlets thrown up by the Estates-General and had them bound for easy reference. As minister, he amassed extensive personal archives and supported archival research by experts, like Dupuy and Godefroy. In his *Testament politique*, Richelieu refers to his habit of 'listening a great deal' and to his 'monstrous hearing'. According to Retz, he was the best-informed minister in the world. Once he had achieved power he was better placed still to gather information and disseminate his own ideas. Aubery states that the cardinal used to send a bookseller abroad regularly to find out who was writing pamphlets against him. At his *lever* he would receive couriers from different parts of France or Europe and then call a secretary to draft memoranda for distribution to printers. He would arrange for news, suitably doctored, to be publicized at the Pont-Neuf.[1]

169

Richelieu's share of pamphleteering took various forms. Sometimes he provided the general idea for a pamphlet, at other times he would touch up a text he had inspired. There was nothing haphazard about his propaganda: it was carefully designed in form and content to promote an idea or create a mood. The cardinal believed that this could be more effectively achieved by means of many small pamphlets rather than one large book. Much of the pamphleteering he sponsored was aimed at whipping up anti-Spanish feeling. Controlling public opinion was, of course, a two-way process. To secure unanimous support for his policies, Richelieu needed to stifle criticism, and this he did with a fair measure of success.

Under Henry IV the press had been relatively free but under Richelieu it was subjected to a brutally oppressive regime. In 1624 censorship was tightened up. On 10 July an edict forbade the printing of 'letters, memoirs or instructions concerning affairs of state' without a permit from a secretary of state sealed by the Great Seal. At the Assembly of Notables (1626–27) Richelieu suggested heavier penalties for publishers of defamatory libels.[2] Such measures proved reasonably effective. Most of the pamphlets published in France in Richelieu's time supported the government; those taking an opposite view emanated from abroad. The cardinal stretched the concept of *lèse-majesté* to include any publication critical of the government. Anyone who dared to publish 'ill-digested' writings about current affairs risked imprisonment or death. Two pamphleteers were, in fact, beheaded during his administration. Hunting down such writers was among the duties of Isaac de Laffémas, 'the cardinal's hangman'.[3]

Richelieu employed more writers to boost his administration than any other statesman of his day. They included Mathieu de Morgues, who began by supporting the cardinal but, after the Day of Dupes, became his bitterest and most persistent critic in print. Another was François Langlois, *sieur* de Fancan, who acted as a kind of press secretary to Richelieu, recruiting fellow-writers and giving them their instructions. For ten years, we are told, he used to talk to the cardinal each day for two to three hours. He had wide-ranging ideas, many useful contacts abroad and a vigorous style. Among his pet hates were Spain and the *dévots*. He disapproved of the forceful conversion of heretics, adhering to the proverb that 'it is sometimes better to let a child go snotty than to tear off its nose'.[4]

In September 1625 a particularly effective denunciation of Richelieu's foreign policy, called *Admonitio ad regem*, was published abroad. It denounced Louis XIII's alliances with heretical powers as contrary to Scripture. His ministers, it declared, were wrong to suggest that the war with Spain was purely secular. They called themselves Catholics, but were really atheists who mocked God under guise of serving the public good. No one, claimed the pamphlet, had the right to force Catholics to serve heretics; if a king bore arms against his faith, his subjects were in duty bound to resist him.[5] Richelieu could not allow such a tract to go unanswered. He turned first to Fancan whose *Le miroir du temps passé* began a series of officially inspired defences of French policy.[6] There is evidence that Richelieu helped to shape its contents. The pamphlet identifies the *dévot* faction with the former *Ligueurs* and accuses them of subverting the state in the name of religion. It lists instances of treason by the Catholic League, of interference in French politics by Jesuits and papal envoys and of ultramontane efforts to counter French diplomacy in various parts of Europe. Fancan's main objective was to show that the *dévots* were using religion to advance the cause of Spanish hegemony.

Among the many pamphlets inspired by Richelieu during the 1620s the most interesting was the *Catholique d'État* (May 1625).[7] It has been ascribed to an ex-Protestant, Jérémie Ferrier, but seems to have been a joint effort by a group that included Ferrier, Father Joseph, Bérulle and possibly several more high-ranking ecclesiastics. Richelieu himself may have supervised the work and retouched it at the end. Its main purpose is to refute the suggestion that French policy, notably the war with Spain and the alliance with heretical powers, is unchristian. It also disputes the right of the king's subjects, including theologians, to question the righteousness of royal policies. The Spaniards are the true enemies of God. They pose as the defenders of the faith but, in reality, they separate politics from religion. It is the king of France who defends the faith by taking them at their true worth. 'The enemies of our kings,' the author writes, 'are the enemies of God; therefore they must be ours'. And the subject is bound to obey the king, because that is required by his faith; nor is he allowed even to criticise: 'Subjects may not censor nor judge in order to determine the justice or injustice of the arms of their kings; their role is merely obedience and fidelity'. The *Catholique d'État* cites biblical precedents in support of its contention that heretical powers are legitimate and that Catholic rulers may ally with them as circumstances determine. A clear distinction is drawn between public and private morality: 'The justice of kingdoms has other laws than the justice that is exercised between private persons.' It is for the king and his ministers to decide what is right or wrong in matters of state; their subjects are not in a position to know.

Three principal themes run through the many government pamphlets produced between 1624 and 1627: the restoration of royal authority and the condemnation of Spain abroad and of the *dévots* at home. Henry IV is acclaimed as the restorer of the king's authority in France and Louis XIII is the continuator of that noble task. Between them they have turned France from a languishing state into a triumphant one. The king is seen as the prime mover of national life and his authority is sometimes identified with the operation of reason. The Spaniards are criticised for their pride, ambition and unscrupulousness. They are accused of aiming at world domination and of using religion to achieve this end. The pamphlets also attack those 'great Catholics whose zeal is merely on their lips' – hypocrites who support the cause of Spain while pretending to defend Catholicism. The horrors of the Wars of Religion are vividly recalled by the pamphlets, and a direct line of descent is traced from the League to the *dévot* faction. The activities of the League are closely linked to those of the Jesuits, who are blamed for the assassination of Henry IV.

Thuau has argued that the pamphlets sponsored by Richelieu clearly point to a laicization of French political thought. Religious justifications for political actions are increasingly set aside in favour of justifications arising out of the national interest or reason of state. While the pamphleteers still do not see France as a secular state, they separate the interests of state and religion more clearly than ever before.[8] W F Church disagrees. In his view, Richelieu was very far from being a Machiavellian. The religious character of the French state was too deeply rooted for this to be even possible. The exigencies of politics may have forced Richelieu to resort to Machiavellian measures, but, Church maintains, 'his fundamental ideals and objectives were utterly remote from those of the astute Florentine'.[9]

After the Day of Dupes, Richelieu was able to set up a far more effective propaganda machine than would have been possible before. He assumed the role of 'schoolmaster of the French people' and surrounded himself with a group of obedient writers. They included Boisrobert, Paul Hay du Chastelet and Jean Chapelain. After serving as an *avocat* in the Parlement of Rouen, Boisrobert became a court poet and a kind of literary agent to the cardinal. He played a leading role in the foundation of the *Académie française*. Hay du Chastelet was also an ex-*parlementaire*. He was regularly employed by Richelieu to answer his critics and was a founder member of the Academy. Chapelain succeeded Malherbe as official poet. He liked to stress his devotion to Richelieu, calling him 'this divine man'. After 1630 the group of writers employed by Richelieu became to some extent institutionalized with the founding of the *Académie française* and of the *Gazette*.

While the creation of the Academy was undoubtedly intended to enhance the intellectual and artistic prestige of France, it also had a political motivation.[10] According to Chapelain, Richelieu was determined that only his known servants should be members of the Academy. Some he employed to revise his speeches, others to check his theological writings, others still to write pamphlets in defence of his policies. Such a use of the Academy was publicly criticised, and the Parlement expressed its concern by delaying registration of the letters patent setting it up. The government denied that in founding the Academy it had been animated by any political *arrière-pensée*, but the public remained sceptical. It was widely believed that the academicians were being paid to support the cardinal's actions. The earliest critic of the Academy in its political role was Mathieu de Morgues:

In truth, [he wrote] I have never seen a man more unfortunate in his eulogies than His Eminence who has never been esteemed by an upright man nor praised by an able and learned writer. He has recognized his poverty, and in order to overcome it he has established

a school or rather an aviary of Psapho, the Academy. . ..
There assemble a great many poor zealots who learn to
compose frauds and to disguise ugly acts and make oint-
ments to soothe the wounds of the public and the Cardinal. He promises some advancement to and gives small
favours to this rabble who combat truth for bread.[11]

Extreme as it was, this criticism was undoubtedly correct
in pointing to Richelieu's political use of the Academy. Its
founder members included Paul Hay du Chastelet, Jean Sirmond, Jean de Silhon and Guez de Balzac, all of whom spoke
in support of Richelieu at meetings of the Academy. Later
additions to the membership show that the cardinal continued
to keep a tight rein on its composition.

The 1630s also witnessed the creation of an official press. A
French periodical, *le Mercure françois*, already existed when
Richelieu came to power. Founded in 1605, it was the
official compilation of news of the court and Crown. It
was directed by Father Joseph from 1624 until his death
in 1638. But its ability to influence public opinion was
limited by the fact that it only appeared once a year.
The need for a more regular and frequent newspaper
was met by the creation of the *Gazette*.[12] The editor was
Théophraste Renaudot, a physician and philanthropist, who,
like Richelieu, hailed from Poitou. The *Gazette* was not
the first French newspaper. It had been forestalled by a
weekly called *Nouvelles ordinaires* edited by three members
of the Corporation of Printers and Booksellers. They sued
Renaudot, who appealed to Richelieu, with the result that,
on 18 November, he was given the monopoly of publishing
news. In February 1635, his privileges were confirmed. He
and his heirs were authorized to publish the *Gazette* 'fully,
peaceably and perpetually, without suffering or permitting
any trouble or obstacle to the contrary to be made or inflicted
upon them'.

In sheer volume Renaudot was the most important pub-
lisher in Paris during the period 1633 to 1644. His *Gazette*
appeared each Saturday. It was four pages long at first, then
grew to eight and even twelve pages. It was not aimed at the
majority of Frenchmen either by content or price (the twelve
pages cost four *sous*), but a reader could pay a monthly fee
and read it in a shop or at a stand on the Pont-Neuf. Also in

1631 Renaudot launched a *Recueil*, bringing together all the year's back numbers. This proved so popular that it became an annual. In March 1634 he also began to publish *Relations extraordinaires*, covering special events. This appeared more than once a month, often each week. By 1644 Renaudot ran at least four presses. With three working at full capacity, he could produce 1,200 to 1,500 copies of the *Gazette* in one day.

Renaudot saw himself as a mere recorder of events. Pressures of time, he explained, did not allow him to check the accuracy of every news item that reached him. What he passed on as fact sometimes turned out to be merely rumour. He liked to think of himself as objective, but in selecting items for publication he tried to glorify the monarchy. The *Gazette* was filled with news of the royal family and of happenings at court. Dispatches from wherever the king might be at the time were a regular feature. Louis XIII's life was presented as a catalogue of all the heroic and Christian virtues, which his subjects were meant to emulate. Richelieu too was portrayed as a superhuman being.[13]

However objective Renaudot may have aspired to be, the news he offered to the public was unquestionably slanted in favour of the government: for example, news of the confusion that attended Marie de' Medici's life in exile was clearly intended to be in marked contrast to the unity and repose that she had left behind in France. Following France's declaration of war on Spain in May 1635, the *Gazette* had to assist in mobilizing the country. Bad news was excluded from its pages or delayed. Thus a two months' silence followed the capture of Corbie by Spain on 15 August 1636, whereas only three days elapsed before its recapture was reported on 17 November. Although armies in the seventeenth century were notoriously ill disciplined, atrocities, according to the *Gazette*, were only committed by France's enemies, never by her own forces or those of her allies. Equally partisan was Renaudot's treatment of economic questions. The *Gazette* constantly reminded its readers of the Dutch challenge to French economic interests. Many of its stories reflected Richelieu's interest in foreign trade. One of its longest economic articles was an enthusiastic description of the French colony in Acadia. 'This enterprise,' it declared, 'is to be valued above all by relieving us, we hope, of all the able-bodied beggars in France.'[14]

Richelieu's influence on the *Gazette* ranged from making theoretical suggestions to assigning specific articles to particular individuals and to writing and editing complete dispatches himself. His critics believed that the *Gazette* was 'corrected and seasoned according to His Eminence's taste'. This was an exaggeration, but he undoubtedly gave as much detailed attention to his contributions to the *Gazette* as to all his other writings. Thus, in August 1642, he wrote to Sublet de Noyers and Chavigny, whom he often employed as intermediaries with the *Gazette*: 'it is most important to give Sr Renaudot the letter you have sent to the provincial officers and ambassadors. I beseech you to give it to him so well written and so well punctuated that he will print everything necessary, without a single error.'[15] On 15 September 1635 Richelieu advised Chavigny after a naval battle near Genoa: 'I ask you to tell Renaudot not to print anything about this action until I send him the relation. I have seen one that is unsatisfactory as it hurts all our galley captains.' Two days later he sent the promised account: 'I send you the account of the battle of the galleys as it must be given to Renaudot; I have corrected certain matters which harm all the captains, including those who performed best.'[16]

Even reports sent by the king were corrected by the cardinal before they appeared in the *Gazette*. Renaudot could expect editorial interference from Richelieu up to the last minute. On 4 June 1633, for instance, Richelieu sent an article for that morning's *Gazette* which had already been half printed and distributed; it had to be recast to accommodate the cardinal's piece.[17] Richelieu controlled the *Gazette* through a number of intermediaries, who have been described as 'an editorial committee composed of men devoted to the monarchy'. They included Father Joseph, Chavigny and Pierre d'Hozier. Father Joseph provided the *Gazette* with news supplied by Capuchin missionaries in Abyssinia, China, Japan and India.[18] Chavigny was entrusted with direction of the *Gazette* when Richelieu was not in Paris. Pierre d'Hozier placed his network of European contacts at Renaudot's disposal.

The Academy and the *Gazette* were only two of the means by which Richelieu tried to shape public opinion in the 1630s. Literature in general became increasingly politicised. Thus, in poetry, Louis XIII and Richelieu were eulogized by Malherbe. He wrote a sonnet in praise of Richelieu's admission to and presidency of the king's council as well as a famous ode celebrating Louis XIII's campaign to punish the rebels of La Rochelle. In 1633 a group of poets, centred on Malherbe, published two collections of verses in praise of the king and the cardinal. Richelieu enjoyed being the object of adulation. Tallemant tells us that the cardinal once deleted the word 'hero' from a dedication to himself, substituting the word 'demi-god'.

Richelieu also mobilised the support of historians.[19] In 1631 Sirmond wrote a biography of the cardinal of Amboise, Louis XII's chief minister, which was in reality a panegyric of Richelieu. Another parallel frequently drawn at the time was that between Richelieu and Cardinal Jiménez de Cisneros, the famous minister of the Catholic Kings of Spain. Such comparisons served to justify Richelieu's administration and to demonstrate its superiority. Historians looking for justification of Richelieu's foreign policy liked to evoke the example of King Henry IV.[20] Sometimes the cardinal shared in writing a historical work. Scipion Dupleix, for example, tells us that Richelieu supplied him with information that he would not have been able to get elsewhere. Dupleix was the ablest and most prolific of Richelieu's historian-apologists. His most important work is his *Histoire de Louis le Juste treizième de ce nom* (1635). Although the king's achievements are duly praised, it is Richelieu who is given the palm. After reviewing the failures of earlier ministers, Dupleix writes: 'But since Cardinal Richelieu has had the government of the state in hand, all these defects have ceased because of the precise remedies that he has applied to them with superhuman prudence.' The historian sees Richelieu as divinely chosen and inspired: 'God, by a singular grace towards this monarchy, has given us a Frenchman who sincerely and tenderly prizes his fatherland and deserves not only to be cherished and honoured but also venerated, since his Royal Majesty himself honours him.'[21]

The theatre, too, fell under the cardinal's influence.[22] From 1635 onwards it underwent a revival in France sponsored by the state. The king decided, in 1635, to maintain permanently three companies of players, and, in 1641, he issued a declaration upholding the social respectability of the acting profession. Richelieu himself wrote a play (*la*

Comédie des Tuileries) but insisted on Chapelain taking the credit. Other writers from whom the cardinal commissioned plays were the so-called Five Authors (including Corneille), Boisrobert and above all Desmarets. In 1641 a tragi-comedy by Desmarets, called *Mirame*, was staged to celebrate the opening of the theatre at the Palais-Cardinal. Clearly inspired by Anne of Austria's affair with the Duke of Buckingham, it was evidently intended to bring the pro-Spanish lobby at court into ridicule. Another play by Desmarets, called *Europe*, was an allegorical glorification of Louis XIII's foreign policy. Richelieu also commissioned François Hédelin, *abbé* d'Aubignac, to write a treatise on the theatre. Though written in 1641 this was not published till 1657. The author praised the didactic value of drama. It could teach people things which they might otherwise resist, such as a taste for war, glory, the heroic virtues and 'some tincture of moral virtue'. By occupying the minds of idlers it kept them out of mischief.

Alongside these varied literary activities the flood of pamphlets defending Richelieu's policies continued to pour out of the printing shops. Many of those published in the early thirties were concerned with the revolt of Marie de' Medici and Gaston d'Orléans. Four published in 1631 were by Jean Sirmond. The *Coup d'État de Louis XIII* praised the king for retaining the services of Richelieu and resisting pressure from the *Grands*, who had been in league with Spain. It praised the cardinal for rediscovering the art of ruling like Tiberius or Louis XI. The *Défense du roi et de ses ministres* refuted Gaston's letter of 30 May 1631 which had expounded his grievances. *Les entretiens des Champs Elysées* (1631) took the form of a conversation among deceased statesmen and soldiers. Among them was Henry IV, who congratulated Louis XIII on keeping his indispensable minister. *La réponse au libelle intitulé: Très humble, très véritable et très importante Remontrance au Roi* (1632) refuted the work of Mathieu de Morgues, Richelieu's bitterest critic in print. *L'Hellébore pour nos malcontents* showed Gaston's aristocratic followers to be self-seeking, envious and greedy. Finally, Hay du Chastelet's *Observations sur la vie et condamnation du maréchal de Marillac* portrayed the unfortunate marshal as a 'muddler, a go-getter, an extortionist, a peculator and a thief of the king's money'. It was also a condemnation of the *dévots* in general.

Government pamphlets of the thirties justified Richelieu's administration on religious, practical and historical grounds. They pointed to the fact that his policies had been approved by the king, whose sovereignty was divine. One pamphlet held that it was impious to question a king's decisions and that his ministers shared in this immunity from criticism. Obedience to Richelieu, in short, was equated with submission to the king. 'Ministers,' wrote Sirmond, 'are to the sovereign as its rays are to the sun.' Achille de Sancy compared Richelieu's relationship with Louis XIII to that between Moses and God. Just as God had commanded his people through Moses, so the cardinal acted for the king over his subjects. Such eulogies of a royal minister were unprecedented in French history. It is not to be wondered at, therefore, that Richelieu tended to equate criticism of his policies with the crime of *lèse-majesté*. An important landmark in the history of French polemic in the thirties was Hay du Chastelet's *Recueil de diverses pièces pour servir à l'histoire*. This brought together dozens of documents and earlier pro-Richelieu tracts. The cardinal paid for its publication and Hay secured formal approval of his work by the Academy. The preface stressed the joint responsibility of the king and the cardinal for policy-making.[23]

In respect of the actual conduct of policy, the cardinal's pamphleteers stressed the need to maintain order in the kingdom and to suppress any potentially disruptive elements. With the queen-mother and Monsieur in mind, Sirmond wrote:

> No matter who causes the trouble, there is no obligation so great nor consideration so just that it should prevent forestalling the beginning and arresting the progress of the evil influence of the persons from whom it comes and from whom one suspects that it comes. I make no exception in this; it is subject to none.[24]

In doing his duty by preserving the state, the ruler might well be obliged to override all other considerations: 'The safety of the state is the supreme law.' Another pamphleteer, Sancy, justified Richelieu's foreign policy as the necessary price to be paid for securing law and order at home. Although it imposed sacrifices on the people, the benefits of war far outweighed its disadvantages.

In addition to pamphlets, government propaganda offered theoretical works to a more sophisticated readership. One of the most important was *Le Prince* by Guez de Balzac (1631). The author, whilst focusing his work on Louis XIII, eulogised Richelieu's policies:

> After the king, you are the perpetual object of my mind. I hardly ever divert it from the course of your life, and if you have followers more assiduous than me . . . I am certain that you have no more faithful servant nor one whose affection springs more from the heart and is more ardent and natural.

Balzac sees the renovation of the French state following the chaos of the civil wars as Louis XIII's greatest achievement:

> I can hardly believe my own eyes and impressions, when I consider the present and recall the past. It is no longer the France that until recently was so torn apart, ill and decrepit. No longer are the French the enemies of their country, slothful in the service of their prince and despised by other nations. Behind their faces I see other men and in the same realm another state. The form remains but the interior has been renewed.

Balzac saw the king as uniquely inspired by the Almighty. 'Most of his great decisions,' he writes, 'have been sent to him from heaven. Most of his resolutions stem from a superior prudence and one inspired immediately by God.' The equity of the king's actions, according to Balzac, was assured by his divine inspiration. Consequently, he was ready to approve even morally questionable measures that the king might have to take for the public good. Given the choice between individual rights and collective security, Balzac preferred the latter. He viewed as lawful any measure, even an arbitrary execution, required for political survival:

> a drowning man seizes anything he can, be it a drawn sword or a hot iron. Necessity divides brothers and unites strangers. It unites Christian and Turk against Christian; it excuses and justifies all that it creates. The law of God has not abrogated natural law. Self-preservation is the most pressing if not the most legitimate of duties. In extreme peril one disregards

propriety, and it is no sin to defend oneself with one's left hand.[25]

One of the ablest writers who consistently supported Richelieu was Jean de Silhon, whose *Ministre d'État* was published in 1631. This lays down the qualities needed by the perfect minister, and Richelieu is repeatedly used to illustrate this ideal. Silhon believed that rulers should be better than their subjects. Not only should they have superior intelligence; they should also acquire greater dexterity in matters of government. Although such qualities were not always present in sovereigns, Silhon believed that Louis XIII had them in full. He had been sent by God to end disorder and serve as a model of perfection. He had picked as Chief Minister a paragon of reason and virtue. While Silhon believed that politics should be conducted justly and equitably, he stressed the minister's obligation to defend the state's interests:

> let the minister remember that the principle of his conduct and the primary motive of his actions should be the good of the state and the interests of the prince, that he has no other law to follow nor path to take, and that he is never permitted to deviate from it, provided that he never offends justice.

Yet Silhon held that ethical standards were different in public and private affairs. It was impossible, he argued, for ministers to be limited by conventional standards of morality when defending the interests of the state. But if anyone could rule equitably, Richelieu, according to Silhon, was such a person: he had attained the highest order of intelligence and moral qualities so that even his sense of nobility and glory were subordinate to reason and virtue. In foreign affairs, Silhon argued that deception was necessary to counter the self-interested actions of princes. But he felt sure that in Richelieu's hands it would be used only with justice and for lawful ends. The cardinal had successfully served both church and state: he had crushed the Huguenots and, at the same time, had resisted ultramontane influences in the kingdom.[26]

Of all the theoretical works published in support of Richelieu following the Day of Dupes, the most important was Cardin Le Bret's *De la Souveraineté du Roy* (1632). Le Bret was a jurist who served as councillor of state throughout Richelieu's ministry. He was employed by the cardinal on various missions at home and abroad and was one of the judges who sentenced marshal de Marillac to death. *De la Souveraineté du Roy* stands in the direct line of evolution from Bodin, who first developed the concept of sovereignty, to the absolutists of Louis XIV's reign. Le Bret starts from the premise that the king personally holds in perpetuity all public authority in the realm directly from God and is accountable only to Him. No official has any authority in his own right; he is merely the king's instrument, acting in his name. Even the Parlement has no jurisdiction of its own, only a delegated power. All legislation is the work of the king who 'alone is sovereign in his realm and sovereignty is no more divisible than a point in geometry'. But Le Bret did not favour despotism: he urged the absolute monarch to exercise power with moderation. In practice this required a close co-operation between the various organs of government. Thus royal co-operation with the provincial Estates and Estates General was likely to benefit all concerned. There was also value in the process whereby the parlements remonstrated against new legislation. As far as taxation was concerned, Le Bret argued that the king should never take a man's property for his own use alone, only for the public good.[27]

Le Bret considered the possibility of power being wielded by a tyrant. In his opinion, royal commands that were contrary to divine law should not be obeyed, but a seemingly unjust act aiming at the good of the state ought not to be resisted. This rule applied equally to a preventive war. Le Bret's basic authoritarianism is most clearly expressed in his treatment of *lèse-majesté* which Church has called 'a landmark in the history of the concept'. Le Bret lists three kinds of *lèse-majesté*: slander against the prince, attacks on his life and conspiracy against the state. What he has to say about slander is particularly interesting because of the importance attached to this matter by Richelieu. Slander is identified by Le Bret with sacrilege, and the examples he cites show that almost any criticism of the prince or his policies, whether serious or in jest, qualifies as *lèse-majesté*. The rigorous suppression of all offences against the Crown Le Bret believes to be entirely in accord with the highest law since the prince, in carrying out such a suppression, is only doing his divinely appointed duty.[28]

The final period of Richelieu's administration was marked by sharper exchanges between his critics and defenders. The cardinal's chief critic among the pamphleteers was Mathieu de Morgues. On 3 June 1635 he was sentenced to death *in absentia* by the *Chambre de l'Arsenal* in Paris. He had been charged with plotting against the state and the cardinal's life. In reality, he had simply criticised French policy in print. In his *Catholicon françois* Morgues accused Richelieu of manipulating religion for political ends:

> You make use of religion as your preceptor Machiavelli showed the ancient Romans doing, shaping it, turning it about one way after another, explaining it and applying it as far as it aids in the advancement of your designs. Your head is as ready to wear the turban as the red hat, provided the Janissaries and the Pashas find you sufficiently upright to elect you their Emperor.[29]

This prompted a reply by Sirmond, called *Advis du françois fidelle aux malcontents nouvellement retirés de la Cour*. He accused the *grands*, who had gone into exile, of placing their personal interests above those of the state and urged them to submit to Louis XIII and accept Richelieu's policies which had been approved by the king. This was followed by another diatribe from de Morgues. His *Derniers advis à la France par un bon Chrestien et fidèle citoyen* (1636) opens with a blistering attack on Richelieu's foreign policy: 'his anger has brought the Goths into the state; his madness has called the Poles, Cossacks, Croats and Hungarians into France and has brought us enemies, wars, and disorders such as France has never seen since her beginning'. The solution recommended by de Morgues is the tyrant's overthrow:

> All good Frenchmen, open your eyes to see what a miserable condition you are in; open your minds to foresee the great desolation that menaces you. Do not permit a puny man, sick in body and mind, to tyrannize over the bodies and minds of so many sane persons, nor an apostate monk [Father Joseph], his principal counsellor, to treat you as galley slaves. Cast off these two evil instruments.[30]

The most resounding controversy of the mid-thirties regarding Richelieu's foreign policy was precipitated by Jansenius's

Mars Gallicus (1635).[31] This based its argument on the unqualified supremacy of religious values. In his preface Jansenius declared that all true Catholics deplored the French policy of making war on the defenders of Catholicism in alliance with heretics. He discounted arguments in favour of the superior sovereignty and prestige of Louis XIII among European rulers. He examined and rejected the usual argument invoked by the French to justify their alliance with heretical powers. The Dutch and the Swedes, in Jansenius's opinion, were seeking to advance their heresy by injuring the Spaniards. By helping them the French were obeying their king but endangering their souls. The argument that a French king could do no wrong cut no ice with Jansenius. French policy, he claimed, was contrary to immutable Christian principles and ought to be resisted.

In the face of such an attack Richelieu felt constrained to provide the reading public with rebuttals. He commissioned Denis Cohon, bishop of Nîmes, to produce a reply but was evidently dissatisfied with the result. Far more effective was Daniel de Priézac's *Vindiciae Gallicae adversus Alexandrum Patricium Armacanum theologum* (1638). It has been described as 'one of the most valuable studies of reason of state to be published with Richelieu's sanction during the later years of his tenure of power'.[32] Priézac's appointment to the French Academy in 1639 may be taken as evidence that the cardinal approved of his work. Priézac's treatise contains few new ideas, but argues its case cogently. The author emphasizes the Christian character of the French monarchy and describes the great services of French kings to the Christian cause. He claims that the French monarchy is the most genuinely Christian in all Europe. Focusing on foreign policy, he insists that treaties with heretics for defensive purposes are sanctioned by divine law, and cites biblical examples to support his view. Since all powers conduct their foreign policy without regard for religion, all must be judged alike; it is not fair to criticise France alone. 'A war is just,' writes Priézac, 'when the intention that causes it to be undertaken is just.' In his view, Louis XIII's war with the Habsburgs is such a war since he undertook it not in order to gain territories but to protect the oppressed, preserve the realm and defend the Catholic faith. As for the king's subjects, they must not question his motives: 'it in no way belongs to those who are born to obey to insinuate themselves into affairs of state and to scrutinize its principal maxims, nor to inquire why the prince undertakes war'.[33]

Despite his onerous ministerial responsibilities, Richelieu found time to supervise two major literary productions: his *Mémoires* and his *Testament politique*. There has been a good deal of discussion as to the authenticity of both, but it is now generally agreed that they were conceived by the cardinal. The actual writing, however, was done by his secretaries, all of them mediocre men, who were close enough to Richelieu to know his views but who would never have dared to intrude themselves into whatever they were writing.[34] The *Mémoires* were intended to be a lengthy and comprehensive account of Richelieu's ministerial career, but the project was never completed, presumably because it was far too ambitious. As they stand, the *Mémoires* are a chronologically arranged collection of summaries of documents, letters and fragments of all sorts linked by a commentary. Facts predominate; ideological issues are barely touched on. Divine right sovereignty and the need for a powerful Chief Minister are taken for granted. God, it is repeatedly stated, has chosen Richelieu to guide France through a perilous era and has directed his efforts. In foreign policy, the *Mémoires* show the cardinal's resolve to preserve Christian justice among the nations. His opponents are invariably depicted as enemies of the French state.[35]

The *Testament politique* undoubtedly received closer personal attention from Richelieu.[36] Certain parts, indeed, can only have been written or dictated by him; namely, the dedicatory epistle and certain passages where errors are admitted. Nor can the general plan, many of the ideas and even some of the maxims have come from any other source. Whereas the *Mémoires* were conceived on a grand scale, the *Testament politique* deliberately focuses on the essentials of Richelieu's achievement and on his recommendations for the future. It is addressed to Louis XIII, and we cannot be sure that it was originally aimed at a wider readership although this does seem likely, given the cardinal's known desire to perpetuate his fame and glory. Be that as it may, the *Testament politique* is an invaluable source for modern scholars, for it sets forth more explicitly than other documents many of Richelieu's basic assumptions.

The French state, as seen by the *Testament politique*, is a hierarchical, corporate and organic structure of individuals and groups occupying specific stations and making distinctive contributions to the nation's life and advancement. This whole edifice rests on the assumption that human beings, even if they are all equal in the sight of God, are on earth profoundly unequal. They are differentiated by varying aptitudes and abilities; also by their assignment, usually by birth, to a particular social slot. The main purpose of monarchy is to ensure that every man plays his divinely appointed role, however lowly. This can best be achieved by removing any threat to social stability. Thus Richelieu advocates a reduction in the number of institutions of higher learning on the ground that an excessive number of educated men can unfit them for social responsibility. It can cause economic decline, reduce the scope of military recruitment and fill the nation with wranglers who disrupt families and ruin the peace of the realm.

The *Testament politique* has much to say about the role of the clergy in national life. It advocates the reform of appointments, jurisdiction, discipline and much else. Turning to the nobility, it recognises its financial hardships and general decline, but it is sympathetic to its code of honour and looks to ways of restoring the nobility to its former lustre and traditional functions. The Third Estate is divided into two groups: the royal office-holders and the common people. With regard to the first, Richelieu would like to eliminate abuses that obstruct the proper administration of justice. They include venality, but Richelieu thinks its abolition could create more problems than it would solve. An urgent need is the appointment of well-qualified judges of high personal integrity. As for the common people, Richelieu has hard things to say. They must not be too comfortable, otherwise they may be tempted from the path of duty. 'They must be compared to mules which, being accustomed to burdens, are spoiled by long rest more than by work.' This statement has often been adduced as evidence of Richelieu's heartlessness. But he does not advocate oppression of the lower orders as a principle. He thinks they should be taxed fairly. All that he is advocating is the proper functioning of society so that all can benefit.

The importance of discipline is repeatedly stressed by the *Testament politique*. It is made necessary by the volatility of the French people, their disrespect for rules, their love of intrigue and their willingness to place self-interest above national interest. Richelieu ascribes the discomfitures of his ministerial predecessors to their failure to impose discipline. This must be done – harshly, if necessary – for the sake of the common good. Any hint of trouble from a nobleman must lead to his banishment regardless of any other consideration. The Parlements too must stop meddling in affairs of state. They should stick to judging lawsuits between private individuals and abstain from presenting remonstrances and refusing to register laws.

The *Testament politique* lists the qualities needed by a minister. Choosing well-qualified ministers is among the king's most important duties before God. Richelieu thinks ecclesiastics are good ministerial material since they have fewer personal interests than laymen. He also argues the case for having a single supreme minister, rather than several of equal rank. 'There is nothing more dangerous in the state,' he writes, 'than several equal authorities in the administration of affairs.' The primary purpose of monarchy is to establish God's kingdom on earth and the greatest influence for good is the example set by the king himself. Christian kings and statesmen are bound to rule according to God's law which is revealed to them by reason. This not only demonstrates God's existence as Creator; it points to the means whereby God's precepts can be made effective in human affairs.[37]

. . .

NOTES AND REFERENCES

1. Thuau E 1966 *Raison d'État et Pensée politique à l'époque de Richelieu.* Paris, A Colin, pp. 169–74.
2. Ibid., pp. 175–77.
3. Ibid., p. 176.
4. Ibid., p. 177; Church, W F 1972 *Richelieu and Reason of State.* Princeton, NJ, Princeton University Press, pp. 98–100, 116–20. See also Geley, L. 1984 *Fancan et la politique de Richelieu de 1617 à 1627.* Paris; and Fagniez, G. 1911 'Fancan et Richelieu' in *Revue historique* CVII: 59–78, 310–22; CVIII: 75–87.
5. Church *Richelieu and Reason of State*, pp. 123–26.

6. Ibid., p. 127; Thuau, *Raison d'État et Pensée politique*, pp. 194–95.

7. Ibid., pp. 182–93; Church *Richelieu and Reason of State*, pp. 128–39.

8. Thuau, *Raison d'État et Pensée politique*, pp. 203–8.

9. Church, *Richelieu and Reason of State*, pp. 8n, 11.

10. Fumaroli M 1987 'Les intentions du Cardinal de Richelieu, fondateur de l'Académie française' in *Richelieu et la Culture*. Paris, CNRS, pp. 69–78; Thuau, *Raison d'État et Pensée politique*, pp. 219–20.

11. Church, *Richelieu and Reason of State*, p. 348. I have corrected the quotation. Church writes 'aviary of Sappho', but Morgues's original text reads 'volière de Psaphon'. Psapho was an ancient Greek tyrant. See below p. 192.

12. Solomon H M 1972 *Public Welfare, Science and Propaganda in Seventeenth-Century France: The Innovations of Théophraste Renaudot*. Princeton, NJ, Princeton University Press, pp. 100–22; Feyel G 1987 'Richelieu et la *Gazette* aux origines de la presse de propagande' in *Richelieu et la Culture*. Paris, CNRS, pp. 103–23.

13. Solomon, *Public Welfare*, p. 129.

14. Ibid., pp. 131–33, 143–44.

15. Avenel DLM (ed.) 1874 *Lettres, instructions diplomatiques et papiers d'état du Cardinal de Richelieu*. Paris, vol. VII, pp. 91–2.

16. Ibid., vi. 175–76, 179–81.

17. Solomon, *Public Welfare*, p. 149.

18. For a critical assessment of Father Joseph's involvement with the *Gazette*, see Feyel 'Richelieu et la *Gazette*', p. 122 n 15.

19. Ranum O 'Richelieu, l'Histoire et les Historiographes' in *Richelieu et la Culture*, pp. 125–37.

20. Thuau *Raison d'État et Pensée politique*, p. 224.

21. Church *Richelieu and Reason of State*, pp. 463–71.

22. Couton G 'Richelieu et le théatre' in *Richelieu et la Culture*, pp. 79–101; Mesnard, J. 1985 'Richelieu et le théatre' in *Richelieu et le Monde de l'Esprit*. Paris, pp. 193–206. Hall, Hugh Gaston, 1990, *Richelieu's Desmarets and the Century of Louis XIV*. Oxford: Clarendon. See also below pp. 193–4.

23. Thuau *Raison d'État et Pensée politique*, pp. 226–29.

24. Church *Richelieu and Reason of State*, pp. 344–45.

25. Ibid., p. 221.

26. Ibid., pp. 238–52; Thuau *Raison d'État et Pensée politique*, pp. 252–63.
27. Church *Richelieu and Reason of State*, pp. 261–68; Thuau *Raison d'État et Pensée politique.* pp. 266–68.
28. Church *Richelieu and Reason of State*, pp. 268–76; Thuau *Raison d'État et Pensée politique*, pp. 275–78.
29. Church *Richelieu and Reason of State*, p. 376.
30. Ibid., p. 378.
31. Ibid., pp. 383–89.
32. Ibid., p. 394.
33. Ibid., pp. 398–99.
34. Ibid., p. 472; Deloche M 1912 *La maison du Cardinal de Richelieu.* Paris, pp. 100–39.
35. Church *Richelieu and Reason of State*, pp. 473–80. Two editions of the *Mémoires* are available: Petitot, 10 vols, Paris, 1823; Société de l'Histoire de France, 10 vols. Paris, 1907–31.
36. The best edition of the *Testament politique* is by André L., Paris, 1947.
37. Church *Richelieu and Reason of State*, pp. 480–95.

Chapter 12

RICHELIEU AS PATRON
OF LETTERS AND THE ARTS

· · ·

PATRON OF LETTERS

Though trained in a rhetorical tradition and renowned as a public speaker, Richelieu was keenly interested in the written word. As bishop of Luçon he wrote religious books, and, even after becoming chief minister, he continued to write, dictate, annotate and read. But, as he did not dispose of enough time to commit all his thoughts to paper himself, he surrounded himself with scribes of different sorts to whom he assigned tasks. He was probably the first French statesman to commission memoranda and reports which might be used to determine policies and justify them before posterity. In France today he is perhaps best remembered as the founder of the *Académie française* whose main task is to ensure that the purity of the French language is preserved.

Richelieu rose to power against the background of a lively literary debate between humanists and modernists. The humanists, who were mainly *parlementaires*, magistrates and clergy, looked back for inspiration to the literatures of ancient Greece and Rome, and more recently to the works of Ronsard and the Pléiade. The modernists followed the lead of the poet Malherbe, who loathed Ronsard and admired only those ancient poets whom the humanists despised. Writing in 1623, Théophile de Viau described the imitation of ancient authors as larceny and called for the banishment of literary archaisms: language, he claimed, needed to be clear, direct and significant. As others joined the modernist movement, its principles were defined more precisely. The aim of art, the modernists claimed, was to give pleasure; poets should follow their own natures; and reason should be their guide, not the authority of the ancients. Some modernists adopted a style emphasising effect at the expense of truth. But this baroque phase of modernism soon petered out. By 1630 it had been replaced by a new aesthetic which, paradoxically, took its cue from Ronsard, who in his last years had advocated a style that was grand but not inflated. It was among writers of the age of Richelieu, not under Louis XIV, that classicism developed in France. One of its earliest exponents was Chapelain, who regarded evenness, balance and discretion as the most desirable literary qualities. Another was Guez de Balzac, who argued that modernism meant re-interpreting the ancients, not breaking with them.[1] It was in the midst of this classical revival that Richelieu founded the *Académie française* in 1634.

In 1629 a group of men of letters took to meeting regularly at the house of Valentin Conrart, one of the king's secretaries, in Paris. They would talk about literature, read their own books to each other, exchange court gossip, go for walks and take refreshments. The ethos of their meetings was different from that of sixteenth-century academies which had hoped to influence the court and turn the king into the prince of a new golden age. Conrart's academy, though in touch with the court, offered an escape from it; but Richelieu got wind of its activities. One of his literary assistants, Boisrobert, commissioned from Conrart and his friends a series of panegyrics dedicated to the king and the cardinal. Richelieu was so pleased by their efforts that he invited them henceforth to meet under his authority. This embarrassed some of the members who were clients of Richelieu's enemies. They wished to decline. But Chapelain warned them of the possible consequences of such an action. The cardinal, he said, was 'not used to encountering resistance or to suffer it with impunity'. He might take a refusal as an insult and dissolve the society. Rather than face this risk, Conrart and his friends 'humbly thanked His Eminence' who promptly instructed them to give their society a set of statutes. The *Académie Conrart* soon grew in size. Among its new members were some of Richelieu's propagandists and also two ministers of state: Abel Servien and Pierre Séguier. By 1642 it comprised a fair cross-section of French literary life without giving preponderance to any particular movement.

The new society called itself *Académie française* in imitation of the Roman Academy founded by Pomponio Leto, a famous academy of Renaissance Italy. But, unlike Pope Leo X who had taken a full part in the activities of the Roman academy, neither Richelieu nor Louis XIII ever set foot in the French academy. They left this task to the Keeper of the Seals. By remaining aloof Richelieu may have hoped to dispel the notion that the world of letters was falling under the power of the state. His presence too might have intimidated the members, and it would certainly have compromised his own social standing, for men of letters in early seventeenth-century France were less highly esteemed socially than humanists had been at the court of the Valois kings.

The aims of the new academy were outlined in a *Projet* by Nicolas Furet. This argued that the political and military restoration of the state would not be complete until the language in which its commands were expressed and its glory proclaimed was wrested from the barbarians. The aim of the academy was to give the new Augustan age, which Richelieu had revived in France, a tongue as beautiful, universal and lasting as Cicero's Latin. Its first task was to compile a dictionary and a set of rules for rhetoric and poetry. A set of statutes drawn up by Hay du Chastelet was taken by a deputation to the cardinal at Rueil. He welcomed the academicians 'with so much grace, politeness, majesty and sweetness that all those present were ravished'. He may have impressed them even more by striking out of the statutes a clause requiring each member to revere his memory and virtue.

But the academy soon ran into difficulties. The Parlement was afraid that it would encroach upon its own powers of censorship and viewed itself as the best-qualified arbiter of the French language. Consequently, it delayed registration of the letters patent (dated 27 January 1635) founding the academy until 10 July 1637. It also amended the statutes in order to restrict the academy's literary jurisdiction. Meanwhile, the academy came under fire from Richelieu's enemies. Mathieu de Morgues called it 'Psapho's aviary' after a Greek tyrant who, having trained birds to speak his name, sent them to the four corners of the world. Saint Evremond denounced the administrative pedantry which Richelieu had introduced into the world of letters. But the cardinal, undeterred by these criticisms, instructed the academicians to deliver speeches –

one each week – on topics of their own choice. He did not press them, however, to start work on the dictionary or the rules of rhetoric and poetry foreseen in the statutes.[2]

It is doubtful if Richelieu ever imagined the prestige which the *Académie française* would acquire and retain over the centuries. He was much more interested in the theatre. Whereas he failed to provide the Academy with a permanent home (it moved from house to house until it settled at the Louvre in 1672), he pressed for the construction and completion of the theatre in the Palais-Cardinal, wishing it to be the most luxurious and the best-equipped technically yet seen in France. Nor did he keep as far away from playwrights as he did from academicians; he liked their company and even counted himself among them. Desmarets de Saint-Sorlin captured his highest favour by writing three plays almost under his very eyes. Pending completion of his theatre, Richelieu commissioned a group of 'Five Authors' to provide plays for the court theatre. They were generously rewarded for writing plays around plots suggested by himself. They included *La comédie des Tuileries*, *L'Aveugle de Smyrne* and *La grande Pastorale*. He may have had a hand in the two plays by Desmarets, *Mirame* and *Europe*.

Richelieu's interest in the theatre was not confined to its role in political propaganda. It was in this literary field rather than in those of language or eloquence, where he had been forestalled by others, that he could be truly creative. It was largely thanks to his patronage that the acting profession acquired social respectability after 1635. Indeed, it was as bold for a cardinal to be a theatrical patron as it was for him in his foreign policy to ally with Protestant powers. For prejudice against plays and actors remained strong within the French church.[3]

A controversial blemish on Richelieu's patronage of the theatre was a famous dispute involving Pierre Corneille, the greatest French playwright of the age. It followed the première of his play *Le Cid* early in 1637. Inspired by a Spanish romance, its action unfolded in three different places over two days, and it contained more than one plot. Thus it was not a tragedy, but a tragi-comedy, and, as such, it may have displeased Richelieu, who favoured tragedy as the kind of theatre best able to set a high moral tone. This, however, is mere supposition; the known facts suggest otherwise.

Within a month of its première *Le Cid* was performed three times at the Louvre and twice at the Palais-Cardinal. The cardinal asked to see Corneille, who gave him a copy of the Spanish work that had inspired him. On 24 March Corneille's father was ennobled by the king. Soon afterwards, however, Scudéry accused Corneille of breaking the rules of tragedy. On receiving no reply, Scudéry asked the *Académie française* to adjudicate. His action may have been spontaneous, but it may also have been instigated by Richelieu, for when Corneille agreed to have his play examined by the academy, he said that he was obeying the cardinal's wishes. Be that as it may, Chapelain prepared the judgement: while criticising *Le Cid* on matters of principle, he commended it for many details. Richelieu, however, thought this verdict too lenient and ordered Chapelain to revise it. After more delays the academy published its definitive judgement: while defending 'true knowledge' against 'sweet illusion', it acknowledged that *Le Cid* had 'uncommon graces'.[4]

Wiser for his experience, Corneille dedicated *Horace* to Richelieu in 1641. Even so, a commission that included five academicians required him to alter the play's ending. But Corneille, after some tergiversation, kept to his original text. In a trilogy of plays written after Richelieu's death he offered a harsh indictment of public authority. His verdict on the cardinal was as follows:

Il m'a trop fait de bien pour en dire du mal,
Il m'a trop fait de mal pour en dire du bien.[5]

(He has done me too much good for me to speak ill of him,
He has done me too much harm for me to speak well of him.)

Even a brief survey of Richelieu's literary patronage needs to mention his magnificent library, containing more than 6,000 titles. It was built around two important collections. The first comprised more than 800 Syriac, Arab, Turkish and Persian manuscripts which had been acquired by Savary de Brèves, a French ambassador to Constantinople. They were purchased from his heirs by Louis XIII and given to Richelieu. The other was the public library of La Rochelle, which had been founded by Protestant clergy in 1604, and contained many works by the principal reformers. This was taken over by Richelieu after the fall of La Rochelle. The proportions of books according to subject in his library were as follows: theology, 30.41%; law, 4.13%; science, 5.14%; medicine, 4.25%; literature, 19.67%; history and geography, 25.33%; miscellaneous, 11.07%. The cardinal owned no books in English or German, but many in Italian, Spanish and eastern languages, especially Hebrew. He left his books to the Sorbonne, where they remained until they were transferred to their present home, the *Bibliothèque nationale*.[6]

Richelieu was interested not only in collecting books but also in their production. The quality of French printing had declined during the Wars of Religion; it failed to compete with the finest productions of the Dutch presses. Richelieu looked for ways of multiplying publications that were 'useful to the glory of the king, the progress of religion and the advancement of letters'. In particular, he instructed Sublet de Noyers to set up a royal printing press. This had to be done surreptitiously so as not to provoke opposition from printers and booksellers in general. Sublet's efforts resulted in the establishment of the *Imprimerie royale* in the autumn of 1640. It was housed in the Grande Galerie of the Louvre and directed by Sébastien Cramoisy, who had served Richelieu for many years. The first books to be published by the new press comprised works by classical authors as well as religious works by St Bernard, St Ignatius and St François de Sales. Richelieu gave generous subsidies to the press during the first three years of its existence, and Cramoisy paid tribute to his support by reprinting his *Les principaux points de la foi* and *L'instruction du chrétien*. Significantly, the press declined after the deaths of Richelieu and Louis XIII.[7]

. . .

RICHELIEU AS BUILDER

Richelieu was a great builder. Not only did he build a number of houses and palaces – even a town – for his own convenience and as evidence of his social pre-eminence, but he also supervised the construction of several royal buildings, including fortifications. As the scion of a provincial aristocratic family that had hit upon hard times, the cardinal was brought up in modest surroundings. There was nothing grand about the château of Richelieu as he first knew it. On visiting his bishopric of Luçon for the first time, he was shocked by his accommodation.

> I am very poorly housed, [he wrote] for there is no-where to light a fire because of the smoke; as you can see. I do not need a harsh winter; the only remedy is patience. I assure you that I have the worst bishopric in France [*le plus crotté*] and the most disagreeable. . .there is nowhere to stroll: no garden, no path, nothing, so that my house is a prison.[8]

The cathedral was in an even worse state: it had lost its steeple, its walls were cracked and it had been stripped of statues, paintings, tapestries and candelabra; only the altars remained. Richelieu promptly carried out improvements to his palace and agreed to contribute a third of the cost of restoring the cathedral.[9] But it was in his capacity as Marie de' Medici's *surintendant* that he made his apprenticeship as master of the works, for one of his duties was to supervise the building of her new residence in Paris, the Luxembourg palace. This brought him into contact with architects and builders, like Salomon de Brosse and Charles de Ry, and painters and sculptors, like Rubens and Berthelot.

Once Marie de' Medici had been restored to favour in 1620, Richelieu began to acquire property. In 1623 he bought the château of Limours. But after only three and a half years he sold it to the king, who wanted it for his brother Gaston. In 1628 Marie de' Medici gave Richelieu the château of Bois-le-Vicomte in gratitude for his part in the capture of La Rochelle, and Richelieu carried out improvements to the building and park. But Bois-le-Vicomte was inconveniently situated for a minister who needed to be within easy reach of the court, so Richelieu rented the château of Fleury-en-Bière, where he often stayed over a period of ten years. Then, in 1633, he bought the château of Rueil, near Paris. With the help of the architect, Jacques Le Mercier, and the builder, Jean Thiriot, Richelieu carried out embellishments to both château and park. The château also needed to be enlarged so as to accommodate his numerous household. Even so, it was never a large house. John Evelyn, who visited Rueil in 1644, wrote:

> The house is small, but fairly built in form of a castle, moated around. The offices are towards the road, and over against it are large vineyards, walled in. But though the house is not of the greatest, the gardens about it are so magnificent that I doubt whether Italy has any exceeding it for all rarities of pleasure.[10]

The gardens at Rueil were especially famous on account of their artificial grottoes and ingenious waterworks.[11] The *Fontaine du Dragon* was described by Evelyn as a 'basilisc of copper which managed by the fountaniere casts water neere 60 feet high, and will of itself move round so swiftly, that one can hardly escape wetting'. Richelieu also liked tall trees, and planted a handsome row of horse-chestnuts alongside the lake at Rueil. Among the flowers in the formal parts of the garden he liked the tulips particularly. Rueil was Richelieu's favourite residence. He relished its peaceful atmosphere, and lived there whenever the court was at St Germain.[12]

Although Richelieu was at heart a countryman, his ministerial responsibilities obliged him to spend much time in Paris. On 9 April 1624, after becoming a royal councillor, he bought the *hôtel* d'Angennes (or de Rambouillet) in the rue St Honoré. It was situated near the Louvre in an area ripe for development. The cardinal also bought the neighbouring *hôtel* de Sillery with a view to demolishing it and leaving an open space in front of his new residence. The *hôtel* d'Angennes consisted of several buildings with a courtyard in front and a garden at the rear. In February 1628 Richelieu commissioned Le Mercier to build a new wing and a chapel. As director-general of the king's new fortifications, Richelieu was able to pull down what remained of the wall of Charles V and use the land to enlarge his garden. The rest he leased as forty-two building plots to a speculator. Meanwhile, he carried out extensive alterations to his palace. Another wing, which was added in 1634, contained a *salle de gardes* of 180 square metres with a monumental fireplace flanked by two life-size statues of prisoners in chains as well as by figures of Peace and Justice. In 1637 work began on a theatre intended for the performance of 'comedies of pomp and display'. In 1642, shortly before his death, the cardinal commissioned the building of a library. In brief over a period

of fifteen years the old *hôtel* d'Angennes was radically trans-
formed into the Palais-Cardinal at a cost of roughly 400,000
livres. It survives today as the Palais-Royal.[13]

Among the interior decorations of the Palais-Cardinal were
two series of paintings showing all the buildings put up by
Richelieu. The most spectacular was undoubtedly the château
of Richelieu in Poitou. In 1621, following the death of his
elder brother, the cardinal repurchased the small ancestral
fief. Three years later, after becoming chief minister, he
began to enlarge it. But it was not until after the Day
of Dupes in November 1630 that he decided to rebuild
the ancestral château and to create a new town nearby.
In 1631 the lordship of Richelieu became a duchy, and
soon it was enlarged again after the cardinal had acquired
the royal domain of Chinon (1633) and the lordship of
Champigny-sur-Veude (1635).[14]

Stylistically, the château of Richelieu held few surprises. It
was designed by Le Mercier, who clearly drew his ideas from
the palaces of Luxembourg and Fontainebleau. It was a vast
structure grouped around three courtyards of which nothing
remains today, except one of the pavilions and the entrance
gateway. Visitors in its heyday were mainly impressed by
the array of statues and busts which made Richelieu one
of the finest sculpture galleries in Europe. Oddly enough,
the cardinal was not among these visitors. He never set foot
at Richelieu again after visiting it in 1632 at the start of the
works. When someone urged him to go there, he replied
that 'even if he were only ten leagues away from Richelieu
he would not be tempted to go there as long as the king's
business beckoned him elsewhere'.[15] As for the town, reason
determined its plan: a rectangular grid through the middle
of which ran a central main street. At each end of this street
was a square, one containing the market house and the other,
the church. The houses were uniform in design and of brick
with stone quoins. The land on which the town stood was
given by Richelieu but the public buildings were paid for out
of the revenue of the *Ponts et chaussées* while the houses were
paid for by the cardinal's friends, local officials and various
partisans. The cardinal had hoped that his new town would
become a thriving administrative, commercial, cultural and
religious centre. It was given fiscal and commercial privileges to attract inhabitants, but it was too closely tied to the

fortunes of its founder, and his death, in 1642, proved fatal to its prospects. In 1644 a visitor noted: 'in the town itself, one sees no trade, no population; everything seems dead'.[16] Little seems to have changed in the town, as it is today.

According to Aubery, Richelieu's earliest biographer, of all the buildings put up by the cardinal the one which he held most at heart was the Sorbonne.[17] This assertion finds confirmation in a letter written by Richelieu to Sainctot in December 1627. 'Although I have many expenses in hand,' he wrote, 'I am as keen to continue building this house without interruption as I am to pay as little as possible for the destruction of La Rochelle's fortifications.'[18] In September 1642 he assured Sublet de Noyers that he was less interested in the greatness of his house than he was in that of the Sorbonne.[19] Its rebuilding was, in fact, an event of major importance in French architectural history. As an anonymous panegyric put it in 1643, the cardinal had turned the Sorbonne into 'a superb palace of theology and a mausoleum for his ashes'.[20] It was in 1626, four years after becoming *proviseur*, that Richelieu began to rebuild the college at his own expense. At first he planned to rebuild the colleges of the Sorbonne and Calvi around the old fourteenth-century chapel, giving this a new façade. But in 1633 he adopted another, far more ambitious, project, which entailed the complete restructuring of the Latin quarter around a new chapel of monumental dimensions. The demolition of the old Sorbonne began in 1626, and the first stone of the new structure was laid in Richelieu's absence by François de Harlay on 18 March 1627. A year later, in June 1628, the doctors and students informed Richelieu of the progress made so far. Each day, they reported that Parisians came in large numbers to admire the new building. By 1629 the great hall of disputations, the library and the doctor's quarters were finished. In March 1634 Richelieu commissioned Le Mercier to build the new church, and in May 1635 he laid the first stone.[21] The two façades were the most striking feature of Le Mercier's design: one looked towards the street and the other faced the college courtyard. As rapid progress was made on building the church, houses nearby were swept away to clear its approaches. By the time Richelieu died, the bulk of the work was finished. In his will he asked to be buried in the church under a monument designed by Le Mercier. But a protracted dispute between the college authorities and the cardinal's niece delayed his burial till 1694, more that fifty years after his death.[22]

Richelieu built not only for himself but also for the king. At first his interest in royal building was limited to supervising the fortifications protecting France from foreign invasion. After 1636, however, as the threat to the frontiers lessened, but especially after the Dauphin's birth in 1638 had guaranteed monarchical continuity, Richelieu added his full weight to the continuation of a royal building programme that had been initiated by Henry IV and Sully.[23] He supervised alterations at the château of Fontainebleau as well as two projects in Paris. Le Mercier was asked to continue the Square Court at the Louvre begun by Lescot in the mid-sixteenth century. While adhering to Lescot's style, he added the Pavillon de l'Horloge, giving it an additional storey and a square dome. The other Parisian project was a new square with an equestrian statue of Louis XIII in the middle.

Richelieu was far too busy with affairs of state personally to supervise the building works associated with his name. He relied heavily on deputies. These included Sainctot for the Sorbonne, archbishop Sourdis for the château and town of Richelieu, Léonor d'Étampes for the library of the Palais-Cardinal and Sublet de Noyers and d'Argencourt for the fortifications in Picardy. They signed the contracts, negotiated with builders, kept a close watch on work in progress, checked on building materials, controlled expenditure and decided most matters of detail.[24] Though Richelieu sometimes signed a contract, he was normally represented. No major decision, however, was taken without his approval. He allowed his deputies considerable discretion, for he believed that, being on the spot, they were best able to decide. Thus, in November 1627, he wrote to Noyers: 'I have seen the contracts for the fortifications which I do not understand too well, but I am happy to accept whatever you and Monsieur d'Argencourt decide.'[25]

· · ·

RICHELIEU AS PATRON OF THE ARTS

In all of his buildings, whether public or private, Richelieu made full use of painters and sculptors. He used them not merely to beautify his buildings, but also to glorify the ruling dynasty and to proclaim his own achievements as servant of the Crown. In all his residences there were galleries of portraits, of which the most famous was the *Galerie des hommes illustres* at the Palais-Cardinal. This comprised portraits by Philippe de Champaigne and Simon Vouet of great servants of the monarchy from abbot Suger to Richelieu himself. Another series of portraits was in the room where Richelieu displayed his collection of porcelain, and a third in the library. At Limours, portraits of the king and queen were surrounded by those of princes and noblemen. At Bois-le-Vicomte there were portraits of kings and queens, and, at Richelieu, the queen's wardrobe was adorned with portraits of Louis XIII and his family, and of statesmen. There was also 'an emblem of the joy felt by the city of Paris at the birth of the future King Louis XIV'.[26] Tapestries in the king's apartment depicted the Trojan war, and the painted ceilings told the story of Achilles. The gallery of the château was decorated with paintings of twenty battles fought during Richelieu's ministry. In a frieze above, an equal number of smaller paintings represented battles of the ancient world. Over a fireplace in the antechamber was a painting of Hercules defeating the Hydra. It bore the motto '*Armandus Richeleus/Hercules Admirandus*'. Richelieu's own apartment was adorned with portraits of his ancestors and of great European princes. The fireplace in the gallery was flanked by equestrian portraits of the king and Richelieu. About half of the fifty paintings at Rueil were portraits. The room where Richelieu dined had two portraits of the Dauphin.[27]

Richelieu commissioned many portraits of himself in the course of his career, most of them from Philippe de Champaigne, a native of the Spanish Netherlands. Various reasons have been suggested for the favour shown to this artist by Richelieu. It may have pleased him to take under his wing an artist who had once been the subject of the king of Spain, but more probably he was impressed by Champaigne's skill, especially his use of colour. Richelieu also liked men of spirit, and Champaigne once dared to refuse his order to reside at the château of Richelieu so as to supervise the decorations there. Such a show of independence was all too rare among the cardinal's entourage, and it seems to have pleased him. In artistic matters, however, Champaigne was wholly subservient to his patron's wishes.

Richelieu first commissioned Champaigne in 1628 to paint an *Adoration of the Shepherds* for the abbey of St Benoît-de-Quincey, near Poitiers, doubtless in thanksgiving for the fall of La Rochelle. The painting (now at the Wallace Collection in London) was one of only two religious pictures painted by Champaigne for Richelieu. In 1635 he undertook the decoration of parts of the Palais-Cardinal and later of the dome of the Sorbonne chapel. In both he deferred to Richelieu's programmes. Thus in the *Galerie des hommes illustres* he aimed to show that France's greatness was founded by churchmen and soldiers, Richelieu being an uncommon blend of the two. At the Sorbonne, he chose a Mannerist treatment of the dome, which echoed work in progress on the dome of St Peter's at the time of Richelieu's visit in 1606–7. Most of the easel paintings commissioned from Champaigne by Richelieu were portraits of himself of which twenty-four survive. None betrays any sign of age or illness in the sitter despite the passage of time. This is because Richelieu asked Champaigne to retouch all his portraits so as to conform to one painted in 1640. Except for three portraits, all of them show the cardinal standing and in full-length. Normally, churchmen were portrayed seated: only rulers and statesmen were shown full-length and standing. Clearly, Richelieu wanted to be of their company.[28]

Richelieu's treatment of Rubens and his patronage of artists representing sharply contrasted, even contradictory, styles have been adduced as evidence of his lack of discrimination. The charge, however, can be rebutted. If Richelieu had really disliked Rubens or his art, he would not have commissioned the artist to paint two pictures for his study. Yet it is true that, as Marie de' Medici's *surintendant*, the cardinal prevented Rubens from finishing the decoration of the *Galerie Henri IV* at the Luxembourg palace, which might have proved an even greater masterpiece than the *Galerie Médicis*. But Richelieu's attitude may have been prompted by political rather than aesthetic considerations. For Rubens was not just a painter; he was also a skilled diplomat deeply committed to the Habsburg cause. The cardinal had reason to suspect that the artist's studio was a nest of political intrigue.

As for the charge that Richelieu patronised artists of different schools, this is undeniable. Thus he employed Vouet, the pioneer of Baroque in France, Stella and Poussin, who were perhaps the most classical painters of the century, and Vignon, who resumed and extended the Mannerist tradition. But the cardinal cannot be criticised for failing to recognise artistic categories devised since his day. Rather, should he be given credit for throwing his net out widely in his search for talent. He was not content simply to use artists with established reputations; he looked for younger men with distinctive talents to offer. Champaigne was 36, La Hyre 33 and Le Brun 22 when the cardinal discovered them.

At the same time, it has to be said that Richelieu had difficulty divorcing art from politics. Among the artists he employed were several from Lorraine. Thus he invited Jacques Callot to execute two large engravings depicting the sieges of La Rochelle and the Île de Ré, and owned paintings by Claude Deruet and Georges de La Tour. It is possible that Richelieu enjoyed all these works on account of their intrinsic merits, but Lorraine also lay at the heart of his political preoccupations, and it is likely that he used his artistic patronage as a means of building up a francophile attitude within the duchy.[29]

If paintings were the main decorative element at the Palais-Cardinal, sculpture was much in evidence at the château of Richelieu. Above the entrance stood an equestrian statue of Louis XIII by Berthelot. In niches flanking the gateway were two ancient statues of Hercules and Mars. On the dome above the gate stood a bronze statue of Fame with a trumpet in each hand, also by Berthelot. Around the main courtyard were many statues, busts and vases in niches. A visitor noted 'gods on all sides in the walls' while another described the château as 'the Pantheon with all the Roman court'. Some visitors thought the abundance of sculpture was intended to mask irregularities in Le Mercier's building, but it seems more likely that it was to give grandeur to Richelieu's ancestral home. In his public buildings the cardinal used sculpture to glorify the Bourbon monarchy. Thus the altar-piece in the Sorbonne chapel is a veritable triumphal arch. It is decorated with bronze angels carrying censers, with the symbols of

justice and election and with large statues of Charlemagne
and St Louis bearing the king's features. Similar statues of
the emperor and the king adorned the altar of St Louis-des-
Jésuites. At the same time Richelieu was anxious to publicise
the royal image. Thus he resumed work on the plinth of
Henry IV's statue at the Pont-Neuf, giving it five bas-reliefs
in bronze (three by Bordoni, one by Boudin and another
by Tremblay). Soon afterwards, Richelieu ordered an equestrian statue of Louis XIII which was unveiled in 1639. He
was, it seems, more reticent about commissioning statues
of himself than paintings. At Richelieu, his political role
was symbolized merely by two rostral columns of variegated
marbles. The earliest portrayals of the cardinal, apart from
paintings, were medals designed by Guillaume Dupré or Jean
Warin.

Richelieu seems to have been interested in sculpture. Once,
on a visit to Albi, he refused to believe that the finely chiselled
rood and choir screen were actually of white stone. Taking
a ladder, he climbed a few steps and scraped away with
a trowel to find out for himself if the stone were really
plaster.[30] But even if this famous anecdote does suggest
a measure of personal curiosity, it remains true that the
cardinal's taste in sculpture was eclectic. The contemporary
sculptors he patronized fell into two sharply contrasted
categories. A number worked within the well-established
tradition of French realism (for example, Thomas Boudin,
Barthélemy Tremblay, Germain Gissey), while others practised the newer, more grandiloquent Italian style (such as
Jacques Sarrazin, Simon Guillain, Christophe Cochet and
Pierre Biard). Richelieu commissioned Biard to carve a bust
of Louis XIII for the château of Limours, but later expressed
a preference for the work of Guillaume Berthelot, who had
been trained in Rome before entering the service of Marie
de' Medici. He commissioned from Berthelot statues for
the château of Richelieu and for the Sorbonne chapel.
The cardinal's taste for Italianate sculpture culminated in
a commission sent to Bernini through Mazarin and cardinal
Antonio Barberini. The great Italian master began work
on a marble statue of Richelieu, using some 'profiles' he
had been sent from Paris. This was never completed, but
Bernini did do a bust of Richelieu, which is now in the
Louvre.[31]

. . .

RICHELIEU AS ART COLLECTOR

Richelieu was the first private individual in France to collect works of art on a massive scale. Many survive in museums all over the world. They include Michelangelo's *Slaves*, paintings by Mantegna, Perugino and Lorenzo Costa that had once adorned the *studiolo* of Isabella d'Este, Poussin's *Bacchanalia*, and the famous marquetry table now in the *Galerie d'Apollon* at the Louvre. Although Richelieu, unlike Mazarin, had not been brought up in a particularly aesthetic environment, his interest in art seems to have developed early in his career. In 1624 Marie de' Medici suggested to the duke of Mantua that he might gratify the cardinal by sending him 'some excellent pictures'. The Mantuan ambassador, writing in the same year, described Richelieu as 'a great collector of rare pictures'.[32] During his first visit to North Italy in 1629–30 the cardinal much admired the duke of Savoy's picture gallery at Rivoli. Some of his earliest art acquisitions were probably included in Marie de' Medici's gift of the Petit-Luxembourg. As Richelieu's political stature grew, he received many more gifts. Thus Michelangelo's *Slaves* were given to him by Henri duc de Montmorency shortly before his execution. A painting attributed to Sebastiano del Piombo came from the same source. Others gifts to the cardinal were more spontaneous. Thus, in 1633, Alfonso Lopez, a Jewish businessman, asked his agent in Provence to buy anything 'curious and rare', so that it might be given to Richelieu. When Mazarin returned from Rome as nuncio in 1644 he brought him gifts from Antonio Barberini. They included four paintings by Titian, Pietro da Cortona, Giulio Romano and Antonini, a cassock and some small tables and bureaux 'full of a thousand galantries of perfume'.[33] Mazarin was accused by one of his many critics of using his pension to make gifts to Richelieu, who 'like a God did not want anyone to approach him empty-handed'.[34]

Richelieu also purchased works of art on a large scale. Thus in 1638 he acquired the collection of marshal Créqui, who had spent much time in Italy as a diplomat. He competed with other notable collectors of the age – the king of England, the duke of Parma and Marie de' Medici – in acquiring treasures from the Gonzaga collection. He failed to get the famous cartoons by Mantegna, now at Hampton Court, but did succeed in getting the masterpieces from Isabella d'Este's *studiolo*. In March 1633 the papacy allowed him to take away from Rome sixty statues, sixty busts, two heads and five vases.

However, Richelieu's political preoccupations did not allow him enough time to hunt for art treasures. He had to rely on intermediaries. Lord Arundel, one of the greatest connoisseurs of the age, helped him buy sculpture, allowed him to acquire the collection of a palace in Rome and supplied him with information about eighty busts on sale in different parts of Italy. In 1633 Cardinal Barberini, the nephew of Pope Urban VIII, helped Richelieu buy several works of art. Normally, however, Richelieu was assisted by 'creatures' of the Barberini, such as the Frangipani or Mazarin. Within France, one of his principal artistic agents was Alfonso Lopez. Another was archbishop Sourdis, who supervised the works at Richelieu: he advised the cardinal on the choice of artists and of subjects for the decoration of the château. But Richelieu kept a close watch on the progress of his collection, especially on items intended for his ancestral château. In 1636 he asked for two paintings by Poussin to be brought to him at Amiens in the midst of a military campaign, thereby showing the importance he attached to direct contact with works of art.[35]

Richelieu's importance as an art collector is only beginning to be appreciated. The rediscovery of a probate inventory of 1643 has shed light on his collection at the Palais-Cardinal.[36] As was customary, the inventory takes no account of paintings that were part of the fabric, such as murals. Consequently, it omits the portraits of the *Galerie des hommes illustres*, also works by Vouet, Champaigne, Poussin and Le Brun. Of the 262 pictures listed in the inventory 84 are given precise attributions. Most of them are by Italian artists, including Leonardo da Vinci, Raphael and Correggio. The Venetians – Giovanni Bellini, Titian, Lotto and the Bassanos – are particularly well represented, as are Bolognese artists of the sixteenth century (Guercino, Guido Reni and Carracci). Among the relatively few French artists in the list are Philippe de Champaigne, Poussin and de la Tour. There are a few Dutch works (Rubens, Pourbus) and only one German, a *Nine muses* ascribed to Dürer. Most of the pictures are religious, but there are also many landscapes.[37]

Richelieu collected other works of art than pictures and sculpture. At the Palais-Cardinal, he had about 400 pieces of china valued at 1,732 *livres*, including a great urn and two sizeable Chinese dishes. There were also twenty-two objects of crystal valued at more than 5,000 *livres*. Two items were especially precious: a large basin with bands of enamelled and finely chiselled gold, and a large vase of rock crystal, also enriched with enamelled gold. Among valuable items in the green apartment were four clocks, a Copernican sphere and a terrestrial globe. There were also two tortoise-shell tables, an Indian cabinet, and several Chinese cabinets and chests inlaid with mother-of-pearl and precious stones. In other rooms of the palace stood a table of black marble bearing a nautical device in the centre and several tables of marquetry, including one inlaid with jasper, lapis lazuli, cornelian, agate and jade. Among furniture bequeathed by the cardinal to Louis XIII were three beds. One of them, valued at 45,000 *livres*, was eventually taken to the Louvre where it was used by Queen Christina of Sweden in 1656. Among numerous tapestries at the Palais-Cardinal there were about a dozen valued at between 3,500 and 32,000 *livres*. At Rueil, the tapestries were less valuable. The cardinal's dining room was adorned with a Gobelins tapestry depicting Guarini's poetic drama, the *Pastor Fido*.[38]

Silver and jewellery also figure in the inventory of the Palais-Cardinal. At his death, Richelieu owned 54 dozen dishes of silver or silver gilt. His collection also included chandeliers, basins, salt-cellars, sweetmeat dishes, baskets, flagons, fruit-bowls, ewers, nefs and buckets. The entire collection was valued at 237,000 *livres*. Ecclesiastical silver consisting of crosses, basins, censers, aspersoria and paxes was worth an additional 10,000 *livres*. The cardinal, it seems, regarded his collection of silver not merely as a luxury but as collateral for state loans in times of necessity. He informed Bullion, in 1640, that he owned silver worth 150,000 *livres* in Paris and jewellery to the same value which might be used for this purpose. But the jewellery listed in the inventory of the Palais-Cardinal is valued at only 58,000 *livres*. This is easily explained: excluded from the inventory is the large, heart-shaped diamond which Richelieu left to the king in his will. This may have been the diamond bought from Lopez for 75,000 *livres*. The cardinal left the rest of his jewels and precious stones to his niece, the duchesse d'Aiguillon.

Did Richelieu really enjoy works of art or did he merely collect them as status symbols? Was he, in short, a true connoisseur? That he was genuinely interested in some of the arts is beyond doubt: he liked literature, especially the theatre, and was fond of gardens. But it seems that in his day-to-day existence he did not feel the need to contemplate the works of art in his collection. The inventories of the Palais-Cardinal and of the château of Rueil indicate a degree of austerity in his private apartments in sharp contrast to the magnificence of his collections. He had a *St Jerome* by La Tour and a painting by Fouquières of the château of Richelieu. Otherwise, most of the pictures were mediocre. The furniture, apart from the bed, some armchairs and stools, was not much better than that in the servants' quarters. At Rueil, the story was much the same. Simplicity was the keynote of the cardinal's private life-style. This suggests that his personal taste in the arts was more subdued than his public patronage. 'It is in the end difficult,' writes Honor Lévi, 'to dismiss the notion that Richelieu's collections represented not so much a personal aesthetic taste as a desire to publicise the external signs of the political power that nourished his soul.'[39]

. . .

NOTES AND REFERENCES

1. Adam A 1974 *Grandeur and Illusion: French literature and society, 1600–1715*. Harmondsworth Penguin, pp. 142–53.
2. Fumaroli M 1985 in *Richelieu et le monde de l'esprit*. Paris, Imprimerie nationale, pp. 217–35.
3. Ibid., pp. 233–35; Couton G. in Mousnier R. (ed.) 1987 *Richelieu et la culture*. Paris, CNRS, pp. 79–101.
4. Adam A 1972 in *Richelieu*. Paris, Hachette, pp. 214–18.
5. Fumaroli *Richelieu et le monde de l'esprit* p. 235.
6. Flouret J 1985 in *Richelieu et le monde de l'esprit*, pp. 249–51.
7. Grinevald P-M 1985 in *Richelieu et le monde de l'esprit*, pp. 23–48; Thuillier J. 1987 in Mousnier (ed.) *Richelieu et la culture*, pp. 163–74.

8. Avenel DLM (ed.) *Lettres, instructions diplomatiques et papiers d'état du Cardinal de Richelieu*. i. 24.

9. Lacroix L 1890 *Richelieu à Luçon*. Paris; reprint 1986, pp. 73–74.

10. Evelyn J 1879 *Diary*, Bray W. and Wheatley H.B. (eds.) London, vol. I, pp. 56–7.

11. Woodbridge K 1986 *Princely Gardens*. London, Thames & Hudson, pp. 148–58.

12. Babelon J-P 1985 in *Richelieu et le monde de l'esprit*, p. 80.

13. Bercé Françoise in ibid., pp. 61–6.

14. Mignot C. in ibid., pp. 67–74; Battifol L 1937 *Autour de Richelieu*. Paris, pp. 143–205.

15. Aubery A 1660 *Histoire du Cardinal Duc de Richelieu*. Paris, p. 614.

16. Brackenhoffer E 1925 *Voyage en France, 1643–1644*. Paris, pp. 219–32.

17. Aubery *Histoire du Cardinal Duc de Richelieu* pp. 614–15.

18. Grillon P 1977 *Les papiers de Richelieu*, Paris, Pedone, vol. 2, p. 690.

19. Mignot in *Richelieu et le monde de l'esprit*, p. 87; Battifol *Autour de Richelieu* pp. 95–141.

20. Cited by Mignot in *Richelieu et le monde de l'esprit*, p. 88.

21. Blunt A 1957 *Art and Architecture in France, 1500–1700*. Harmondsworth, p. 115.

22. Mignot in *Richelieu et le monde de l'esprit*, p. 92.

23. Ibid., p. 58.

24. Mignot in Mousnier (ed.) *Richelieu et la culture*, pp. 142–43.

25. Avenel 1856 *Lettres, instructions diplomatiques et papiers d'état du Cardinal de Richelieu*. Paris vol. II, p. 736.

26. Lévi Honor in Mousnier (ed.) *Richelieu et la culture*, p. 177.

27. Schloder J in *Richelieu et le monde de l'esprit*, p. 120.

28. Dorival B in ibid., pp. 129–34; and in Mousnier (ed.) *Richelieu et la culture*, p. 153–61.

29. Thuillier in *Richelieu et le monde de l'esprit*, pp. 45–7.

30. Bresc-Bautier G. in ibid., p. 159.

31. Bonnaffé E 1883 *Recherches sur les collections de Richelieu*. Paris, pp. 15–16.

32. Boubli L in *Richelieu et le monde de l'esprit*, p. 110.

33. Dethan G 1968 *Mazarin et ses amis*. Paris, Berger-Levrault, p. 282.

34. Schloder in *Richelieu et le monde de l'esprit*, p. 123.
35. Montembault M in *Richelieu et le monde de l'esprit*, p. 172.
36. Boubli in *Richelieu et le monde de l'esprit*, p. 103. The inventory is in a private collection housed at the château de Saint-Vallier (Drôme).
37. Ibid., p. 106.
38. Lévi in R Mousnier (ed.) *Richelieu et la culture*, pp. 175–84.
39. Ibid., p. 183.

EPILOGUE

Richelieu died on 4 December 1642 at the Palais-Cardinal in Paris. The cause of his death was apparently pleurisy, but he had been in poor health for a long time. Already in May, when he had made his will at Narbonne, he had not been able to sign it. But he had soldiered on for months, being carried about in a litter so huge that it could only enter houses through their windows or breaches in their walls. Even as he lay dying, the cardinal continued to work, giving orders to the secretaries of state sitting at his bedside. Among his visitors was the king. Relations between the two men had been soured by the Cinq-Mars affair, but now they were ready to sink their mutual doubts.

> Sire, [said Richelieu on 2 December] this is my last farewell: in taking leave of Your Majesty I draw comfort from knowing that I leave the kingdom in the highest degree of glory and reputation it has ever known and all your enemies defeated and humbled. The only reward I dare ask of Your Majesty for my pains and services is that it should continue to honour my nephews and kinsmen with its protection and goodwill. I shall give them my blessing on condition that they will never stray from the loyalty and allegiance which they have sworn and will always owe you.

Louis called on the dying Richelieu twice. The first time, he disconcerted observers by laughing loudly as he left the Palais-Cardinal, but on the second occasion he seemed genuinely distressed. It was during this second visit that Richelieu advised Louis to retain the services of Sublet de Noyers and Chavigny and to appoint Mazarin as his successor. The king conceded both requests. On 3 December, as the end drew near, Richelieu was asked if he wished to forgive his enemies. 'I have never had any,' he replied, 'other than those of the state.' On the following day, finding himself alone for a time with his niece, the duchesse d'Aiguillon, who had stayed with him throughout his final illness, he said to her: 'Remember that I have loved you more than all the others.' Then, after being absolved for the second time by Father Léon, the great cardinal breathed his last. His body lay in state for nine days, after which it was carried in a solemn procession to the chapel of the Sorbonne, where it was given a temporary resting place until 1694 when it was transferred to the tomb carved by Girardon in the church choir.[1]

News of Richelieu's death caused rejoicing in France. Father Griffet, writing in 1768, commented: 'He was disliked by the people and I have known old men who could still remember the bonfires that were lit in the provinces when the news was received.' Even the king, it seems, had mixed feelings. According to Monglat, the keeper of his wardrobe: 'Within his heart, he was much relieved and delighted to be rid of him, and he did not conceal this from his familiars.' On 9 December, however, he declared:

> I wish to be constant and firm in following the maxims and advice of the said lord cardinal, for I want all things to remain as they are without change. I intend to have the same ministers and I have brought cardinal Mazarin into my council as he knows better than anyone else the plans and maxims of the said cardinal.[2]

Louis also confirmed Sublet de Noyers and Chavigny as secretaries of state.

Richelieu's disappearance inevitably led to changes at court, for Mazarin's régime was far less strict. In January 1643 Gaston d'Orléans returned and was pardoned by Louis for the sixth time. He was followed by most of the nobles who had gone into exile under Richelieu. Marshals Bassompierre and de Vitry were released from the Bastille. As a Venetian observer noted, these reprieves were likely to lead to more disturbances, 'for such actions are commonly rewarded by ingratitude'. On 20 January 1643 Louis XIII failed to turn up at a solemn mass celebrated at Notre-Dame for the repose of Richelieu's soul. In April, he dismissed Sublet de Noyers as secretary of state for war, replacing him with Michel le Tellier. Shortly afterwards the king fell gravely ill and, on 14 May, he died. An observer commented:

> He has piously completed thirty three years of royal power, but it was very limited in his early years by the tutelage and authority of his mother and in his last years by the domination of the late cardinal who exceeded the limits of the ministry in the exercise of his functions.[3]

Richelieu's will is a matter-of-fact document throwing almost no light on his religious convictions or political ideals. It is concerned essentially with the survival of his name and house at the highest level of wealth and aristocratic respectability. The king, however, is not forgotten. Richelieu had already made several important gifts to Louis in 1636 but they were only to come into effect at his death. They included the Palais-Cardinal, his magnificent mass service, a great diamond and his silver plate. The will now added the *hôtel* de Sillery and a cash bequest of 1.5 million *livres*. This, the cardinal explained, had been vitally useful to him as a contingency fund; he suggested that the king should use it in situations 'which cannot suffer the long-drawn out fiscal procedures'. A curious passage in the will suggests that Richelieu had an uneasy conscience about his former patroness, Marie de' Medici: 'I have never failed to do what I owed to the Queen his mother, despite the calumnies that people have spread about me on this matter.'

The cardinal's provisions regarding the rest of his wealth were dominated by his decision to create two entails, each based on one of his duchies. Entails were widely practised in France to keep patrimonies and estates intact, especially where customary law tended to protect the rights of younger children to a share of their parents' estates. As his 'universal legatee', who was to inherit the title of duc de Richelieu, the cardinal chose his young grand-nephew, Armand-Jean, son of François de Pont Courlay. Anticipating that the latter might feel aggrieved at being set aside in favour of his own son, Richelieu offered him various inducements in the hope of dissuading him from contesting the will. Only by upholding it could he remain a beneficiary. As for François's sister, Marie-Madeleine, duchesse d'Aiguillon, she received a number of valuable bequests, including the château of Rueil; more importantly, she was appointed as administrator of Armand-Jean's person and estate during his minority. Among the obligations laid on the new duke was the building of a town house in Paris for his family, the creation of a library to house the cardinal's collection of books and make them available to scholars, and the completion of the chapel and college of the Sorbonne.

Inevitably, not everyone was pleased with Richelieu's will. Brézé, Condé and Pont Courlay all felt justified in contesting it, but it was energetically defended by Aiguillon. In March 1643 a compromise was achieved which saved the cardinal's estate from massive dismemberment. Condé, however, attacked the will in 1644, and two years later, managed to seize the Fronsac entail. Aiguillon's main responsibility as administrator of her uncle's will was to settle his debts and legacies. She set about securing large cash reserves, totalling 4,080,000 *livres*, which he had carefully stored in different strongholds. But Brézé seized 300,000 *livres* at Saumur, while the king confiscated 1,074,000 *livres* at Brouage and Le Havre. He and Anne of Austria also refused to honour the Crown's debts to the cardinal totalling 1,035,000 *livres*. Moreover, Aiguillon was asked to top up her uncle's legacy to the king with 50,000 *livres*. As a result, the cash reserves at her disposal to settle Richelieu's debts were much reduced. These debts were of two kinds: personal and unforeseen. The personal debts included legacies to servants, household expenses and certain land purchases. They amounted to about 1,568,122 *livres*. The unforeseen debts were made up of claims presented to the duchess after her uncle's death, sometimes long afterwards. Once Brézé and the king had helped themselves to so much of Richelieu's cash reserves, the duchess had difficulty meeting the largest claims. In particular, the rebuilding of the Sorbonne proved a never-ending drain on her resources. Between 1643 and 1648 she paid out about 280,000 *livres*, yet she failed to honour the cardinal's promises, and the Sorbonne's doctors took her to court. She agreed in May 1646 to pay another 250,000 *livres* in four annual instalments, but in 1650 she still owed half this sum and was forced to borrow.[4]

Richelieu, according to Voltaire, was both admired and hated. Both sentiments can be seen running through the entire length of his historical reputation. Hatred was expressed by a host of writers soon after the cardinal's death.

He was the butt of a flood of memoirs, pamphlets, lampoons and satirical verses. All kinds of stories were spread about him. From the beginning he was accused of sacrificing all, including justice, to his insatiable ambition. For the cardinal de Retz, he 'created within the most lawful of monarchies the most scandalous and most dangerous tyranny which may ever have enslaved a state'. Richelieu, according to Retz, 'blasted, rather than governed, the king's subjects'.[5] Michel Le Vassor, in his history of Louis XIII (1712), writes: 'I can look only with horror on a prelate who sacrifices the liberty of his fatherland and the peace of all Europe to his ambition.'

A similar charge was levelled by Voltaire in his *Siècle de Louis XIV* (1751): 'There was fighting since 1635 because Cardinal Richelieu wanted it; and it is likely that he wanted it in order to make himself necessary.' Elsewhere, Voltaire railed against the 'red tyrant', accusing him of injustice and barbarity. In particular, he could not forgive him for sending Urbain Grandier, *curé* of Loudun, to the stake on a charge of being a magician. While accepting that Richelieu had begun to make France formidable internationally, he accused him of neglecting her domestic prosperity. He had left her roads in a poor state and overrun by brigands, and the streets of Paris filthy and full of thieves. He dismissed the *Testament politique* as a work 'stuffed full of errors and misconceptions of every kind'.[6] As for Montesquieu, he called Richelieu a 'wicked citizen' (*méchant citoyen*).

With the advent of the Romantic movement in the nine-teenth century, Richelieu was relentlessly vilified by poets and novelists. Alfred de Vigny in his novel *Cinq-Mars* (1826) subordinated history to his poetic imagination. The ills of France, he suggested in the preface, had all been caused by Richelieu's attack on the power of the nobility.[7] In 1831 Victor Hugo's verse drama, *Marion Delorme*, portrayed Louis XIII as a cipher, the real ruler of France being the tyrannical and bloodthirsty cardinal. Richelieu himself never appears on the stage. His voice, however, is heard from behind a curtain at the end saying, 'No mercy', as the hero, Didier, is about to be executed for breaking the anti-duelling laws. But the least flattering portrait of Richelieu was painted by Alexandre Dumas in his hugely successful novel, *The Three Musketeers* (1844). This shows the cardinal as a man devoid of faith or justice who uses his red robe to conceal his depraved appetites. Louis XIII, in his presence, is little more than a whimpering child.

For the historian Jules Michelet, the cardinal was the 'sphinx in a red robe' whose dull grey eye said, 'whoever guesses my meaning must die', the 'dictator of despair' who 'in all things could only do good through evil', a soul tormented by 'twenty other devils' and torn by 'internal furies'. The cardinal, according to Michelet, 'died so feared that no one dared speak of his death, even abroad. It was feared that out of spite and with a terrible effort of will he might decide to return.'[8] The most sweeping indictment of Richelieu's policies is to be found in Hilaire Belloc's biography of 1930. This presents the cardinal as the creator of modern Europe in which nationalism has taken the place of Catholicism as the state religion. 'We are what we are,' he writes, 'so divided and in peril of dissolution through our division, because Richelieu applied his remote, his isolated, his overpowering genius to the creation of the modern state, and, unwittingly to himself, to the ruin of the common unity of Christian life.'[9]

So much for hatred; there has also been admiration, often as uncontrolled. Sometimes it has come even from Richelieu's harshest critics. Thus Retz paid tribute to the cardinal's two aims of crushing the Huguenots and defeating the Habsburgs. They were as vast in his judgement as those of any Caesar or Alexander; he achieved the first and, at his death, had well advanced the second. The duc de La Rochefoucauld, writing soon after the cardinal's death, argued that the private complaints prompted by the severity of his rule were as nothing compared to the greatness of his achievements: the fall of La Rochelle, the ruin of the Huguenot party and the defeat of the Habsburgs. In 1698 La Bruyère, in a speech to the *Académie française*, described Richelieu as a genius who had explored the mysteries of government; in pursuing the public interest he had forgotten his own.

For Aubery, author of the earliest history of Richelieu's administration, the cardinal was like a torch that had burnt itself out in the service of others. He had loved the State better than his own life. Tender by nature, he had shown compassion to the French people while promoting Louis XIII's greatness at home and abroad. Father Griffet (1758) also saw saintly qualities in the cardinal. We owe him the story

216

of Peter the Great's visit to Richelieu's tomb. As the tsar stood before the effigy, he exclaimed: 'Great man, if you were alive today, I would shortly give you half my empire on condition that you would teach me how to govern the other half.'[10] For Michelet (even he!) the cardinal's earthly genius was comparable to Galileo's heavenly vision. He was 'the most serious man of his time' who had successfully resisted the forces of ultramontane obscurantism.

But it was in Napoleon's wake that the cardinal's reputation as the founder of French absolutism came into its own. For J Caillet (1860) he was no less important as an administrator than as a statesman. His 'powerful genius' gave momentum to the energies of the French nation, which, after being contained or misdirected for a long time, were about to perform wonders. Nothing in Caillet's estimation was more entrancing than the sight of Richelieu disputing every moment of his life with sleep or death in order to dedicate it to the greatness of France.[11] Essentially the same view is expressed in the first volume of Hanotaux's huge work (1893): 'he dedicated himself to a great task: the completion of French unity through the final establishment of the king's absolute authority and the ruin of the house of Spain. He lived for that alone.'[12] In the late nineteenth century, the rights and wrongs of Richelieu's foreign policy were discussed in the light of France's defeat by Prussia in 1871 and her loss of Alsace-Lorraine. Whereas Germans accused him of unwarranted aggression, Frenchmen claimed that he had only given France her 'natural frontiers'.

In 1932 a French diplomat, the comte de Saint Aulaire, answered Belloc's sweeping condemnation of the cardinal. In his view Richelieu, far from unleashing the forces of darkness in Europe, had inaugurated an age of renewal tied to the security and greatness of France. The Treaty of Westphalia had saved Europe's liberties, and the cardinal had only used absolutism as an expedient forced upon him by circumstances, not as a dogma; he had strengthened France's ancient institutions wherever possible. He was one of humanity's prophets.[13] The age of the dictators did not spare Richelieu praise that he might not have welcomed. 'To him,' writes Bailly (1934), 'was due the resplendent glory of the French monarchy during the seventeenth and eighteenth centuries. We cannot discover in past history another example of national recovery so swift and magnificent. Fascism alone, at the present day, can present us with a similar achievement.'[14]

Even today it is difficult for the historian to achieve a dispassionate assessment of Richelieu. For he had great qualities, but also enormous faults. He was intelligent, resourceful, single-minded, energetic, cultivated and devout, but, at the same time, insatiably ambitious, proud, ruthless, grasping, vindictive and at times heartless. His policies too are sharply contrasted. Whereas at home he crushed the Huguenots, depriving them of their military and political privileges, abroad he allied with Protestant powers against the Catholic house of Habsburg. This exposed him to the charge of being unprincipled or of putting politics before religion. But he probably would not have recognised the distinction, for he regarded the French monarchy as divinely chosen to bring peace to Christendom. The Habsburgs, on the other hand, were in his judgement merely using religion as a pretext for enslaving Europe.[15] He saw his alliance with foreign Protestant powers simply as a means whereby France might accomplish more easily her sacred mission.

Furthermore, the cardinal viewed his own rise to power and wealth as the prerequisite of France's greatness. And, as Richelieu himself claimed, he did fulfil the promises he had made to Louis XIII. In the course of his ministerial career he ruined the Huguenot party, humbled the great nobles and raised the king's international prestige. In achieving these results the cardinal was often assisted by good fortune. For example, the death of Gustavus Adolphus in battle rid him of an embarrassing ally. But, as J H Elliott points out, Richelieu deserves credit for recognising good fortune and exploiting it. He had a 'keen sense of anticipation, which enabled him on so many occasions to get his timing right'.[16] The cardinal was also successful in other respects. He gained new territories for France, promoted her development as a maritime power, and founded the *Académie française*. At the same time, he steadily built up his own wealth and raised the status of his family to the highest aristocratic level.

But an assessment of Richelieu, to be fair, must take his shortcomings into account. He was less successful in his policies than is often assumed. His record as a military administrator has been severely criticised of late. His attempts to set up a French empire overseas were by and large a failure. His efforts to promote monastic reform in France were counter-productive. And his achievement, such as it was, was extremely precarious. The ruin of the Huguenots was limited to the loss of their military and political privileges. They could no longer rebel, but they survived as a religious minority subject to persecution by church and state. The problem of the religious division of France remained until Louis XIV revoked the Edict of Nantes in 1685. As for the nobles, they may have been humbled by Richelieu, but they survived as a serious threat to royal authority. As soon as the cardinal was out of the way, they returned from exile and resumed their opposition to the government. From 1649 until 1652 France had to face another aristocratic rebellion. Richelieu's foreign policy was more successful in the long term. He did not live long enough to witness the French victory at Rocroi, the Peace of Westphalia or that of the Pyrenees. None of these events was necessarily inevitable. Rocroi has been described as 'an unexpected reversal of events on the north-eastern frontier, which had hitherto favoured Spanish arms'.[17] But, even if one assumes that Richelieu had virtually won the war for France by the time of his death, the price he had to pay for this result is not easily condoned. His decision to take France into the Thirty Years War, though possibly justified in nationalistic terms, imposed upon her people, more especially the peasantry, an intolerable tax burden. As the costs of war soared, the Crown had to use force to extract contributions from people already hard-pressed by famine and plague. The result was an upsurge of popular unrest which threatened to destroy the kingdom from within. In spite of savage repression, the revolts spilled over into the minority of Louis XIV. The war also revealed some of the fundamental administrative weaknesses of the ancien régime, notably its dependence on office-holders, who had purchased their offices and could not, therefore, be dismissed. They were often corrupt or lethargic so that the government had to bypass or replace them by commissioners dismissible at will. These *intendants* were not invented by Richelieu, who was no creative genius, but by using them as regular agents of the central government he paved the way for Louis XIV's 'absolutism'. To this extent the cardinal may be regarded as the founder of absolutism. Not all historians, however, are convinced of the effectiveness of this system of government, even under Louis XIV.[18]

Richelieu, as we have seen, was a master propagandist. He did all that was possible to ensure that posterity would remember his achievement. For a long time his efforts were rewarded, but in the light of much recent research a question mark now hangs over the cardinal's reputation. We may well ask ourselves whether he was truly as great or as successful as he would have had us believe. His principal achievement, in my estimation, was to have remained in power for eighteen years in spite of countless attempts by powerful enemies to overthrow him. To some extent he was helped by his status. A cardinal who enjoyed the backing of the church would have been less easy to remove than a nobleman. But Richelieu actively contributed to his own survival. He did so by persuading Louis XIII that no one other than himself could serve the monarchy so well; by suppressing with exemplary harshness all opposition; by employing hard-working and loyal 'creatures' dependent on his patronage; and by building up a power base comprising lands, offices and benefices on a massive scale for himself and his family. By remaining in power for so long Richelieu was able to pursue policies consistently which, in the end, achieved some of the aims he had set himself, but only, it must be stressed, in the short term. The French monarchy was stronger and more widely respected in 1642 than it had been in 1624. But soon after Richelieu's death, France was again plunged into civil chaos. The Fronde has been interpreted as a revolt against Richelieu's 'revolution in government'.[19] It began as a revolt of the office-holders, angered by the Crown's encroachments on their rights and privileges, and was soon followed by another, this time of the upper nobility. But the rebels failed to get their act together and the monarchy eventually emerged from the upheaval stronger than before.[20] Thus was Richelieu fortunate, even in death.

. . .

NOTES AND REFERENCES

1. Chevallier P 1979 *Louis XIII*. Paris, Fayard, pp. 628–32; Carmona M 1983 *Richelieu*. Paris, Fayard, pp. 692–94;

Burckhardt C J 1971 *Richelieu and his Age*. London, Allen & Unwin, vol. III, pp. 455–60.

2. Chevallier *Louis XIII*, p. 631.
3. Ibid., p. 646.
4. Bergin J 1985 *Cardinal Richelieu: power and the pursuit of wealth*. New Haven, CT, Yale University Press, pp. 256–92.
5. Retz, Cardinal de 1956 *Mémoires*. Paris, Gallimard, pp. 66–70; Salmon J H M 1969 *Cardinal de Retz: the anatomy of a conspirator*. London, Weidenfeld & Nicholson, pp. 58, 87–8.
6. Voltaire n.d. *Siècle de Louis XIV*. Paris, Garnier, pp. 18, 588–89.
7. Honour H 1981 *Romanticism*. Pelican Books, p. 201.
8. Michelet J n.d. *Richelieu et la Fronde*. Paris, Calmann-Lévy, p. 235.
9. Belloc H 1930 *Richelieu*. London, Benn, pp. 8, 25–6.
10. Mousnier R 1972 'Histoire et mythe' in Adam A *et al. Richelieu*. Paris, Hachette, p. 246.
11. Ibid.
12. Ibid., p. 248.
13. Saint Aulaire, Comte de 1932 *Richelieu*, Paris, Dunod, pp. 240–43.
14. Bailly A 1936 *The Cardinal Dictator*. London, Cape, p. 265.
15. Weber H 1986 'Dieu, le roi et la chrétienté: Aspects de la politique du Cardinal de Richelieu' in *Francia: Forschungen zur Westeuropaïschen geschichte*, Sigmaringen, Jan Thorbecke.
16. Elliott J H 1984 *Richelieu and Olivares*. Cambridge, Cambridge University Press, p. 155.
17. Parrott D 1987 'French military organization in the 1630s: the Failure of Richelieu's Ministry' *Seventeenth-Century French Studies* IX: 153.
18. Mettam R 1988 *Power and Faction in Louis XIV's France*. Oxford, Blackwell.
19. Lloyd Moote A 1971 *The Revolt of the Judges*. Princeton, NJ, Princeton University Press, p. 35.
20. See my *The Fronde* (Historical Association, rev. edn, 1986).

BIBLIOGRAPHICAL ESSAY

A useful critical bibliography is contained in Tapié V-L 1974 *France in the Age of Louis XIII and Richelieu*, translated and edited by Lockie D McN, Macmillan. For a more up-to-date, albeit shorter, bibliography see the 1984 edition published by Cambridge. Also useful is Church W F 1965 'Publications on Cardinal Richelieu since 1945: a Bibliographical Study' in *Journal of Modern History* 37. The bibliography contained in Mandrou R 1970 *La France aux XVIIe et XVIIIe siècles*, Presses Universitaires de France, is excellent for the economy and society. Two helpful bibliographical aids are Barbier F 1987 *Bibliographie de l'Histoire de France*, Masson, and Taylor B 1989 *Society and economy in Early Modern Europe, 1450–1789: A Bibliography of post-war research*, Manchester.

The amount of primary sources, both manuscript and published, for the reign of Louis XIII is huge. Anyone wishing to explore them should first consult Emile Bourgeois and Louis André, 1913–35, *Les sources de l'histoire de France au XVIIe siècle*, 8 vols; also the bibliography in Préclin E and Tapié V-L 1949 *Le XVIIe siècle*, Presses Universitaires de France. A large number of original documents concerned with the administration of Richelieu may be found in four compilations: Avenel D L M (ed.) 1853–77 *Lettres, instructions diplomatiques et papiers d'état du Cardinal de Richelieu*, 8 vols; Hanotaux G (ed.) 1880 *Maximes d'état et fragments politiques du Cardinal de Richelieu*; Société de l'histoire de France (ed.) 1907–31, *Mémoires du Cardinal de Richelieu*, 10 vols; and Grillon P (ed.) 1975–85 *Les Papiers de Richelieu*, Pedone, 6 vols so far, covering the period 1624 to 1631. The best edition of Richelieu's *Testament politique* is by André L 1947, Laffont. For a selection from this work in an English translation see Hill H B 1965 *The Political Testament of Cardinal Richelieu*, Wisconsin.

Many contemporary memoirs are also available in print, but need cautious handling. Among the more important are those of de Bassompierre F, de La Rochefoucauld F, de Montchal C, Montglat, Madame de Motteville, Phélypeaux de Pontchartrain P, de Rohan H, de Saint-Simon L, Vittorio Siri and Tallemant des Réaux. Particularly important for the history of popular revolts during Richelieu's administration is Mousnier R (ed.) 1964 *Lettres et mémoires adressés au chancelier Séguier (1633–1649)*, 2 vols, Presses Universitaires de France.

For royal legislation see Isambert F A (ed.) 1822–33 *Recueil général des anciennes lois françaises depuis l'an 420 jusqu'à la révolution de 1789*, 29 vols.

Collections of extracts in English from contemporary archive material are Bonney R 1988 *Society and Government in France under Richelieu and Mazarin, 1624–61*, Macmillan, and Shennan J H 1969, *Government and Society in France, 1641–1661*, Allen & Unwin.

Readers requiring a background knowledge of French history in the early modern period should begin by consulting Parker D 1983 *The Making of French Absolutism*, Arnold; Briggs R 1977 *Early Modern France*, Oxford; Goubert P 1969–73 *L'Ancien régime*, 2 vols, Colin (vol. 1 has been translated into English: Weidenfeld, 1969); Mandrou R 1975 *Introduction to Modern France 1500–1640*, Arnold; Mousnier R 1979 *The Institutions of France under the Absolute Monarchy*, Chicago; Ranum O 1968 *Paris in the Age of Absolutism*, Wiley.

For the religious background see Delumeau J 1977 *Catholicism between Luther and Voltaire: a new view of the Counter-Reformation*, Burns & Oates. Interesting essays on witchcraft, popular revolts, church and state, Jansenism and Catholic reform are in Briggs R 1989 *Communities of Belief: Cultural and Social Tension in Early Modern France*, Clarendon.

The classic history of Richelieu's administration is Hanotaux G and Duc de la Force 1893–1946 *Histoire du Cardinal de Richelieu*, 6 vols, Firmin-Didot/Plon. It is of uneven quality and inevitably somewhat out of date. Generally sound and still useful as a factual narrative is Mariéjol J H 1906 *Henry IV et Louis XIII*, vol. 6, pt. 2 of Lavisse E *Histoire de France*. The best general account of the reign of Louis XIII in English is Tapié V-L 1974 *France in the Age of Louis XIII and Richelieu*, Macmillan; and new edn, 1984 Cambridge. It is a very balanced work: Richelieu may be its hero, but his limitations are recognised. The age is described as 'a contrast between magnificence and dire poverty, between things that were beautiful and things that were infamous'. This verdict is as acceptable today as in 1952, when the work was originally published in France. A brief survey of the reign is provided by Méthivier H 1964 *Le siècle de Louis XIII*, Presses Universitaires de France.

The best recent biography of King Louis XIII is Chevallier P 1979 *Louis XIII*, Fayard. This uses evidence provided by foreign ambassadors resident in France, and its account of the Day of Dupes supersedes that of Mongrédien G 1961. Lloyd-Moote A 1989 *Louis XIII the Just*, California, is a trifle wordy and suffers from too much psycho-history. The author argues that Louis, 'far from being the do-nothing king ridiculed in Alexandre Dumas's *Three Musketeers*, or, as recent serious scholarship has reinterpreted him to be, the shadowy "collaborator" of his great minister Richelieu', was a highly effective monarch. Elizabeth Marvick 1986 *Louis XIII: the Making of a King*, Yale, sets out to interpret the evidence contained in the diary of the young king's doctor, Jean Héroard (edited by Madeleine Foisil, Fayard, 1989 2 vols). Unfortunately, the interpretation is wholly Freudian and, therefore, questionable.

Biographies of Richelieu are numerous and variable in quality. The most recent in French is Carmona M 1983 *Richelieu: l'ambition et le pouvoir*, Fayard. It runs to nearly 800 pages and is packed with facts, but it only reaches Richelieu's ministerial career on p. 403 and is weak on interpretation. The final chapter, after listing the pros and cons, chooses to sit on the fence. The same author's 1984 *La France de Richelieu*, Fayard, fills in some of the background, not always accurately (the section on taxation is unreliable).

Among biographies of Richelieu in English, three deserve to be singled out: Hilaire Belloc 1930 *Richelieu*, Benn, is memorable mainly as a diatribe against the cardinal, who is blamed, along with Bismarck, for all that was wrong in the world of the thirties. Far more serious, albeit little more than a lively essay, is Wedgwood C V 1962 *Richelieu and the French Monarchy*, Hodder & Stoughton; Burckhardt C J 1971 *Richelieu and his Age*, 3 vols, Allen & Unwin, is uneven in quality and at times irritatingly diffuse; Treasure G R R 1972 *Cardinal Richelieu and the Development of Absolutism*, Black, is essentially a textbook, sensibly analytical in approach, but marred by misprints and factual slips.

Outstanding among recent works on the cardinal is Bergin J 1985 *Cardinal Richelieu: Power and the Pursuit of Wealth*, Yale. This is a truly original work based on hitherto unused records in Paris and elsewhere. It demonstrates beyond dispute that Richelieu was 'an unquestioning believer in the propriety of matching power and wealth quite closely'. Elizabeth Marvick's 1983 *The Young Richelieu*, Chicago, suffers from the same Freudian slant as her more recent work on Louis XIII. It has been carefully researched and contains much information on the cardinal's antecedents, relatives and upbringing but its interpretation of Richelieu's leadership relies on too much guess-work. Adam A *et al.* 1972 *Richelieu*, Hachette, contains some interesting essays, including one by Blet P on the cardinal's faith and another by Mousnier R on his reputation through the ages. Richelieu's personal religion is discussed by Orcibal J 1948 'Richelieu, homme d'église, homme d'état, à propos d'un ouvrage récent' *Revue d'histoire de l'église de France* 34.

Among older works on Richelieu containing much that is perceptive the following stand out: Battifol L 1937 *Autour de Richelieu*, and 1934 *Richelieu et le roi Louis XIII*, Calmann-Lévy. The cardinal's household is examined in Maximin Deloche 1912 *La maison du Cardinal de Richelieu*, which partly rests on an expense account of 1639 (reprinted in full in an appendix).

Richelieu's education and career as bishop of Luçon are examined in Lacroix L 1890 *Richelieu à Luçon: sa jeunesse, son épiscopat*. For his role at the Estates-General of 1614, see Hayden J M 1974 *France and the Estates-General of 1614*, Cambridge.

The council of state to which Richelieu was admitted in 1624 and its relationship with other councils are discussed by Mousnier R 'Le conseil du roi de la mort de Henri IV au gouvernement personnel de Louis XIV'. This first appeared in 1947 but has been included with other important papers by the same author in 1970 *La plume, la faucille et le marteau*, Presses Universitaires de France. Mousnier has consolidated his views on the administration in 1974–80 *Les institutions de la*

France sous la monarchie absolue, 2 vols, Presses Universit-aires de France. The first volume of this work is available in English (see above). The cardinal's relations with the king and his reliance on government through 'creatures' are examined by Orest Ranum 1963 *Richelieu and the Councillors of Louis XIII*, Oxford. This book also contains chapters on the secre-taries of state and superintendants of finance. For Richelieu's relations with Father Joseph, see Fagniez G 1894, *Le Père Joseph et Richelieu*, 2 vols, and Huxley A 1941 *Grey Eminence*, Chatto & Windus.

Whereas French historians generally accept the idea that Louis XIII's monarchy was absolute, some English-speaking historians have cast doubt on this. A classic statement of the traditional French view is Pagès G 1926 *La monarchie d'ancien régime*. The argument must inevitably hinge on the meaning of the term 'absolutism'. For a good discussion of recent writings on the subject, see Bonney R 1987 'Absolutism: what's in a name?' *French History* I. For Richelieu's contri-bution to the concept of reason of state, see Thuau E 1966 *Raison d'état et pensée politique à l'époque de Richelieu*, Colin; and Church W F 1972 *Richelieu and Reason of State*, Princeton. Whereas Thuau thinks Richelieu helped to secularize political thought, Church argues persuasively that the cardinal 'never lost sight of higher ends of a religious nature'. By adhering closely to the chronology of events, Church seeks 'to dem-onstrate that the growth of the concept of reason of state in France during this period roughly paralleled and was inspired by the politics that Richelieu undertook for the benefit of the French state'. Hildesheimer F 1985 *Richelieu: une certaine idée de l'état*, Publisud, is an excellent brief ac-count. On Richelieu's writings in general, Deloche M 1920 *Autour de la plume du Cardinal de Richelieu*, Société française d'imprimerie et de librairie, is essential. The cardinal's role as a propagandist, more particularly his influence on the *Gazette*, is discussed by Solomon H M 1972 *Public Welfare, Science and Propaganda in Seventeenth Century France: the Innovations of Théophraste Renaudot*, Princeton.

Absolutism in practice could not be implemented through office-holders who had bought their offices and become too independent of the Crown; it required the use of commis-sioners revocable at the king's will. This came about with the increased use of *intendants*. Their origins and duties are examined in Bonney R 1978 *Political Change in France under Richelieu and Mazarin 1624–1661*, Oxford. Major obstacles in the path of a fully fledged absolutism were the Parlements and provincial Estates. On this, see Shennan J H 1968 *The Parlement of Paris*, Eyre & Spottiswoode, and Kettering S 1978 *Judicial Politics and Urban Revolt in Seventeenth Century France*, Princeton. This work focuses on relations between the central government and the parlement of Aix. The same author's 1986 *Patrons, Brokers, and Clients in Seventeenth-Century France*, Oxford, is very important. Of great interest on absolutism at a provincial level is Beik W 1985 *Absolutism and society in seventeenth-century France*, Cambridge. This cites archbishop Montchal of Toulouse, who accused Richelieu of being 'a usurper who put pride above service and literally wore out the king with his misguided projects'. On the cardinal's bypassing of the ordinary lawcourts in hounding his political opponents, see Kitchens J H 1982 'Judicial commissions and the parlement of Paris' *French Historical Studies* 12. Perhaps the only historian who does not believe that Richelieu promoted absolutism is Russell Major J. His 1980 *Representative Government in Early Modern France*, Yale, is a mine of information on the French provincial estates, but its contention that it was Marillac, not Richelieu, who wanted to impose centralisation on the estates through an extension of the system of *élections* is controversial. The use of commissioners was a more effective way of centralising government than the multiplication of office-holders.

A considerable embarrassment to Richelieu on becoming chief minister was the rebellion of the Huguenots in the west and south of France. The build-up of tension on the eve of his coming to power is described by Lublinskaya A D 1968 *French Absolutism: the crucial phase, 1620–1629*, Cambridge. The climax of the struggle was the siege of La Rochelle. Richelieu's success here has been traditionally ascribed to his military skill, but Parker D 1980 *La Rochelle and the French monarchy: Conflict and Order in Seventeenth-Century France*, Royal Historical Society, shows that deep divisions existed among the Rochelais, notably between the oligarchy controlling the town and the bourgeois. Conflicting economic interests, not merely religion, had an important part to play. For a traditional account of the siege, see de Vaux de Foletier F 1931 *Le siège de La Rochelle*, Firmin-Didot. The English expedition to the Ile de Ré is described in Lockyer R 1981 *Buckingham*, Longman. A good account of the role of the Huguenots in France before and after the peace of Alès is in Menna Prestwich 1985 *International Calvinism 1541–1715*, Oxford.

Richelieu claimed to have lowered the pride of the high nobility. But, as Orest Ranum shows, 1963 'Richelieu and the Great Nobility: Some aspects of Early Modern Political Motives' *French Historical Studies* 3, the cardinal aimed to restore order and obedience among the *grands*, not to diminish their power and prestige. One way in which they could be obedient was by abstaining from duelling, which had become a veritable plague. The standard work on this is Billacois F 1986 *Le Duel dans la société française des XVIe et XVIIe siècles*, EHESS (an English translation is due from Yale, 1990). Also useful are Herr R 1955 'Honor versus Absolutism: Richelieu's Fight against Duelling' *Journal of Modern History* 27, and Kiernan V G 1986 *The Duel in European History*, Oxford. Erlanger P 1971 *Richelieu and the Affair of Cinq-Mars*, Elek, argues that Richelieu saved the Bourbons from a Merovingian end. Few historians have credited the aristocratic plotters with motives of an unselfish kind. An exception is Constant J-M 1987 *Les conjurateurs: le premier libéralisme politique sous Richelieu*, Hachette. Also favourable to the king's turbulent brother is Dethan G 1959 *Gaston d'Orléans conspirateur et prince charmant*. Historians are not in complete accord about the causes of aristocratic unrest in early seventeenth-century France. Various reasons are suggested by Bitton D 1969 *The French Nobility in Crisis 1560–1640*, Stanford, and Deyon P 1964 'A propos des rapports entre la noblesse française et la monarchie absolue pendant la première moitié du XVIIe siècle' *Revue historique*, 231. An English translation of this important article, which shows that despite its exemption from the *taille*, the aristocracy was under increasing fiscal pressure, is in Coveney P J 1977 *France in Crisis 1620–1675*, Macmillan. But Wood J B 1980 *The Nobility of the Election of Bayeux 1463–1666*, Princeton, shows that in this area at least the nobility was not in a state of tension. See also his 1976 'The Decline of the Nobility in Sixteenth and Early Seventeenth Century France: Myth or Reality' *Journal of Modern History* 48. Other recent works on the nobility include Constant J-M 1985 *La vie quotidienne de la noblesse française aux XVIe et XVII siècles*,

Hachette, and Labatut J-P 1972 *Les ducs et pairs de France au XVIIe siècle*, Presses Universitaires de France.

A major criticism of Richelieu's policy is that he subordinated the well-being of ordinary Frenchmen to the pursuit of an aggressive foreign policy which culminated in a costly war with the Habsburgs. For the European background, the following can be recommended: Parker G 1979 *Europe in Crisis, 1598–1648*, Fontana; Cooper J P (ed.) 1970 *The Decline of Spain and the Thirty Years War, 1609–48/59*, Cambridge; and Pennington D H 1970 *Seventeenth Century Europe*, Longman. On the Valtelline crisis, see Parker G *The Army of Flanders and the Spanish Road, 1567–1659*, Cambridge; also Pithon R 1960 'Les débuts difficiles du ministère de Richelieu et la crise de la Valtelline' *Revue d'histoire diplomatique* 74. The significance of the Mantuan war in changing Olivares's perception of France is underlined by Stradling R 'Olivares and the origins of the Franco-Spanish War, 1627–35' *English Historical Review* 101. More controversially, he suggests that Olivares came to favour a pre-emptive strike against France before she declared war in 1635. See also Parrott D 'The Causes of the Franco-Spanish War of 1635–59' in Black J 1987 *The Origins of War in Early Modern Europe*, Donald. Still of fundamental importance is Pagès G 1937 'Autour du "Grand Orage": Richelieu et Marillac: deux politiques' *Revue historique* 179. This points to the crucial importance of Richelieu's advice to the king following the capture of Pinerolo in 1630. Thereafter France became committed to war with the Habsburgs. Among the best studies of this conflict are Pagès G 1939 *La guerre de Trente Ans*, Payot (English translation 1970, A & C Black), and Parker G 1984 *The Thirty Years War*, Routledge.

France's relations with Sweden come under authoritative scrutiny in Roberts M 1953–58 *Gustavus Adolphus: A History of Sweden 1611–32*, Longman. On this too see Weibull L 1934 'Gustave Adolphe et Richelieu' *Revue historique* 174. Franco-Spanish relations loom large in Elliott J H 1986 *The Count-Duke of Olivares: the Statesman in an Age of Decline*, Yale. Whereas Richelieu may be accounted a successful statesman, Olivares was a tragic failure. The personalities, careers and policies of the two chief ministers are skilfully compared in Elliott J H 1984 *Richelieu and Olivares*, Cambridge. For Richelieu's designs along France's eastern border see Battifol L 1921 'Richelieu et la question de l'Alsace' *Revue historique*

138; Weber H 1968 'Richelieu et le Rhin' *Revue historique* 239; and Zeller G 1926 *La réunion de Metz à la France*. For a critical re-appraisal of Richelieu's conduct of military operations, see Parrott D 1987 'French military organization in the 1630s: the Failure of Richelieu's Ministry' *Seventeenth-Century French Studies* IX.

Insolvency in various degrees was a constant feature of the French monarchy in the ancien régime. Although Richelieu was chief minister, he tended to leave financial policy-making to others. The complexities of the French fiscal system and the financiers upon whom the Crown relied for loans are lucidly described by Dent J 1973 *Crisis in Finance: Crown, financiers, and society in Seventeenth-century France*, David & Charles. For an overall view of the royal finances, the only reliable guide is Bonney R 1981 *The King's Debts*, Oxford. This shows that 1630 marked a turning-point, 'after which the abuses in the financial administration reached disastrous proportions'. In particular, office-holders were exploited more than ever before. The essential work on them is Mousnier R 1971 *La venalité des offices sous Henri IV et Louis XIII*, Presses Universitaires de France.

An oppressive royal fiscality was the main cause of popular unrest under Richelieu. The first historian to attempt an overall view was Porchnev B F 1963 *Les soulèvements populaires en France de 1623 à 1643*, SEVPEN, but his Marxist interpretation has been challenged by Mousnier R 1958 'Recherches sur les soulèvements populaires en France avant la Fronde' *Revue d'histoire moderne et contemporaine* 5. An English translation of this article, along with one of Porchnev's preface, are contained in Coveney P J (see above, p. 228). A lucid account of the Porchnev–Mousnier debate is Salmon J H M 1967 'Venality of Office and Popular Sedition in Seventeenth Century France' *Past and Present* 37. Fundamentally important works on popular revolts in three regions are Bercé Y-M 1974 *Histoire des Croquants*, 2 vols, Droz; Madeleine Foisil 1970 *La révolte des nu-pieds et les révoltes normandes de 1639*, Presses Universitaires de France; and Pillorget R 1975 *Les mouvements insurrectionnels de Provence entre 1596 et 1715*, Pedone. See also Bercé Y-M 1987 *Revolt and Revolution in Early Modern Europe*, Manchester, and Goubert P 1986 *The French Peasantry in the Seventeenth Century*, Cambridge.

Although Richelieu disclaimed any knowledge of finance, he had definite views on how France's economy should be run. Still the best account of these views is Hauser H 1944 *La pensée et l'action économiques du Cardinal de Richelieu*, Presses Universitaires de France. In particular, the cardinal wanted to build up France's maritime power. A critical assessment of his achievement in this sphere is Boiteux L-A 1955, *Richelieu: grand maître de la navigation et du commerce de France*, Ozanne. For a more favourable assessment, see Lacour-Gayet G 1911 *La marine militaire de la France sous les règnes de Louis XIII et de Louis XIV*, Champion. An important aspect of Richelieu's economic programme was to establish French settlements in Canada and the Caribbean. Excellent on the former is Trudel M 1973 *The Beginnings of New France, 1524–1663*, Toronto. The place of industry in Richelieu's economic thinking is discussed by Zeller G 1964 'L'industrie en France avant Colbert' in *Aspects de la politique française sous l'ancien régime*, and Nef J U 1957 *Industry and Government in France and England, 1540–1640*, Cornell.

Cultural aspects of Richelieu's ministry are admirably covered by two works: 1985 *Richelieu et le monde de l'esprit*, Imprimerie nationale, a collection of learned papers given in celebration of the quatercentenary of the cardinal's birth; and Mousnier R (ed.) 1987 *Richelieu et la culture*, CNRS. They deal authoritatively with such aspects as Richelieu's architectural commissions, his collections of paintings, sculpture and crystal, his relations with certain artists, his library, his interest in the theatre and his theological works. Less up-to-date yet still excellent on the cardinal's artistic patronage in general is Blunt A 1957 *Art and architecture in France 1500–1700*, Pelican History of Art. On Richelieu's gardens, see Woodbridge K 1986 *Princely Gardens: the origins and development of the French formal style*, Thames & Hudson. For a lucid, albeit not always historically up-to-date, survey of the literary background, see Adam A 1974 *Grandeur and Illusion: French literature and society 1600–1715*, Penguin.

A most important recent publication is Bergin, J., 1991 *The Rise of Richelieu*, New Haven, CT.& London. Drawing on original sources, some used for the first time, the author discusses Richelieu's family history, his choice of career, his university studies, his record as a bishop, his writings and the milieux he frequented.

GLOSSARY

Aides. Range of indirect taxes primarily on drink.

Bailliage. The basic unit of royal administration at the local level, administered by the *bailli*. Equivalent to a *sénéchaussée*.

Ban et arrière-ban. The traditional proclamation to muster the nobility for military service. Such proclamations were used under Louis XIII as an indirect method of taxing the nobility by requiring them to provide for substitutes.

Bureau des finances. Such *bureaux* were created in the *généralités* (q.v.) in the sixteenth century. They were administered by a number of *trésoriers généraux*.

Cahier de doléances. Representatives of each estate drew up a *cahier de doléances* on the convoking of Estates General, listing their grievances and wishes.

Chambre de l'édit. A chamber within a *parlement* comprising an equal number of Catholic and Protestant judges, who were to try cases between members of the two religions. Also called *chambre mi-partie*.

Commissaire An official provided with a *commission* to undertake particular duties in a province.

Crue. A new or increased direct tax.

Curia regis. The original body through which the medieval king took counsel and dispensed justice.

Dérogeance. Loss of status by nobles participating in certain occupations such as retail trade.

Dévot. A member of an extreme Catholic party opposed to the policies of giving toleration to the Huguenots at home and of fighting the Catholic house of Habsburg abroad.

Droit annuel. A kind of premium which enabled an *officier* to transmit his office in return for one-sixtieth of its estimated value. Also called the *Paulette*.

Droits aliénés. Right to 'shares' in proceeds of the *taille* sold by the Crown to individuals in return for cash.

Échevin. A member of a municipal corporation.

Écu. A gold crown whose value depended on its declared value in terms of the money of account, the *livre tournois*. On the foreign exchange market it was valued at 3 *livres*.

Élection. Basic unit of fiscal administration for the *taille*, staffed by *élus* forming a court of the same name.

Élu. An official forming part of the staff of an *élection*.

Enquêtes. One of the three main chambers of the Parlement of Paris.

Épargne. The central treasury. Its full name was *Trésor de l'épargne*.

Gabeleur. Popular name for a tax-collector.

Gabelle. Salt-tax levied at varying rates in five areas, a sixth being exempt.

Généralité. A financial area under the jurisdiction of a *bureau des finances*. There were about twenty in the early seventeenth century.

Grands. A collective name for the highest nobles.

Grenier à sel. A warehouse where salt was stored and taxed before it could be sold.

Intendants. Special commissioners sent into the provinces by the Crown, who became the most important royal agents in the localities from the 1630s.

Laboureur. A prosperous peasant-farmer.

Lettres de maîtrise. Diploma of mastership in a trade.

Ligueur. A member of the Catholic League, founded in opposition to the Huguenot party led by Henry of Navarre in the 1570s. After 1589 it opposed his accession to the throne as King Henry IV.

Lit-de-justice. Ceremony in which the king could personally enforce registration of edicts in the parlements or other sovereign courts.

Livre. Money of account. 1 *livre*= 20 *sous*; 1 *sou*= 12 *deniers*.

Maîtres des requêtes. Officials attached to the royal council and under the control of the chancellor. Most *intendants* held such an office.

Noblesse d'épée. The nobility of the sword, heirs of the traditional 'ancient' nobility, which performed military service as feudatories of the king.

Noblesse de robe. Nobility deriving from office in the higher appointments of the judiciary and administration.

Office. A permanent government post (as distinct from a *commission*, which was temporary). It was often sold and entailed a measure of ennoblement.

Officier. The holder of an *office*. Best translated as 'office-holder'.

Parlement. The highest court of law under the king, also responsible for registering royal edicts and with administrative duties. Apart from the Parlement of Paris, there were nine provincial parlements: Toulouse, Grenoble, Bordeaux, Dijon, Rouen, Aix, Rennes, Pau (1620) and Metz (1633).

Parlementaire. A magistrate serving in a parlement.

Paulette. See *Droit annuel*.

Pays d'élections. Provinces subdivided into *élections* (q.v.) for tax-paying purposes. They were for the most part without representative estates and made up the core of the French kingdom.

Pays d'états. Provinces with representative estates responsible for levying taxes. The principal ones were Languedoc, Brittany, Burgundy and Provence.

Présidial. One of the courts (*présidiaux*) set up in 1551 to relieve the pressure of appeals to the parlements from the *bailliages*. Sometimes they could serve as courts of first instance.

Rentes. A government bond commonly issued on the security of municipal revenues. A *rentier* was a person living off such an investment.

Seigneurie. The basic economic unit in rural France. The obligation of the tenants to the *seigneur* involved a complex of rights, services and dues. A *seigneur* enjoyed rights of jurisdiction of varying degrees within his lands, albeit subject to appeal to a royal court.

Sénéchal. An official in charge of a *sénéchaussée*. Equivalent to the *bailli*.

Sol pour livre. A 5 per-cent sales tax introduced in 1640 and made applicable to both *pays d'élections* and *pays d'états*.

Subsistances. A tax paid by townspeople to exempt them from housing troops in winter quarters.

Taille. The principal direct tax, levied in two main forms: the *taille personnelle*, levied on the unprivileged in the north, and the *taille réelle*, levied on non-noble land in the south.

Taxe des aisés. A wealth tax.

Traitants. Financiers who had signed a contract or *traité* with the crown to levy taxes, sell offices, etc.

Traites. Customs duties charged on goods crossing the external or some internal borders of the kingdom.

Trésoriers de France. Financial officials who staffed the *bureau des finances* in each *généralité*.

Valet de chambre. A title conferring membership of the king's household. It was purely honorific and entailed no domestic duties.

LIST OF DATES

1585 Birth of Richelieu (9 Sept.).

1589 Assassination of Henry III (1 Aug.); accession of Henry IV.

1590 Death of François du Plessis, Richelieu's father (10 July).

1594 Richelieu admitted to Collège de Navarre, Paris (Sept.).

1598 Edict of Nantes (13 April); Peace of Vervins between France and Spain (2 May).

1601 Birth of the future Louis XIII (27 Sept.).

1607 Richelieu consecrated as bishop in Rome (17 April); becomes bachelor of theology (29 Oct.).

1608 Richelieu arrives at Luçon (21 Dec.).

1610 Assassination of Henry IV (14 May); regency of Marie de' Medici.

1614 Treaty of St Menehould between Marie de' Medici and prince of Condé (15 May); majority of Louis XIII proclaimed (2 Oct.); opening of the Estates-General in Paris (27 Oct.).

1615 Richelieu's speech to the Estates-General (23 Feb.); marriage of Louis XIII and Anne of Austria in Bordeaux (28 Nov.).

1616 Peace of Loudun between Louis XIII and Condé (3 May); Concini ministry formed, including Richelieu as secretary of state (30 Nov.)

1617 Concini assassinated (24 April); Louis XIII assumes power with Luynes; Richelieu dismissed and confined to his see of Luçon (15 June).

1618 Richelieu exiled to Avignon (7 April); Bohemian revolt marks start of Thirty Years War (May); publication of Richelieu's *Instruction du Chrétien*.

1619 Marie de' Medici escapes from Blois (22 Feb); first war between Louis XIII and his mother; ended by Peace of Angoulême (30 April).

1620 Second war between Louis XIII and his mother; 'battle' of Ponts de Cé (7 Aug.); Peace of Angers (10 Aug.); Louis XIII annexes Béarn to France (19 Oct.).

1621 Death of Philip III of Spain (31 March); accession of Philip IV with Olivares as chief minister; end of Twelve Year Truce between Spain and United Provinces (9 April); Louis XIII fights the Huguenots; death of Luynes (14 Dec.).

1622 Richelieu becomes a cardinal (5 Sept.); Peace of Montpellier (18 Oct.).

1623 Richelieu renounces see of Luçon (19 May).

1624 Richelieu enters council of state (29 April); La Vieuville dismissed; Richelieu becomes chief minister (13 Aug.); Franco-Swiss army expels papal garrisons from Valtelline (Nov.).

1625 Marriage by proxy of Charles I and Henrietta Maria, Louis XIII's sister (11 May); fall of Breda (10 June).

1626 Peace of La Rochelle with Huguenot rebels (5 Feb.); Treaty of Monzón between France and Spain (5 March); Chalais arrested (8 July) and executed (19 Aug.); marriage of Gaston d'Orléans and Mlle de Montpensier (5 Aug.); Richelieu becomes *Grand Maître et surintendant de la navigation et du commerce* (Oct.); Assembly of Notables meets in Paris (Dec.); Richelieu's plan of reform.

1627 Franco-Spanish alliance (20 March); duel of Bouteville and Les Chapelles (14 May); Buckingham lands on Île de Ré (20 July); siege of La Rochelle begins (12 Sept.);

death of Vincenzo II duke of Mantua (26 Dec.); duke of Nevers claims his succession.

1628 Spain besieges Casale (May); Buckingham assassinated (23 Aug.); fall of La Rochelle (28 Oct.); dispute over succession to duchy of Mantua.

1629 *Code Michau*; French invade Piedmont (6 March); Edict of Alès (28 June); *seigneurie* of Richelieu becomes a *duché-pairie* (26 Nov.); Richelieu is appointed the king's lieutenant-general in Italy (29 Dec.).

1630 Pinerolo captured by French (29 March); Richelieu's memorandum on the affairs of Italy (13 April); Mantua captured by Imperial army (18 July); serious illness of Louis XIII (Sept.); Treaty of Regensburg (13 Oct.); Franco-Spanish peace at Casale (26 Oct.); Day of Dupes (10–11 Nov.); fall of Marillac and triumph of Richelieu.

1631 Treaty of Bärwalde between France and Sweden (23 Jan.); Gaston d'Orléans leaves France – goes first to Orléans, then to Lorraine; first number of Renaudot's *Gazette*; Marie de' Medici escapes from Compiègne to Spanish Netherlands (18–19 July); Swedish victory at Breitenfeld (17 Sept.).

1632 Gaston d'Orléans marries secretly Marguerite de Vaudémont (3 Jan); Treaty of Vic between France and Lorraine (6 Jan.); Marshal de Marillac executed (10 May); Gaston d'Orléans invades Languedoc, then signs Treaty of Béziers (29 Sept.); duc de Montmorency executed (30 Oct.); Gaston d'Orléans flees to Spanish Netherlands; death of Gustavus Adolphus at Lützen (16 Nov.).

1633 League of Heilbronn between Sweden and German princes (23 April); France occupies Lorraine (20 Sept.).

1634 Sweden defeated at Nördlingen (6 Sept.); Peace of Écouen between Louis XIII and Gaston d'Orléans (1 Oct.).

1635 Foundation of the *Académie française* (Jan.–Feb.); first performance of *Comédie des Tuileries* (10 March); first stone laid of new Sorbonne chapel (15 May); France declares war on Spain (19 May); unrest in Bordeaux and Périgueux (May–June); Rohan victorious in Valtelline.

1636 Corbie lost to Spain (15 Aug.), then recaptured (14 Nov.); revolt of the *Croquants*.

1637 *Croquants* defeated at La Sauvetat (1 June).

1638 Birth of future Louis XIV (5 Sept.); French defeated at Fuenterrabía (7 Sept.); fall of Breisach to Bernard of Saxe-Weimar (18 Dec.); death of Father Joseph (18 Dec.).

1639 French capture Hesdin (29 June); revolt of *Va-nu-Pieds* in Normandy (July); death of Bernard of Saxe-Weimar (16 July); unrest in Rouen; Cinq-Mars becomes *grand écuyer* (15 Nov.); defeat of *Nu-Pieds* at Avranches (30 Nov.).

1640 Suppression of *Va-nu-Pieds* (Jan.); Catalan revolt (June); Arras captured (10 Aug.); Portuguese revolt (Dec.); alliance between France and Catalonia (16 Dec.).

1641 Edict forbidding Parlement to meddle in state affairs (21 Feb.); Treaty of Paris between France and Lorraine (29 March); defeat and death of comte de Soissons at La Marfée (9 July); siege of Sedan (5 Aug.).

1642 Foundation of Ville-Marie at Montréal (8 May); death of Marie de' Medici in Cologne (3 July); French occupy Perpignan (10 Sept.); execution of Cinq-Mars and De Thou (12 Sept.); death of Richelieu (4 Dec.).

1643 Death of Louis XIII (14 May); accession of Louis XIV; France defeats Spain at Rocroi (19 May).

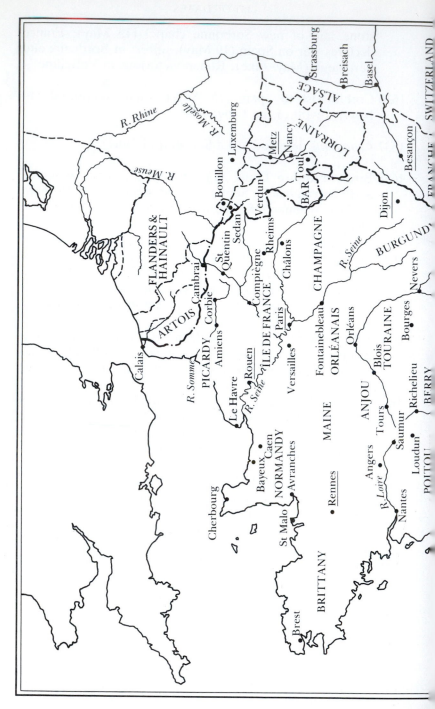

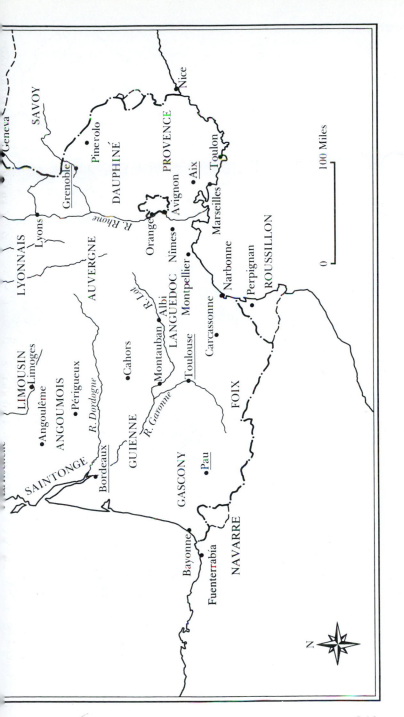

1. France in 1630 (towns underlined are seats of parlements)

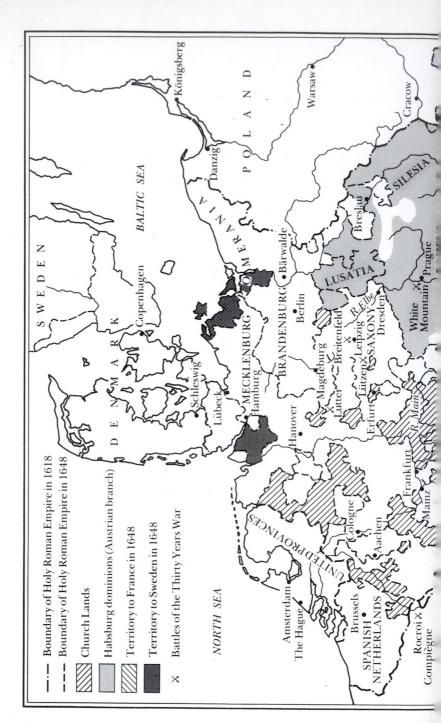

Legend:

- — · — Boundary of Holy Roman Empire in 1618
- — — — Boundary of Holy Roman Empire in 1648

Church Lands

Habsburg dominions (Austrian branch)

Territory to France in 1648

Territory to Sweden in 1648

× Battles of the Thirty Years War

Map labels:

NORTH SEA

BALTIC SEA

SWEDEN

DENMARK

Copenhagen

Schleswig

Lübeck

Hamburg

MECKLENBURG

POMERANIA

BRANDENBURG

Berlin

Bärwalde

Danzig

Königsberg

POLAND

Warsaw

Cracow

SILESIA

Breslau

LUSATIA

Prague

White Mountain ×

Dresden

SAXONY

Leipzig

Lützen ×

Breitenfeld ×

Erfurt

Magdeburg

Lutter ×

Hanover

R. Elbe

Frankfurt

R. Main

Mainz

Cologne

Aachen

UNITED PROVINCES

Amsterdam

The Hague

Brussels

SPANISH NETHERLANDS

Rocroi ×

Compiègne

2. Europe in c. 1618

INDEX

and theatre, 177–8, 193–4, 197, 208
and trade, 159–61, 165, 175
and women, 46, 48
his benefices, 27–9
his building projects, 29, 46, 195–200
his character, 42–3, 47, 218
his collections, 201, 205–8
his 'creatures', 21–3, 39, 220
his death, 62, 117, 125, 157, 164, 194–5, 199, 207, 211, 214, 216, 219
his debts, 214
his eloquence, 3, 9
his enemies, 33, 40, 42, 46, 93–4, 191, 212
his estate, 213–14
his friends, 44–5
his health, 3–4, 41–2, 109, 211
his household, 29, 42, 44, 46, 196, 214
his income, 25, 27–9
his interest in church reform, 45, 186, 219
his interest in the sea, 139, 149, 151, 155–6, 158, 218
his interests, 42
his lands, 25–7, 29, 46, 49, 196, 214
his library, 23, 46, 194–5, 197, 200–1, 214
his memoirs, 13, 52, 185
his patronage of the arts, 200–4, 208
his patronage of printing, 202–3
his physique, 41
his private fortune, 24, 29, 46–7, 218
his probate inventory, 206–7
his naval reforms, 34, 90, 156–9
his religious views, 4, 44, 46, 69–70, 80–1, 183, 213
his *rentes*, 27, 29
his reputation, 41, 47, 214–16, 220
his residences, 166, 196–8, 201
his secretaries, 28, 185

his severity, 42–3, 50, 53, 58–9, 61, 129, 137, 186–7, 215, 220
his *Testament politique*, 45, 49, 52, 84, 129, 155, 160, 166, 169, 185–6, 215
his unpopularity, 116, 212
his use of propaganda, 52, 77, 137, 169–70, 172–4, 176–7, 179–80, 193, 201, 203–4, 220
his will, 23, 199, 211, 213–14
his writings, 4, 6, 45, 69, 80–1, 84, 173, 176–7, 185, 190, 195
Richelieu, château of, 26, 29, 196, 198, 201, 203–4, 206, 208
  manor of, 2
  town of, 26, 198
Riga, 158
Rivoli, 205
Roanne, 37
Rochefoucauld, François, duc de la, 62, 216
Rocroi, battle of [1643], 219
Rohan family, 65
Rohan, Henri, duc de, 58, 71–3, 76, 79, 107, 110, 152
Roissy, Urbain de, 164
Roman Academy, 192
Romanov, Michael, Tsar, 160
Rome, 3, 35, 204–6, *see* Papacy
Ronsard, Pierre de, 190–1
Rouen, 130, 132, 166
  parlement, 67, 132, 173
Roussillon, 117
Roye, 108
Rubens, Peter Paul, 196, 202, 206
Rueil, château of, 26, 29, 42–3, 55, 192, 196–7, 201, 207–8, 213
Ry, Charles de, 196

Sainctot, Pierre de, 199
Saint Aulaire, comte de, 217
St. Benoît de Quincey, abbey of, 202
St. Cyran, Jean Duvergier de Hauranne, *abbé* of, 46, 137

256